ACTIVITY & TEST PREP WORKBOOK

SIDE by SIDE

THIRD EDITION

BOOK 4

D0077627

Steven J. Molinsky • Bill Bliss

with

Carolyn Graham

Contributing Authors

Jennifer Bixby • Dorothy Lynde • Elizabeth Handley

Illustrated by

Richard E. Hill

Side by Side, 3rd edition
Activity & Test Prep Workbook 4

Copyright © 2009 by Prentice Hall Regents
Addison Wesley Longman, Inc.
A Pearson Education Company.
All rights reserved.
No part of this publication may be reproduced, stored in a retrieval system, or transmitted in any form or by any means, electronic, mechanical, photocopying, recording, or otherwise, without the prior permission of the publisher.

Pearson Education, 10 Bank Street, White Plains, NY 10606

Editorial director: *Pam Fishman*
Vice president, director of design and production: *Rhea Banker*
Director of electronic production: *Aliza Greenblatt*
Production manager: *Ray Keating*
Director of manufacturing: *Patrice Fraccio*
Associate digital layout manager: *Paula Williams*

Associate art director: *Elizabeth Carlson*
Interior design: *Elizabeth Carlson, Wendy Wolf*
Cover design: *Elizabeth Carlson, Warren Fischbach*

Photo credit: *p. T27, Michael Newman/PhotoEdit*

The authors gratefully acknowledge the contribution of Tina Carver in the development of the original *Side by Side* program.

ISBN 978-0-13-040640-8; 0-13-040640-6

Printed in the United States of America
2 3 4 5 6 7 8 9 10 – V011 – 14 13 12 11

Contents

*Listening scripts and answer keys for the achievement tests are provided in *Side by Side Plus* Teacher's Guide 4.

| draw | fly | ride | speak | take |
| drive | grow | sing | swim | write |

1. My son Timmy ___swims___ very well.

___He's swum___ for many years.

2. Rita ___takes___ guitar lessons. ___She's___
___taken___ lessons for many years.

3. Harry ___drives___ a truck. ___He's___
___driven___ a truck for many years.

Ciao!

4. I _____ Italian. _____

_____ Italian for many years.

5. My wife and I _____ in a choir.

_____ in a choir for many years.

6. Glen _____ poetry. _____

_____ poetry for many years.

7. Abigail _____ her bicycle to work.

_____ it to work for many years.

8. Dave _____ cartoons. _____

_____ cartoons for many years.

9. Fran _____ airplanes for

Trans-Globe Airlines. _____

_____ airplanes for
Trans-Globe Airlines for many years.

10. My grandfather _____ beautiful

flowers in his garden.

_____ beautiful flowers in his
garden for many years.

B A LITTLE WHILE AGO

do	eat	feed	give	go	see	take	write

1. A. ___Have___ the employees ___gone___ on strike yet?

   B. Yes, ___they have___. ___They went___ on strike a little while ago.

2. A. _____ Alice _____ a break yet?

   B. Yes, _____. _____ a break a little while ago.

3. A. _____ you _____ your homework yet?

   B. Yes, _____. _____ it a little while ago.

4. A. _____ you and Susie _____ breakfast yet?

   B. Yes, _____. _____ breakfast a little while ago.

5. A. _____ Frank _____ out the paychecks yet?

   B. Yes, _____. _____ them out a little while ago.

6. A. _____ Monica _____ her report yet?

   B. Yes, _____. _____ it a little while ago.

7. A. _____ you _____ the cats yet?

   B. Yes, _____. _____ them a little while ago.

8. A. _____ Thomas _____ his new son yet?

   B. Yes, _____. _____ him a little while ago.

C LISTENING

Listen and decide what is being talked about.

1. a. songs *(circled)*
   b. clothes

2. a. a horse
   b. a letter

3. a. a language
   b. a book

4. a. a concert hall
   b. a lake

5. a. e-mail
   b. my new bicycle

6. a. cartoons
   b. newspaper articles

7. a. a movie
   b. inventory

8. a. a van
   b. a letter

9. a. friends
   b. flowers

Activity Workbook   **3**

D IN A LONG TIME

| be | do | eat | get | give | go | ride | see | swim | take | write |

1. A. _____Have_____ you and your husband _____taken_____ a walk on the beach recently?

   B. No, ___we haven't___. _____We haven't taken_____ a walk on the beach in a long time.

2. A. _____ Emily _____ a letter to her grandparents recently?

   B. No, _____. _____ to her grandparents in a long time.

3. A. _____ your husband _____ a raise recently?

   B. No, _____. _____ a raise in a long time.

4. A. _____ you _____ bowling recently?

   B. No, _____. _____ bowling in a long time.

5. A. _____ people _____ in the lake outside of town recently?

   B. No, _____. _____ there in a long time.

6. A. _____ your car _____ at the repair shop recently?

   B. No, _____. _____ at the repair shop in a long time.

7. A. _____ you and your wife _____ a movie recently?

   B. No, _____. _____ a movie in a long time.

8. A. _____ Diane _____ her motorcycle recently?

   B. No, _____. _____ it in a long time.

9. A. _____ you _____ at a nice restaurant recently?

   B. No, _____. _____ at a nice restaurant in a long time.

10. A. _____ George _____ anything interesting recently?

    B. No, _____. _____ anything interesting for a long time.

11. A. _____ I _____ you any difficult tests recently?

    B. No, _____. _____ us a difficult test in a long time.

Listen. Then clap and practice.

A.   Have you gone   to the zoo?

B.   Yes,   I have.

       I went   to the zoo   last May.

  And how about   you?   Have you gone there,   too?

A.   No, I haven't.   I'm going   today.

A.   Have you seen   the news?

B.   Yes,   I have.

       I saw   the news   at seven.

  And how about   you?   Have you seen it,   too?

A.   No, I haven't.   I'll see it   at eleven.

A.   Have you done   your laundry?

B.   Yes,   I have.

       I did   my laundry   last Sunday.

  And how about   you?   Have you done yours,   too?

A.   No, I haven't.   I'll do it   next Monday.

A.   Have you taken   your driving test?

B.   Yes,   I have.

      I took it   last   November.

  And how about   you?   Have you taken it,   too?

A.   No, I haven't.   I'll take it   in September.

| be | have | know | own | play | sing | want | work | | since | for |

1. A. How long ___has___ Jonathan ___known___ how to ski?

   B. ___He's known___ how to ski ___for___ the past ten years.

2. A. How long _____ your daughter _____ the measles?

   B. _____ the measles _____ last Friday.

3. A. How long _____ you _____ the violin?

   B. _____ the violin _____ several years.

4. A. How long _____ Mr. and Mrs. Chang _____ their own house?

   B. _____ their own house _____ more than a year.

5. A. How long _____ your brother Tom _____ opera?

   B. _____ opera _____ he moved to Italy last year.

6. A. How long _____ your daughter _____ to be a singer?

   B. _____ to be a singer _____ she was ten years old.

7. A. How long _____ you and Kathy _____ at the mall?

   B. _____ at the mall _____ a few months.

8. A. This lecture is extremely long. How long _____ we _____ here?

   B. _____ here _____ more than two hours.

Listen and complete the sentences.

1. (a.) three years.
   b. last year.

2. a. a long time.
   b. they started high school.

3. a. 1999.
   b. fifteen years.

4. a. 1966.
   b. thirty-five years.

5. a. last weekend.
   b. four days.

6. a. I was a young boy.
   b. several years.

7. a. last spring.
   b. three months.

8. a. I moved here.
   b. the past ten years.

9. a. he moved to Boston.
   b. the past twenty years.

H WHAT'S THE QUESTION?

1. _____How long have_____ you _____had a toothache_____?

   I've had a toothache for the past two days.

2. _____ your daughter _____?

   She's wanted to be a teacher since she was a child.

3. _____ your husband _____?

   He's been in the hospital for more than a week.

4. _____ your children _____?

   They've known how to swim since they were young.

5. _____ you and your wife _____?

   We've owned our own home for twenty years.

I WRITE ABOUT YOURSELF

1. I know how to _____.

   I've known how to _____ (since/for) _____.

2. I like to _____.

   I've liked to _____ (since/for) _____.

3. I own _____.

   I've owned _____ (since/for) _____.

4. I want to _____.

   I've wanted to _____ (since/for) _____.

5. I have _____.

   I've _____ (since/for) _____.

6. I'm _____.

   I've been _____ (since/for) _____.

1. A. How long has George been waiting for a taxi?

B. _____He's been waiting for a taxi for_____
half an hour.

3. A. How long have you been feeling sick?

B. _____
the past few days.

5. A. How long have Stacy and Tom been going out?

B. _____
last summer.

7. A. How long have you been doing sit-ups?

B. _____
twenty minutes.

2. A. How long has Julie been practicing the piano?

B. _____
early this afternoon.

4. A. How long have I been talking?

B. _____
an hour and fifteen minutes.

6. A. How long has your car been making strange noises?

B. _____
a few weeks.

8. A. How long has Howard been snoring?

B. _____
midnight.

K LISTENING

Listen and choose the correct answer.

1. a. He bought his TV a few weeks ago.
   b. His TV hasn't been working well.

2. a. She's been going to college.
   b. She's been working at a bank.

3. a. They've been waiting in a restaurant.
   b. They've been shopping in a supermarket.

4. a. Peter and Jane have been going to high school.
   b. Peter and Jane have been dating.

5. a. Their ceiling has been leaking.
   b. Their landlord has been complaining.

6. a. They've been writing all day.
   b. They've been riding their bicycles.

WHAT ARE THEY SAYING?

1. A. Something is the matter with my daughter Debbie.

   B. What seems to be the problem?

   A. She has a fever. And she's crying a lot.

   B. How long _____ *has she been crying* _____?

   A. _____ *She's been crying* _____ since yesterday afternoon.

   B. Can you bring her to see me at 2:00?

   A. Yes, I can. We'll be at your office at 2:00.

2. A. Mr. Burns? We're having some problems in our apartment.

   B. Oh? What's wrong?

   A. The ceiling is leaking. There's water all over the living room.

   B. How long _____?

   A. _____ since Monday morning.

   B. I'm glad you called me. I'll come over right away.

3. A. I'm afraid Michael is having some problems in school.

   B. Oh? What's the matter?

   A. He's been fighting with the other children.

   B. How long _____ with the other children?

   A. _____ with them for the past few weeks.

   B. That's very serious. I'll talk to him about it as soon as I get home.

   A. Thank you. I hope that helps.

(continued)

4.

A. Hello, Charlie? This is Mrs. Graves. I'm afraid I've got some problems with my car.

B. What's wrong with it?

A. The engine is making a lot of noise.

B. How long _____ a lot of noise?

A. _____ a lot of noise since last week.

B. Can you bring it in on Wednesday morning?

A. Wednesday morning? That's fine. See you then.

5.

A. We're having a terrible vacation!

B. That's a shame! What's happening?

A. It's raining. And it won't stop!

B. How long _____?

A. _____ since we arrived here three days ago.

B. That's too bad. I hope it stops raining soon.

A. So do I!

6.

A. I'm having a problem with my neighbors.

B. That's too bad. What's the problem?

A. Their dogs bark all the time. They bark in the morning, they bark in the afternoon, and they bark all night.

B. How long _____?

A. _____ for several weeks.

B. Have you talked to your neighbors?

A. Yes. And they haven't done anything. I'm very frustrated.

WHAT ARE THEY SAYING?

bake	build	do	give	make	see	sell	take	write

1. I'm very tired. _____*I've been giving*_____ piano lessons all day.

   _____*I've given*_____ more than fifteen lessons since this morning.

2. I'm exhausted. _____ cakes since early

   this morning. _____ never _____ so many
   cakes in one day before.

3. We've been busy. _____ tee shirts at the mall

   all afternoon. _____ already _____ more than 75.

4. My children must be tired. _____ sandcastles

   on the beach all morning. Look! _____ already _____
   9 or 10!

5. I need a break. _____ inventory all day.

   _____ never _____ inventory for so many hours before.

6. Dr. Wilson looks very tired. _____ patients

   since 8 A.M. I think _____ more than 20.

7. You must be tired. _____ reports all day.

   _____ never _____ so many reports in one day before.

8. I'm exhausted! _____ smoothies all day.

   Believe it or not, I think _____ already _____ well over a
   hundred since we opened this morning.

9. Okay. You can stop. _____ sit-ups for more

   than an hour. _____ probably _____ more than a hundred.

THEY'VE BEEN WORKING VERY HARD

The Sanchez family is having a big family reunion this weekend. Mr. and Mrs. Sanchez and their children have been working very hard to get ready for the big event.

bake	hang up	look	make	plant	sing	throw out	vacuum	wash	write

1. Mr. Sanchez _____*has been washing*_____ windows. _*He's*_ already _____*washed*_____ more than twenty windows.

2. _____ also _____ carpets. _____ already _____ all the carpets on the first floor of their house.

3. Mrs. Sanchez _____ decorations. _____ already _____ balloons in the living room and the dining room.

4. _____ also _____ casseroles. _____ already _____ five chicken casseroles and five tuna casseroles.

5. Their son, Daniel, _____ flowers and bushes. _____ already

   _____ yellow roses in their yard and two beautiful bushes near the front door.

6. _____ also _____ old newspapers. _____ already

   _____ all the old newspapers that were in their basement.

7. Their daughter, Gloria, _____. _____ already _____ ten apple pies and three dozen chocolate chip cookies.

8. _____ also _____ poems about each member of the family. _____

   already _____ a poem about her brother and a poem about her grandparents.

9. And while they've been working, the whole Sanchez family _____ songs.

   _____ already _____ more than fifty of their favorite songs.

10. Everybody in the Sanchez family is looking forward to the reunion. _____

    forward to it for several months. In fact, they have never _____ forward to
    anything as much as this weekend's family reunion.

1. Last night I was looking forward to having the piece of chocolate cake I *(put)* ____had put____ in the refrigerator. But when I opened the refrigerator, it was gone! Somebody

   (eat) _____ it!

2. Janet was very tired at work yesterday. She was exhausted because her husband

   (snore) _____ all night the night before and she hadn't slept.

3. Fred couldn't eat any lunch yesterday. He *(be)* _____ to the dentist that morning, and his mouth still hurt.

4. I didn't go out with Bill last Saturday night. I was upset because he *(go)* _____ out with my friend Denise the night before.

5. Jerry couldn't read his e-mail yesterday. He *(leave)* _____ his glasses at a concert the night before.

6. The man who delivered my computer couldn't assemble it because he *(assemble)* _____

   never _____ one before.

7. Jack didn't want to go to work yesterday. He was upset because he *(have)* _____ a terrible day at work the day before.

8. I fell asleep in Professor Baker's class yesterday. As soon as he started to speak, I realized

   that he *(give)* _____ the same lecture the week before.

9. We didn't rent *Jungle Adventure* at the video store last night because we *(see)* _____ it twice at the movie theater.

10. Albert didn't buy anything at the mall last weekend because he *(spend)* _____ all his money at the mall the weekend before.

11. I didn't wear my pink-and-purple striped shirt to work yesterday. I wanted to, but then I

    remembered that I *(wear)* _____ it to work a few days before.

12. Frederick wanted to take a day off last week, but he decided that wasn't a very good idea

    because he *(take)* _____ two days off the week before.

13. My children didn't want spaghetti for dinner last night because I *(make)* _____ it for dinner three times the week before.

1.  By the time I (get) ___got___ to the bank, it (close) ___had___ already

     ___closed___.

2.  By the time I (do) _____ my monthly report, my supervisor

     (go) _____ already _____ home.

3.  By the time we (arrive) _____ at the church, Jennifer and Jason

     (get) _____ already _____ married.

4.  By the time we (drive) _____ to the ferry, it (sail) _____

     already _____ away.

5.  By the time my friend (bring) _____ over his hammer, I

     (borrow) _____ already _____ one from my neighbor.

6.  By the time the interviewer from the Blake Company

     (call) _____ me back, I (take) _____ already _____

     a job with the Drake Company.

7.  By the time the doctor (see) _____ my mother, she

     (be) _____ in the emergency room for three hours.

8.  By the time we (find) _____ our seats at the concert hall,

     the symphony (begin) _____ already _____.

9.  By the time my taxi (drop) _____ me off at the train station,

     the train (leave) _____ already _____.

10. By the time I (stop) _____ speaking, I realized that at least

     half the audience (fall) _____ _____ asleep.

1. I came down with the flu last week, and I had to cancel my camping trip. I was so

   disappointed. I *(plan)* _____**had been planning**_____ it for several months.

2. Tom and his girlfriend, Kathy, *(go out)* _____ for more than
   five years. When they broke up last week, everybody was very shocked.

3. Brian injured himself and wasn't able to participate in last week's swimming competition.

   He was extremely disappointed. He *(train)* _____ for it for months.

4. All our neighbors were surprised when the Carters sold their house last month and moved to

   a condominium in Arizona. They *(live)* _____ in our city all their lives.

5. The students in Mr. Frank's eighth-grade English class were upset when he suddenly decided

   to cancel the school play. They *(rehearse)* _____ for it all year.

6. I heard that Jonah got sick and couldn't take the SAT test. What's he going to do? He

   (prepare) _____ for the test since the beginning of the year.

7. I was disappointed that the jewelry store downtown went out of business last month.

   Everybody says the store *(have)* _____ a lot of financial problems.

8. We were all surprised when Brenda quit her job at the bank the other day. She

   (work) _____ there for more than fifteen years.

9. Nobody was surprised when Barry was fired from his job at the Langley Company. He

   (come) _____ to work late, and he *(fall)* _____
   asleep at his desk every afternoon.

10. It's a shame we arrived late for the space launch. We *(look)* _____
    forward to it all year.

11. My daughter Diane played the piano magnificently at her recital last night. I'm not

    surprised. She *(practice)* _____ for the recital for several
    months.

Listen. Then clap and practice.

I had been   planning   to call   Fernando.
By the time   I called,   he had moved   to Orlando.

I had been   hoping   to go out   with Ann.
By the time   I called,   she had left   for Japan.

I   had been thinking of   hiring   Bob.
By the time   I called,   he had found   a good job.

I   had been planning   to see friends   in L.A.
By the time   I got there,   they had moved   away.

S **LISTENING**

Listen to each word and then say it.

bother	both		busy	boss

1. this
2. father
3. they're
4. that
5. weather

6. think
7. birthday
8. Theodore
9. throat
10. Martha

11. music
12. doesn't
13. days
14. because
15. loves

16. sink
17. disappointed
18. guess
19. serious
20. looks

Fill in the missing letters and then read the conversation aloud.

s   th

A. My bro_t_ _h_er _I_ _h_eodore doe__n't __ink he can go to __e __eater wi__ u__ tomorrow becau__e he ha__ a __ore __roat.

B. Ano__ __er __ore __roat? __ __at's terrible! Didn't he ju__t get over one la__t __ursday?

A. __ __at's right. Believe it or not, __ __is is __ __e __ird __ore __roat he'__ had __ __is mon__ __. My poor bro__ __er alway__ get__ __ick when __ __e wea__ __er i__ very cold.

B. I hope it i__n't __eriou__ __ __is time.

A. I don't __ __ink __o. __ __eodore __ays hi__ __ore __ __roat isn't bo__ __ering him too much, but bo__ __ my mo__ __er and fa__ __er __ay he'll have to re__t in bed for at lea__t a few day__. __ __ey're worried becau__e he i__n't eating any__ __ing, and __ __ey don't __ __ink he look__ very heal__ __y.

B. __ __en I gue__ __ he won't be going to __ __e __unday concert ei__ __er.

A. Probably not. And he'__ very di__appointed. He really love__ cla__ __ical mu__ic.

B. Well, I'm __orry our plan__ fell __ __rough. Plea__e tell __ __eodore I hope he feel__ better __oon. Oh, I almo__t forgot. My little si__ter Mar__ __a is having a __mall bir__ __day celebration today at __ __ree __ __irty. Would you like to come?

A. Ye__, of cour__e. __ __ank you very much.

| buy | get | go | have | keep | see | sit | speak | study | take |

1. Angela was late this morning. She

   __should have gotten__ to the train
   station earlier.

2. I'm really upset. I burned my cookies.

   I _____
   them out of the oven sooner.

3. All the students failed Mrs. Baker's math

   exam. They _____
   harder.

4. I got sick because the chili was too spicy.

   I _____ the chicken.

5. Sally went to the beach yesterday, and it

   started to rain. She _____
   to the museum.

6. We hated the science fiction movie in

   Cinema One. We _____
   the drama in Cinema Two.

7. Nobody could hear you at the meeting.

   You _____ louder.

8. I couldn't hear anything she said. I

   definitely _____ closer.

9. I'm sorry I threw away my ex-girlfriend's

   letters. I _____ them.

10. We're sorry we bought the small TV.

    We _____ the large one.

B GOOD ADVICE

1. I'm sorry. I can't read this.
   a. You shouldn't have written so legibly.
   (b.) You should have written more legibly.

2. I was stuck in traffic for two hours this morning.
   a. You should have driven to work.
   b. You shouldn't have driven to work.

3. Janet had a terrible stomachache last night.
   a. She shouldn't have eaten all the ice cream in her refrigerator.
   b. She should have eaten all the ice cream in her refrigerator.

4. Mr. Hopkins was uncomfortable at the beach.
   a. He shouldn't have worn a jacket and tie.
   b. He should have worn a jacket and tie.

5. We didn't like the movie on TV last night.
   a. You shouldn't have watched something else.
   b. You should have changed the channel.

6. Brian is confused in his Advanced Spanish class.
   a. He shouldn't have taken Beginning Spanish.
   b. He should have taken Beginning Spanish.

C YOU DECIDE: *Uncle Charlie's Advice*

should have	shouldn't have

All my life, my Uncle Charlie has always given me advice. He started giving me advice when I was a young boy.

1. Mom was angry because she tripped and fell when she came into my room this morning.

   Well, you should have _____,

   and you shouldn't have _____.

2. My parents were upset because I got a terrible grade on my last English test.

3. I wanted to go to the school dance with Amy, but by the time I asked her, she already had another date.

(continued)

Uncle Charlie was still giving me advice as I got older, got married, and had children.

4. Alice and I went to Hawaii after we got married, and it rained every day.

5. I'm really embarrassed. I ran in a marathon last weekend, and I finished last!

6. My son Ricky borrowed the car and had an accident. HE'S fine, but the car ISN'T!

Even now that I'm retired, Uncle Charlie STILL gives me advice.

7. I looked everywhere, but I couldn't find my glasses this morning!

8. I took my granddaughter to the opera last week, and she didn't like it!

9. I have a terrible backache. I played basketball with some of the kids in the neighborhood.

D WHAT MIGHT HAVE HAPPENED?

| might have   may have |

1. A. I wonder why Louise was late for work this morning.

   B. She *(might / miss)* __might have missed__ the bus.

2. A. What happened to all the ice cream in the refrigerator?

   B. I'm not sure. The children *(may / eat)* ____may have eaten____ it.

3. A. I wonder why Donald isn't wearing his new watch.

   B. He *(may / break)* _____ it.

4. A. I called Aunt Gertrude all morning, and she wasn't home.

   B. She *(might / go)* _____ shopping.

5. A. Lucy didn't come to English class all last week.

   B. She *(may / be)* _____ sick.

6. A. I wonder why Nancy and Larry didn't come to my birthday party.

   B. They *(might / forget)* _____ about it.

7. A. It's 10 o'clock, and the Baxters haven't arrived at the party yet.

   B. Hmm. They *(might / lost)* _____ the directions.

E WHAT'S THE ANSWER?

1. My daughter is sick. She has a bad cold.
   a. She may have played with Timmy. He has a cold.
   b. She should have played with Timmy. He has a cold.

2. I wonder why Bertha didn't want to see the Eiffel Tower when she was in Paris.
   a. She should have seen it already.
   b. She might have seen it already.

3. James arrived late for the meeting.
   a. He should have called to tell us.
   b. He may have been late.

4. Rita decided to study Italian in college.
   a. She might have wanted to learn the language her grandparents speak.
   b. She shouldn't have wanted to learn the language her grandparents speak.

5. I wonder why we haven't seen our next-door neighbors recently.
   a. They should have gone on vacation.
   b. They might have gone on vacation.

6. We didn't like the food at that restaurant.
   a. We shouldn't have gone there.
   b. We may have gone there.

could have

1. Grandma ____could have watched____ anything on TV last night. Why did she watch an old western she had already seen several times?

2. Tom went to his prom last night. He _____ any tuxedo he wanted to. Why did he wear a purple one?

3. I don't understand it. My daughter _____ anybody she wanted to. Why did she marry Herbert?

4. Your friends _____ their bicycles anywhere. Why did they ride them downtown during rush hour? It's very dangerous!

5. I don't understand it. My son _____ anything he wanted to. Why did he become a magician?

6. Those children _____ at the new skating rink in the center of town. Why did they skate on the town pond?

7. Barbara _____ any course she wanted to. I wonder why she's taking first-year French for the fourth time!

8. Richard Rockford _____ in any movie he wanted to. I wonder why he's in this awful movie!

9. You _____ anything you wanted to. Why did you make carrot soup with onions?

10. The Wilsons _____ their new son anything they wanted to. I wonder why they named him Mortimer!

11. Norman _____ his living room any color. I wonder why he painted it black!

12. Those tourists _____ at any restaurant in town. Why did they eat at MacDoodle's?

13. Frank and his wife _____ to a lot of interesting places for their vacation. Why did they go to Greenville?

14. I don't understand it. Sally _____ her composition about anything she wanted to. Why did she write about termites?

Listen. Then clap and practice.

He should have   studied   harder.
He could have   done   his best.
He should have   gotten   a good night's   sleep.
Then he might have   passed   the test.

She shouldn't have   packed   so much clothing.
She didn't need   all   that stuff.
She shouldn't have   taken   four bathing   suits.
One may have   been   enough.

I should have   taken   a shorter   break.
I shouldn't have come back   at three.
I missed   a meeting   at half past   two.
Now my boss   is mad   at me.

They shouldn't have   moved   to the suburbs.
They shouldn't have   bought   a car.
They should have   stayed   in the city,
Where everything's   close,   not far.

We should have   studied   Spanish
Before   we went   to Spain.
We could have   spoken   with the people   there
The minute   we left   the plane.

must have

1. A. Albert has been in a terrible mood all day.

   B. I know. He *(get up)* ___ must have gotten up ___ on the wrong side of the bed this morning.

2. A. Susie has a terrible stomachache.

   B. She *(eat)* _____ too many cookies for dessert.

3. A. I think I know you.

   B. I think I know you, too. We *(meet)* _____ before.

4. A. It's raining, and I can't find my umbrella.

   B. You *(leave)* _____ it at the office.

5. A. I didn't hear a word you said at the meeting.

   B. You didn't? I *(speak)* _____ too softly.

6. A. The boss gave everyone in our office a raise yesterday!

   B. He did? He *(be)* _____ in an excellent mood.

7. A. Ellen and her boyfriend, Bob, have stopped talking to each other.

   B. Really? They *(break up)* _____ .

8. A. Beverly isn't driving an old car anymore.

   B. I know. She *(buy)* _____ a new one.

9. A. Johnny woke up crying in the middle of the night.

   B. I know. I heard him. He *(have)* _____ a bad dream.

10. A. The Gleasons' new living room sofa is beautiful.

    B. I know. It *(cost)* _____ a lot of money!

11. A. When I saw Donna this morning, she looked upset.

    B. Oh, no! She *(do)* _____ badly on her science test.

I YOU DECIDE: *What Must Have Happened at the Millers' House?*

When Barbara and Edward Miller got home last Saturday afternoon, they found their front door was open and everything in the house was out of place. Someone must have broken into their house while they were out!

The first thing they saw was their attractive living room sofa. It was dirty and wet. Someone must have _____ [1]. Then they found their expensive new lamps on the floor. Someone must have _____ [2]. Their beautiful glass bowl from Italy wasn't in its usual place on the piano. Someone must have _____ [3]. Their computer was on, and there was a message on the screen. It said, " _____ _____ [4]." Someone must have _____ _____ [5]. They looked for their fax machine, but they couldn't find it. Someone must have _____ [6].

Then they looked in the kitchen and found that the kitchen cabinets were all open. Someone must have _____ [7]. There was also an empty bottle of soda in the kitchen. Someone must have _____ _____ [8]. And then they found that Barbara's car keys were missing! Someone must have _____ _____ [9]. The door to the back porch was open, and the dog wasn't in the yard. Someone must have _____ _____ [10].

The Millers were very upset. They couldn't believe what had happened while they were out.

1.

What did the Baxters name their new baby boy?

I'm not sure. They might have ...., or they might have ....

Didn't they want to name him after the president?

You're right. Then they must have ....

2.

Where did Elizabeth go on her vacation this year?

I'm not sure. She might have ...., or she might have ....

She sent me a picture of herself on a safari.

Oh. Then she must have ....

3.

What did Howard have for dinner at the restaurant last night?

I'm not sure. He might have ...., or he might have ....

Didn't you see tomato sauce all over his tie?

No, I didn't. Then he must have ....

4.

What vegetables did Martha plant in her garden this year?

The last three times I went to her house, we had carrot juice, carrot cake, carrot cookies, and carrot pie!

I'm not sure. She might have _____ _____, or she might have _____ _____.

Oh. Then she must have _____ _____.

5.

What did Mr. and Mrs. Williams do for their wedding anniversary?

My brother saw them at the most expensive restaurant in town.

I'm not sure. They might have _____ _____, or they might have _____ _____.

Oh. Then they must have _____ _____.

6.

Poor Angela! Her car wouldn't start this morning. How did she get to work?

I think she asked her brother if his bicycle was working.

I'm not sure. She might have _____ _____, or she might have _____ _____.

Oh. Then she must have _____ _____.

(continued)

7.

Why was your brother-in-law, Fred, fired?

I'm not sure. He might have _____ _____, or he might have _____ _____.

Whenever I called him at work, he wasn't there.

Oh. Then he must have _____ _____.

K **GRAMMARRAP:** *What Must Have Happened?*

Listen. Then clap and practice.

Jonathan looks •   • happy.

He must have gotten •   • hired.

Mortimer looks •   • very sad.

He must have gotten •   • fired.

Timothy is •   • quite upset.

He must have failed •   • the test.

Jennifer is •   • smiling.

She must have done •   • her best.

Melanie looks •   • nervous.

She must have lost •   • her keys.

Her dog looks •   • very anxious, too.

He must have gotten •   • fleas.

Marvin came home •   • late last night.

He must have missed •   • the train.

His coat and hat and •   • shoes were wet.

He must have walked • in the rain.

WHAT'S THE WORD?

could have	might have	should have
couldn't have	must have	shouldn't have

1. It's a very cold day. I _____ should have _____ worn a sweater. I'm sorry I didn't.

2. Mrs. Johnson never forgets her appointment with the dentist. But yesterday she forgot. I'm

   sure she _____ been very busy.

3. I _____ called you yesterday. I was in an important meeting all day.

4. Our English teacher was late for class today. He _____ overslept, or the

   bus_____ been late. I'm not sure.

5. Abigail is very absent-minded. Last week she got on the wrong train. She's very lucky. She

   _____ wound up in Canada!

6. I called your apartment all afternoon, and nobody answered. You _____
   gone out.

7. I _____ gone skiing with you last Saturday. I had to take care of my niece.

8. My washing machine is broken. The repairperson said I never _____ tried
   to wash four pairs of sneakers and five pairs of jeans at the same time.

9. I wonder why my cousin Greg didn't want to go to the movie with us last night. He

   _____ seen it already. I'm not sure.

10. We _____ gone sailing on a windy day. We _____
    gotten seasick!

11. You _____ swept your front porch. It looks so clean!

LISTENING

Listen and choose the correct answer.

1. a. He must have gone to bed very late.
   b. He should have been very tired.

2. a. She must have called them later.
   b. She shouldn't have called them so late.

3. a. He should have missed the bus.
   b. He may have missed the bus.

4. a. You could have caught a cold.
   b. You should have done that.

5. a. He might have gotten a promotion.
   b. He must have been disappointed.

6. a. They should have rehearsed more.
   b. They must have remembered their lines.

7. a. She must have been home.
   b. She might have gone away.

8. a. He could have hurt himself!
   b. He shouldn't have hurt himself!

WHAT DOES IT MEAN?

Choose the correct answer.

1. Monica overslept.
   - (a.) She came to work late.
   - b. She stayed at a friend's house.
   - c. She got up too early.

2. My doctor doesn't write legibly enough.
   - a. He doesn't write enough.
   - b. He doesn't write very often.
   - c. I can't read anything he writes.

3. Vincent wound up in jail.
   - a. He was dizzy.
   - b. He asked a police officer to help him.
   - c. He got arrested.

4. Eleanor was almost electrocuted.
   - a. Now she's a senator.
   - b. Now she's in the hospital.
   - c. Now she's an electrician.

5. I owe you an apology.
   - a. I'll pay you back.
   - b. How much did it cost?
   - c. I'm sorry I shouted at you.

6. They ate the entire pizza.
   - a. They ate half the pizza.
   - b. They ate all the pizza.
   - c. They ate just a little pizza.

7. Martha is very understanding.
   - a. She understands everything.
   - b. She's very sympathetic.
   - c. I understand everything she says.

8. He got up on the wrong side of the bed.
   - a. Is he in a better mood now?
   - b. Did he hurt himself?
   - c. He didn't make his bed.

9. Their children refused to go.
   - a. They didn't want to go.
   - b. They wanted to go.
   - c. They went there and returned.

10. We handed over the money.
    - a. We held the money.
    - b. They returned the money.
    - c. We gave them the money.

11. They were having financial problems.
    - a. They were having health problems.
    - b. They were having family problems.
    - c. They were having money problems.

12. Did your landlord evict you?
    - a. Yes. We had to move.
    - b. Yes. We envied them.
    - c. Yes. We enjoyed the apartment.

13. Tony skipped work yesterday.
    - a. He came to work early.
    - b. He didn't come to work.
    - c. He came to work late.

14. We ran up a very large bill.
    - a. We spent a lot of money.
    - b. We were very tired.
    - c. We had never jogged so far.

15. Mrs. Grumble yelled at everybody today.
    - a. She was ecstatic.
    - b. She must have been in a good mood.
    - c. She was very irritable.

16. He didn't act confidently at his interview.
    - a. He didn't arrive on time.
    - b. He didn't talk enough about his skills.
    - c. I can't read anything he writes.

O **LISTENING**

Listen to each word and then say it.

1. f<u>i</u>ll—f<u>ee</u>l
2. f<u>i</u>lling—f<u>ee</u>ling
3. f<u>i</u>t—f<u>ee</u>d
4. h<u>i</u>s—h<u>e</u>'s
5. <u>i</u>t—<u>ea</u>t
6. kn<u>i</u>t—n<u>ee</u>d
7. l<u>i</u>ve—l<u>ea</u>ve
8. l<u>i</u>ving—l<u>ea</u>ving
9. r<u>i</u>ch—r<u>ea</u>ch
10. st<u>i</u>ll—st<u>ea</u>l
11. th<u>i</u>s—th<u>e</u>se
12. w<u>i</u>g—w<u>ee</u>k
13. w<u>i</u>ll—w<u>e</u>'ll
14. T<u>i</u>m—t<u>ea</u>m
15. h<u>i</u>t—h<u>ea</u>t

Listen and complete the sentences.

fill	feel

1. (a) . . . today?
   b. . . . out this income tax form?

still	steal

2. a. . . . cars?
   b. . . . ride your bicycle to work?

this	these

3. a. . . . sneakers?
   b. . . . school?

knitted	needed

4. a. . . . a new sweater.
   b. . . . a new briefcase.

live	leave

5. a. . . . in a small house.
   b. . . . early every day.

living	leaving

6. a. . . . on the third floor.
   b. . . . on the next plane.

his	he's

7. a. . . . very tired.
   b. . . . alarm clock is broken.

It	Eat

8. a. . . . some potatoes instead.
   b. . . . wasn't very fresh.

this	these

9. a. . . . math problems.
   b. . . . homework assignment.

wig	week

10. a. . . . we're going to be busy.
    b. . . . needs a shampoo.

rich	reach

11. a. . . . New York?
    b. . . . and famous?

fill	feel

12. a. . . . it out right away.
    b. . . . a lot better soon.

fit	feed

13. a. . . . the animals very often.
    b. . . . me. They're too small.

It	Eat

14. a. . . . is my favorite recipe.
    b. . . . a little more.

still	steal

15. a. . . . go to high school.
    b. . . . cars anymore.

his	he's

16. a. . . . test was canceled.
    b. . . . getting married soon.

1. A. Did Picasso paint the *Mona Lisa*?

    B. No. The *Mona Lisa* __was painted__ by Leonardo da Vinci.

2. A. Did the Romans build the pyramids?

    B. No. The pyramids _____ by the Egyptians.

3. A. Did the chef serve you dinner at the Ritz?

    B. No. Dinner _____ by four waiters.

4. A. Did Bruce Springsteen compose "Yesterday"?

    B. No. "Yesterday" _____ by John Lennon and Paul McCartney.

5. A. Did Ponce de León discover America?

    B. No. America _____ by Christopher Columbus.

6. A. Did Charles Dickens write *Hamlet*?

    B. No. *Hamlet* _____ by William Shakespeare.

7. A. Did Queen Elizabeth wear this beautiful gown?

    B. No. This gown _____ by Jacqueline Kennedy.

8. A. This movie is incredible! Did Fellini direct it?

    B. No. It _____ by Steven Spielberg.

9. A. Did your parents take this prom picture of you and your girlfriend?

    B. No. This picture _____ by a photographer.

10. A. Did your mother bake this delicious cake?

    B. No. This cake _____ by my father.

YOU DECIDE: *At the Museum*

1. This car *(own)* _____ **was owned** _____

by the president of _____ .

It *(make)* _____

by the _____

Company in _____ .
　　　　　　　　(year)

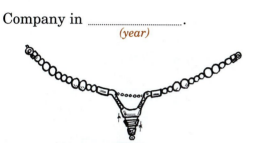

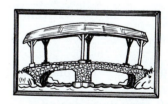

2. This airplane *(fly)* _____

by _____

in _____ . It *(design)* _____
　　　(year)

_____ by _____

_____ .

3. This beautiful necklace *(wear)* _____

_____ by the famous actress

_____ .

It *(give)* _____ to her

by _____ . It *(leave)*

_____ to the museum

by her children.

4. These dinosaur skeletons *(find)* _____

_____ by _____

_____ in Africa

in _____ . Unfortunately, they
　　　(year)

(forget) _____ by the

museum for many years.

5. This letter *(write)* _____

by _____

to _____ ,

but it *(send)* _____ never _____ .

It *(discover)* _____
recently between the pages of an old
book.

6. This impressive bridge *(build)* _____

_____ in _____
　　　　　　　　　　(city)

more than 300 years ago. It *(begin)* _____

_____ in 1520, and it *(finish)*

_____ until 1600.

(continued)

7. This is one of _____'s

earliest operas. It *(compose)* _____

_____ in _____,
(year)

and it *(sung)* _____

for the first time in _____.
(year)

8. This portrait _____

_____

_____

_____

C GRAMMARRAP: *Who Took This Wonderful Photo of Jill?*

Listen. Then clap and practice.

A. Who took   this wonderful   photo of   Jill?

B. I think   it was taken   by her brother   Bill.

A. Who built that   beautiful   house   on the hill?

B. I think   it was built   by my cousin   Phil.

A. Who wrote   this interesting   book   about dance?

B. I think   it was written   by someone   in France.

A. Who drew   the plans for this   elegant   palace?

B. I think they were drawn   by a woman   from Dallas.

A. Who sang   that wonderful   Mexican   tune?

B. I think   it was sung   by a man   from Cancún.

A. Who did   this beautiful   picture   of snow?

B. I think   it was done   by Vincent   Van Gogh.

Aunt Louise is a kind and generous person, but she's a little lazy. She wants to help her friends and family, but she never thinks about helping them until it's too late.

1. A. I'll be glad to help you do the dishes.

   B. Thank you, Aunt Louise, but _____they've_____ already ___been done___.

2. A. Can I set the table for you?

   B. That's very nice of you, but _____ already _____.

3. A. Do you want me to iron the clothes today?

   B. Thanks, Aunt Louise, but _____ already _____.

4. A. I'll be glad to make Grandpa's doctor's appointment.

   B. That's very kind of you, but _____ already _____.

5. A. I think I'll take down the party decorations.

   B. Don't bother. _____ already _____.

6. A. Here. I'll sweep the floor.

   B. I appreciate it, but _____ already _____.

7. A. I'll be glad to buy flowers for the table.

   B. Thank you, Aunt Louise, but _____ already _____.

8. A. Do you want me to hang up the new portrait?

   B. I guess you haven't looked in the hall. _____ already _____.

E **LISTENING**

Listen and decide what is being talked about.

1. (a.) the cookies
   b. the bed

2. a. the train
   b. the movie

3. a. the packages
   b. the letter

4. a. the scarf
   b. the fireplace

5. a. the presents
   b. the children

6. a. the bicycles
   b. the letters

7. a. the song
   b. the portrait

8. a. the books
   b. the cats

9. a. the meeting room
   b. the alarm

F NOTHING IS READY!

☐	make the beds
☐	sweep the porch
☐	prepare the salad
☐	feed the cat
☐	put the children to bed

A. What are we going to do? All our friends will be arriving soon, and nothing is ready. The

beds ____haven't been made___ ¹. The porch _____ ². The salad

_____ ³. The cat _____ ⁴.

And the children _____ ⁵ to bed. I'm really upset.

B. Don't worry. Everything will be okay. We still have some time.

G AT THE HOSPITAL

✔	take Mrs. Johnson's blood pressure
✔	give Ms. Blake her injection
✔	do Mr. Tanaka's cardiogram
✔	tell Mrs. Wong about her operation
✔	send Mr. Bacon home

A. How have all the patients been this morning? Have there been any problems?

B. Everything is fine, Doctor.

A. How is Mrs. Johnson this morning? ____Has____ ¹ her blood pressure ____been taken____ ² yet?

B. Yes, it has. And it wasn't as high as it was yesterday.

A. That's good. And _____ ³ Ms. Blake _____ ⁴ her injection?

B. Yes, she has. And we'll give her another at two o'clock.

A. What about Mr. Tanaka? _____ ⁵ his cardiogram _____ ⁶?

B. Yes. It _____ ⁷ an hour ago.

A. Mrs. Wong looks upset. _____ ⁸ she _____ ⁹ about her operation?

B. Yes. I explained everything to her, and I think she understands.

A. And finally, is Mr. Bacon ready to leave the hospital?

B. He's MORE than ready! _____ ¹⁰ already _____ ¹¹ home!

H CAN WE LEAVE SOON?

- [x] stop the mail
- [x] turn off the lights
- [ ] set the alarm
- [ ] take out the garbage

A. Can we leave soon?

B. I think so. The mail ____has been stopped____ [1], and the lights _____ _____ [2].

A. Great!

B. Wait a minute! _____ [3] the house alarm _____ [4]?

A. No, it hasn't. But don't worry about it. I'll do it right away.

B. And now that I think of it, _____ [5] the garbage _____ [6]?

A. I'm not sure. Why don't I go and see?

I CROSSWORD

Across

2. The paychecks were _____ this morning.

4. Has the kitchen floor been _____ yet?

7. The Christmas presents were _____ in the attic last year.

Down

1. This picture was _____ by my daughter.

2. I hope your homework has already been _____.

3. This dress was _____ by Oleg Cassini.

5. The beds have already been _____.

6. That terrible speech was _____ by the president of our company.

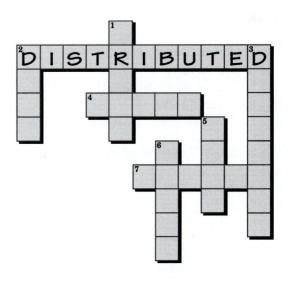

Read and then answer the questions below.

Ernest Hemingway is considered one of the most important modern American writers. He wrote six novels and more than fifty short stories. He also wrote many poems and newspaper articles.

Hemingway's books are lively and exciting. They are full of fighting, traveling, sports, love, and war. Hemingway's life was also lively and exciting.

When he was a young high school student, Hemingway played football, boxed, and wrote for the school newspaper. He ran away from home when he was fifteen years old, but he returned and finished high school in 1917. He never went to college.

Hemingway wanted to fight in World War I, but he was rejected by the army. Instead, he went to war as an ambulance driver and was badly injured.

In 1921, Hemingway went to Paris and started writing seriously. He stayed there for six years. His first novel, *The Sun Also Rises*, was written when he was still in Paris. It made him very famous.

In 1937, Hemingway went to Spain as a journalist to write about the Spanish Civil War. In 1944 he returned to Europe and wrote newspaper articles about World War II. Although he wasn't in the army, it is believed he did more fighting than writing during the war.

What's the Answer?

1. Why is Hemingway considered an important writer?
    a. He wrote many interesting works.
    b. He liked sports.
    c. He lived in many different countries.

2. What *didn't* Ernest Hemingway write about?
    a. Fighting.
    b. Traveling.
    c. Cooking.

3. What did Hemingway do when he was fifteen years old?
    a. He ran a long way.
    b. He left home.
    c. He went to high school.

4. Which of these statements about Hemingway is true?
    a. He finished high school.
    b. He went to college.
    c. He didn't play any sports in high school.

5. Why didn't Hemingway serve in the army?
    a. He wanted to fight.
    b. The army didn't want him.
    c. He didn't want to fight.

6. Which of these statements about Hemingway *isn't* true?
    a. He was a journalist for a while.
    b. He wrote about the Spanish Civil War.
    c. *The Sun Also Rises* was written in Spain.

Mr. and Mrs. Wilson *(rob)* _____were_____ ¹ _____robbed_____ ² last month. Their TV, their

computer, their new VCR, and all of their beautiful living room furniture *(steal)* _____ ³

_____ ⁴. In fact, nothing *(leave)* _____ ⁵ _____ ⁶ in the living room

except the rug. Fortunately, Mrs. Wilson's gold necklace *(take)* _____ ⁷ _____ ⁸.

She was glad because it had been *(give)* _____ ⁹ to her by her husband many years ago.

The thief *(see)* _____ ¹⁰ _____ ¹¹ driving away from the house in a small

blue van. The neighbors called the police, and the man *(arrest)* _____ ¹²

_____ ¹³. He *(send)* _____ ¹⁴ _____ ¹⁵ to jail for seven years.

A day after the robbery, the living room furniture, the computer, the VCR, and the TV

(return) _____ ¹⁶ _____ ¹⁷. The sofa had *(rip)* _____ ¹⁸

_____ ¹⁹, but fortunately everything else was okay.

L LISTENING

Listen and choose the correct answer.

1. (a.) Yes. It's already been
      fixed.
   b. No. It hasn't been
      swept yet.

2. a. Yes. It's already been
      set.
   b. Yes. It's already been
      set up.

3. a. It was written by my
      uncle.
   b. It was taken by my
      wife.

4. a. I'm sorry. They've
      already been sung.
   b. I'm sorry. They've
      already been hung.

5. a. He was hurt in an
      accident.
   b. He was offered a
      better job.

6. a. She's already been
      lent.
   b. She's already been
      sent.

7. a. Yes. It's been
      rejected.
   b. Yes. It's been
      approved.

8. a. She was hired by the
      Blaine Company.
   b. She was fired by the
      Blaine Company.

9. a. They've already been
      hung.
   b. They've already been
      sung.

10. a. Yes. It's already been
      baked.
    b. Yes. It's already been
      set.

11. a. It's already been
      read.
    b. It's already been
      played.

12. a. She's been taken to
      the hospital.
    b. She's been invited to
      a wedding.

YOU DECIDE: *A Famous Composer*

_____ 1 is an extremely talented

composer. She has written many beautiful sonatas. Her

compositions *(perform)* _____have_____ 2 _____been_____ 3

_____performed_____ 4 in Asia, in the United States, and in

_____ 5. Her symphonies are often *(hear)* _____ 6 on the radio.

Ms. _____ 7 started to compose music when she was _____ 8

years old. She *(give)* _____ 9 _____ 10 a composition book for her birthday,

and she knew right away that she wanted to be a composer.

In 1985, she sent some of her sonatas and a symphony to the _____ 11

Symphony Orchestra, but all these early compositions *(reject)* _____ 12 _____ 13.

Ms. _____ 14 was disappointed, but she continued to compose. Finally, in 1994,

several of her sonatas *(recorded)* _____ 15 _____ 16 by the

_____ 17 Symphony Orchestra.

It took many years before Ms. _____ 18's music *(appreciate)* _____ 19

_____ 20. At first, her music *(consider)* _____ 21 _____ 22

strange because it was new and different, and it *(understand)* _____ 23 not easily

_____ 24. Most people couldn't hear the beautiful melodies. Today, of course, Ms.

_____ 25 is highly *(respect)* _____ 26 by composers all over the world.

In 1996, she wrote her most famous symphony called "_____ 27." A year later,

it *(used)* _____ 28 _____ 29 as the music in a very successful movie. Since

then, she has written three other symphonies that *(play)* _____ 30 _____ 31

_____ 32 all over the world.

In 2001, Ms. _____ 33 *(hurt)* _____ 34 _____ 35 badly in a

car accident. She composed a sonata about this terrible accident. In 2002, Ms.

_____ 36 *(choose)* _____ 37 _____ 38 best composer of the

year. She *(invite)* _____ 39 _____ 40 to play her music at the White House

in Washington, D.C.

N WHAT ARE THEY SAYING?

bake	promote	rewrite	take in
clip	repair	set up	wash

1. A. The president is concerned. Is his speech ready?

   B. It'll be ready soon. _____It's_____

   _____being rewritten_____.

2. A. Why are you taking the bus to work?

   B. My car was in an accident. _____

   still _____.

3. A. Is this Bob's Bakery? I'm calling about the cake I ordered.

   B. I'm sorry. It isn't ready yet. _____

   still _____.

4. A. Should I pick up my pants at the tailor's?

   B. Not yet. _____ still

   _____.

5. A. Is Carla going to quit her job at the Internet company?

   B. No. She's decided to stay because

   _____ next week.

6. A. Is the meeting room ready?

   B. Not yet. _____ still _____

   _____.

7. A. What happened to the shirt I wore to the baseball game yesterday?

   B. _____.
   It was very dirty.

8. A. Hello. This is Mrs. Vickers. When is my poodle going to be ready?

   B. Very soon. His hair _____

   _____ right now.

O GRAMMARRAP: *Spring Cleaning*

Listen. Then clap and practice.

The family's   getting organized.

The beds   are being made.

The kitchen's   being swept and cleaned.

The bills   are being paid.

The sheets and towels   are being washed

And dried   and put away.

The rugs   are being vacuumed.

Spring cleaning starts   today.

Good morning, and welcome to your tour of Bob and Betty's Ice Cream Factory. We make the best ice cream in the world, and you're going to see how we do it! You'll learn a lot about how ice cream *(made)* __is__ 1 __made__ 2 at Bob and Betty's! Let's begin.

In this room, cream *(take)* _____ 3 _____ 4 out of our large refrigerators. Then the cream *(put)* _____ 5 _____ 6 into this machine. The cream *(mix)* _____ 7 _____ 8 for about forty minutes in this machine. While the cream is mixing, sugar *(pour)* _____ 9 _____ 10 slowly into the cream by our ice cream makers.

In the next room, the flavors *(prepare)* _____ 11 _____ 12. Today we are making banana nut ice cream. Right now, different kinds of nuts *(chop)* _____ 13 _____ 14 _____ 15 in a large chopper. It's a very expensive machine, but it chops the nuts very quickly. Also, bananas *(slice)* _____ 16 _____ 17 _____ 18 in our new computer-controlled slicing machine.

When the nuts and bananas are ready, they *(add)* _____ 19 _____ 20 to the sugar and cream in a special machine that *(invent)* _____ 21 _____ 22 by Betty a few years ago.

The ice cream *(keep)* _____ 23 _____ 24 in a large cold room until it *(sent)* _____ 25 _____ 26 by trucks all over the country.

That is the end of our tour. Thank you for visiting our factory, and we invite you to go to our tasting room, where our delicious ice cream can *(enjoy)* _____ 27 _____ 28 by all our visitors.

Q WHAT DOES IT MEAN?

Choose the correct answer.

1. I've got to take in my suit.
   - (a.) It's too big.
   - b. It's too small.
   - c. It's too hot.

2. You're required to go to the meeting.
   - a. You might go to the meeting.
   - b. You don't have to go to the meeting.
   - c. You have to go to the meeting.

3. Lois ran up a big phone bill.
   - a. She talked on the telephone a lot.
   - b. She didn't use her cell phone.
   - c. The phone company gave her a phone.

4. Ms. Johnson was promoted.
   - a. She was hired.
   - b. She was given a more important job.
   - c. She was fired.

5. Parking is permitted here.
   - a. You can't park here.
   - b. You can park here.
   - c. You have to park here.

6. Tom is distributing the mail right now.
   - a. He's giving it to everyone.
   - b. He's sending it to everyone.
   - c. He's opening the mail for everyone.

7. I was rejected by Harvard University.
   - a. I'll work there next year.
   - b. I'll be a student there next year.
   - c. I'll attend another college next year.

8. You'll be allowed to vote when you're older.
   - a. You'll be required to vote.
   - b. You'll be permitted to vote.
   - c. You'll want to vote.

9. She was offered the position.
   - a. She was given the job.
   - b. She was told about the position.
   - c. She was taken off the position.

10. Where are the decorations?
    - a. They've already been offered.
    - b. They've already been set.
    - c. They've already been hung up.

11. This is a beautiful portrait.
    - a. Who directed it?
    - b. Who invented it?
    - c. Who painted it?

12. I'm going overseas to work.
    - a. My boss is going to watch me.
    - b. I'm going to work in another country.
    - c. I'm going to work near the water.

13. I'm confident about the future.
    - a. I'm concerned about the future.
    - b. I'm confused about the future.
    - c. I'm positive about the future.

14. My son was chosen "Student of the Month."
    - a. He must be afraid.
    - b. He must be thrilled.
    - c. He must be hung up.

R LISTENING

Listen and choose the correct answer.

1. (a.) When will it be finished?
   - b. When was it finished?

2. a. When will it be ready?
   - b. How long ago did you finish?

3. a. They've been made.
   - b. They're being made.

4. a. I didn't receive mine.
   - b. Someone is distributing them.

5. a. It's being set up.
   - b. It's been set up.

6. a. I see. When will it be ready?
   - b. Good. I'll come over right away.

7. a. When will they be ready?
   - b. How long have they been ready?

8. a. I don't want to disturb them.
   - b. How long ago did you feed them?

A. Complete the sentences.

Ex. My son can swim very well. ___He's___ ___swum___ for many years.

1. Can you speak Chinese? I can speak it very well. _____ _____ it for many years.

2. Can you ride horses? My daughter _____ _____ horses for a long time.

3. When did you take your break? I _____ _____ my break yet.

4. When are you going to eat lunch? I'm hungry. I _____ _____ lunch yet.

5. When are you going to write your composition? I _____ _____ mine yet.

   Bob _____ his composition a little while ago.

6. How long _____ you and your husband _____ married?

7. My daughter _____ _____ studying English for the past few hours.

8. Paul didn't see a movie last weekend. He _____ _____ a movie the weekend before.

9. By the time I got to the plane, it _____ already _____ off.

10. I'm sorry to hear that Debbie and her boyfriend broke up. They _____ _____
    _____ out for several years.

B. Complete the sentences.

could have	might have	must have	should have	shouldn't have

(give)   *Ex.* You ___shouldn't___ ___have___ ___given___ Howard eggs for breakfast. He's
            allergic to them.

(practice)   **1.** Boris has won every chess game he's played today. He _____ _____

            _____ a lot.

(do)   **2.** I don't have anything to wear today. I _____ _____ _____ my laundry.

(leave)   **3.** Timmy can't find his homework. He _____ _____ _____ it at home,

            or he _____ _____ _____ it on the bus. He can't remember.

(build)   **4.** The Ace Corporation _____ _____ _____ their office building
            anywhere. It was a mistake to build it here.

(study)   **5.** You did very well on your test. You _____ _____ _____ a lot.

(wear)   **6.** It's hot in here. I _____ _____ _____ a heavy sweater
to work today.

(feed)   **7.** You _____ _____ _____ Rex. He's been hungry all morning.

(fall)   **8.** Terry shouldn't have stood on that broken chair. She _____ _____
_____.

(spend)   **9.** I _____ _____ _____ ten dollars, or I _____ _____ _____
twelve dollars. I can't remember.

C.   Complete the sentences.

(write)   *Ex.* This poem ____was____ ____written____ in 2001.

(draw)   **1.** This picture _____ _____ by a famous artist.

(repair) **2.** I can't drive my car to work. _____ still _____ _____.

(give)   **3.** My wife _____ _____ _____ a raise twice this year.

(teach)   **4.** Every student should _____ _____ a foreign language.

(do)   **5.** Nobody has to do the dishes. _____ already _____ _____.

(take in) **6.** Your pants aren't ready yet. _____ still _____ _____.

(choose) **7.** Margaret _____ _____ "Employee of the Year."

(make)   **8.** This is a very interesting novel. I think it should _____ _____ into
a movie.

(send)   **9.** Grandma is still in the hospital. She _____ _____ _____
home yet.

D.   Listening

Listen and choose the correct answer.

Ex. (a.) When was it completed?
    b. When will it be completed?

1. a. When will you finish taking them?
    b. When did you finish taking them?

2. a. How much longer will it take?
    b. How long ago did you hang them up?

3. a. They're being made.
    b. They've been made.

4. a. When was it completed?
    b. When will it be done?

5. a. Good. I'll pick it up soon.
    b. When will it be ready?

A. Were you just talking to George and Janet on the phone?

B. Yes. They called from California.

A. How are they?

B. They're fine.

A. The last time I heard from them, they were building a new house. Where are they living now?

B. I don't know _____<u>where they're living now</u>_____ [1]. They didn't say.

A. Where is Janet working?

B. I have no idea _____ [2]. She didn't say.

A. How are their children?

B. I'm not sure _____ [3]. They didn't say.

A. Tell me about George. When will he be starting his new job?

B. I don't know _____ [4]. He didn't say.

A. I really miss George and Janet. When are they going to come to New York?

B. I'm not sure _____ [5]. They didn't say.

A. When will their new house be finished?

B. I don't know _____ [6]. They didn't say.

A. What have they been doing since we saw them last summer?

B. I have no idea _____ [7]. They didn't say.

A. Why haven't they e-mailed us?

B. I'm not sure _____ [8]. They didn't say.

A. This is ridiculous! I'm going to call them tonight. What's their telephone number?

B. I'm sorry. I don't know _____ [9]. They didn't say.

1. A. What does this painting mean?

   B. I have no idea _____ *what this painting means* _____.

2. A. Why does Robert always get to school so early?

   B. I don't know _____.

3. A. When did the ice cream truck come by?

   B. I have no idea _____.

4. A. Where does Margaret work?

   B. I don't remember _____.

5. A. How did Sam break his arm?

   B. I don't know _____.

6. A. Why did Alice rewrite her novel?

   B. I have no idea _____.

7. A. What time does the concert begin?

   B. I'm not sure _____.

8. A. When does the bank open tomorrow?

   B. I have no idea _____.

9. A. What did we do in French class yesterday?

   B. I can't remember _____.

10. A. Where did Mom and Dad go?

    B. I have no idea _____.

11. A. How much does a quart of milk cost?

    B. I don't know _____.

A. Daddy, when did you learn to drive?

B. I can't remember _____ when I learned to drive _____ [1].
It was a long time ago.

A. Why doesn't Grandma drive?

B. I don't know _____ [2].
You'll have to ask her.

A. Daddy, I've been thinking . . . Why is the sky blue?

B. I don't know _____ [3].

A. How do birds learn to fly?

B. I'm not sure _____ [4].

A. Why are clouds white?

B. I don't know _____ [5].

A. What time does the zoo open tomorrow?

B. I'm sorry. I don't know _____ [6].

A. Daddy, do you remember the mouse that was in our attic last winter?

B. Yes, I do.

A. Where is that mouse now?

B. I don't know _____ [7].

A. Daddy, why _____ [8] ?

B. I have no idea _____ [9].

A. Daddy, when _____ [10] ?

B. I don't remember _____ [11].

A. When will we be home?

B. I hope we'll be home soon.

D WHAT ARE THEY SAYING?

1. Do you know _____?
   - (a.) what time it is
   - b. what time is it

2. Could you possibly tell me _____?
   - a. when will the train arrive
   - b. when the train will arrive

3. Can you tell me _____?
   - a. where do they live
   - b. where they live

4. I'm not sure _____.
   - a. how long they're going to stay
   - b. how long are they going to stay

5. I'm sorry. I have no idea _____.
   - a. when will she be back
   - b. when she'll be back

6. Could you possibly tell me _____?
   - a. how I can get there from here
   - b. how can I get there from here

7. I can't remember _____.
   - a. why does she want to talk to me
   - b. why she wants to talk to me

8. Do you have any idea _____?
   - a. whose glasses are these
   - b. whose glasses these are

9. Could you please tell me _____?
   - a. how much this costs
   - b. how much does this cost

10. I don't remember _____.
    - a. what are our plans for the weekend
    - b. what our plans are for the weekend

E LISTENING

Listen and decide what is being talked about.

1. (a.) a bus
   b. a movie

2. a. a word
   b. a person

3. a. a cake
   b. a photograph

4. a. a bicycle
   b. a car

5. a. a movie
   b. a train

6. a. a plane ticket
   b. a VCR

7. a. the packages
   b. the restrooms

8. a. the books
   b. the animals

F GRAMMARRAP: *Do You Know How Long This Flight Will Take?*

Listen. Then clap and practice.

A. Do you know   how long   this flight   will take?

Do you know   what kind of   food   they'll make?

Do you know   what movie   they'll show   on the plane?

Do you know   what time   we'll get   to Spain?

B. I don't know   how long   this flight   will take.

I'm not sure   what kind of   food   they'll make.

I don't know   what movie   they'll show   on the plane.

I have no   idea when we'll get   to Spain.

G YOU DECIDE: *What Are They Saying?*

Answer the questions with any vocabulary you wish.

1. *How much does this bicycle cost?*

A. Can you tell me _____ how much _____
   _____ this bicycle costs _____ ?

B. ....

   ....

2. *Where is the nearest clinic?*

A. Could you possibly tell me _____
   _____ ?

B. ....

   ....

3. *Whose cell phone is this?*

A. Do you have any idea _____
   _____ ?

B. ....

   ....

4. *Why have you been late to work all week?*

A. Could you tell me _____
   _____ ?

B. ....

   ....

5. *When will my dog be ready?*

A. Can you tell me _____
   _____ ?

B. ....

   ....

6.

How long have we been driving?

A. Do you have any idea _____

_____ ?

B. _____

_____

7.

Why is Johnny sitting in a puddle?

A. Can you tell me _____

_____ ?

B. _____

_____

8.

When does the post office open?

A. Do you by any chance know _____

_____ ?

B. _____

_____

9.

What's in the "Chicken Surprise Casserole"?

A. Could you please tell me _____

_____ ?

B. _____

_____

10.

When will you be getting out of here?

A. Do you know _____

_____ ?

B. _____

_____

Listen. Then clap and practice.

A.   What   did he do?

B.   I don't know   what he did.

A.   Why   did he hide?

B.   I don't know   why he hid.

A.   Where   did he go?

B.   I don't know   where he went.

A.   What   did he spend?

B.   I don't know   what he spent.

A.   What   did she say?

B.   I don't know   what she said.

A.   What   did she read?

B.   I don't know   what she read.

A.   Where   was her purse?

B.   I don't know   where it was.

A.   What   does she do?

B.   I don't know   what she does.

A.   What   did they buy?

B.   I don't know   what they bought.

A.   What   did they bring?

B.   I don't know   what they brought.

A.   What   did they sell?

B.   I don't know   what they sold.

A.   Who   did they tell?

B.   I'm not sure   who they told.

I WHAT ARE THEY SAYING?

1. Do you know _____?
   a. whether parking is permitted here *(circled)*
   b. if is parking permitted here

2. Can you tell me _____?
   a. if will the library be open tomorrow
   b. if the library will be open tomorrow

3. Do you by any chance know _____?
   a. whether it's going to rain this weekend
   b. if is it going to rain this weekend

4. Could you please tell me _____?
   a. whether does this bus stop at the mall
   b. if this bus stops at the mall

5. Do you have any idea _____?
   a. if they were upset
   b. whether were they upset

6. Can you possibly tell me _____?
   a. if the bus will be arriving soon
   b. if will the bus be arriving soon

7. Do you know _____?
   a. whether they're coming to our party
   b. if are they coming to our party

8. Can you tell me _____?
   a. whether did I pass the test
   b. if I passed the test

9. Does our superintendent know _____?
   a. if the plumber is coming soon
   b. whether is the plumber coming soon

10. Do you by any chance know _____?
    a. whether I'm going to be fired
    b. if am I going to be fired

J LISTENING

Listen and decide where these people are.

1. a. a beach *(circled)*
   b. a parking lot

2. a. a department store
   b. a laundromat

3. a. a playground
   b. a theater

4. a. a parking garage
   b. a parking lot

5. a. a train station
   b. a gas station

6. a. a classroom
   b. a restaurant

7. a. a bakery
   b. a lake

8. a. a post office
   b. a supermarket

9. a. a zoo
   b. a bank

K GRAMMARRAP: *Gossip*

Listen. Then clap and practice.

A. Do you know   whether David   is dating   Diane?

   Do you know   if Irene   is married   to Stan?

   Can you tell me   if Bob   is in love   with Elaine?

   Do you know   if they really   met   on a plane?

B. I don't know   whether David   is dating   Diane.

   I'm not sure   if Irene   is married   to Stan.

   I can't tell you   if Bob   is in love   with Elaine.

   And I really   don't know   if they met   on a plane.

L RENTING AN APARTMENT

Questions to Ask the Rental Agent

1. Has it been rented yet?
2. Is there an elevator in the building?
3. Does the kitchen have a microwave?
4. Are pets allowed?
5. Is there a bus stop nearby?
6. Does the landlord live in the building?
7. Does the apartment have an Internet connection?
8. _____
9. Can I see the apartment today?

A. Hello. This is Mildred Williams. I'm calling about the apartment at 119 Appleton Street. Can you tell me _____ if it's been rented yet _____ [1]?

B. Not yet. But several people have called. Would you like to see it?

A. Yes, but first I have a few questions. According to the newspaper, the apartment is on the fifth floor. Can you tell me _____ [2]?

B. Yes. As a matter of fact, there are two elevators.

A. I see. And do you know _____ [3]?

B. It has a dishwasher, but it doesn't have a microwave.

A. Also, do you by any chance know _____ [4]?

B. I don't know. I'll check with the landlord.

A. Can you tell me _____ [5]?

B. Yes. The downtown bus stops in front of the building.

A. That's very convenient. Can you also tell me _____ [6]?

B. Yes, he does. And all the tenants say he takes very good care of the apartments.

A. Do you know _____ [7]?

B. Yes, it does. It's a very modern building.

A. And could you please tell me _____ [8]?

B. I'm not sure. I'll have to find out and let you know.

A. You've been very helpful. Do you know _____ [9]?

B. Certainly. Stop by our office at noon, and I'll take you to see it.

YOU DECIDE: *The College Visit*

Ask the Admissions Office

1. How many students go to your school?
2. Do I have to take any special examinations?
3. How do I get an application form?
4. Are the classes difficult?
5. Are the dormitories noisy?
6. What kind of food do you serve in the cafeteria?
7. What do students do on weekends?
8. How much does your school cost?
9. ....
10. ....

Hello. My name is Robert Johnson, and I'm interested in studying at your college. I'd like to ask you a few questions.

Certainly. My name is Ms. Lopez. I'll be happy to answer your questions.

1. Can you tell me _____ how many _____

_____ students go to _____

_____ your school _____ ?

....
....
....

2. Do you know _____

_____

_____ ?

....
....
....

3. Can you tell me _____

_____

_____ ?

....
....
....

(continued)

4. Also, could you tell me _____

_____

_____ ?

_____

_____

_____

5. I've heard the dormitories are large.

Do you know _____

_____ ?

_____

_____

_____

6. Do you by any chance know _____

_____

_____ ?

_____

_____

_____

_____

7. Can you tell me _____

_____

_____ ?

_____

_____

_____

8. I'm a little worried about expenses.

Can you tell me _____

_____ ?

_____

_____

_____

9. Can you also tell me _____

_____

_____ ?

_____

_____

_____

10. And do you know _____

_____

_____ ?

_____

_____

_____

A IF

1. My doctor says that if I exercise every day, _____ healthier.
   a. I'm
   b. I'll be *(circled)*

2. If Alan _____ stuck in traffic today, he'll be late for work.
   a. gets
   b. will get

3. If _____ the lottery tomorrow, I'll have a lot of money.
   a. I'll win
   b. I win

4. If we get to the theater early, _____ to get good seats.
   a. we're able
   b. we'll be able

5. If you decide to apply for a promotion, _____ probably get it.
   a. you'll
   b. you

6. If they _____ to pay the rent next week, their landlord will call them.
   a. forget
   b. will forget

7. If Amanda oversleeps this morning, _____ the bus.
   a. she misses
   b. she'll miss

8. If you _____ for Jack Strickland, you'll have an honest president.
   a. will vote
   b. vote

9. If the weather is warm, _____ to the beach tomorrow.
   a. I'll go
   b. I go

10. If _____ Melanie, I'm sure I'll be happy for the rest of my life.
    a. I'll marry
    b. I marry

B SCRAMBLED SENTENCES

1. late   she'll   lot   tonight.   to   at   If   do,   has   work   Barbara   the   a   office

   _____ If Barbara has a lot to do _____ , _____ she'll work late at the office tonight. _____

2. attic   energetic,   he'll   his   If   this   clean   Tom   weekend.   feels

   _____ , _____

3. cake   about   decide   have   to   If   diet,   I'll   I   dessert.   forget   for   my

   _____ , _____

4. income   weather   tomorrow,   the   home   nice   If   I'll   forms.   stay   isn't   my   tax   fill   out   and

   _____ , _____

5. clinic   see   I   If   I'll   cold   Dr. Lopez.   still   a   go   tomorrow,   have   the   to   and

   _____ , _____

Activity Workbook   **57**

1. If I'm in a good mood, _____.

2. _____ if I'm in a bad mood.

3. If _____,
   he'll speak more confidently.

4. _____, you'll be disappointed.

5. If I can afford it, _____.

6. _____, we'll be very surprised.

7. If I'm invited to the White House, _____.

8. You'll get lost if _____.

9. You'll regret it if _____.

10. _____, you won't regret it.

D **LISTENING**

Listen and complete the sentences.

1. a. . . . I go to a movie.
   (b.) . . . I'll go to a concert.

2. a. . . . I'm on a diet.
   b. . . . I'll stay on a diet.

3. a. . . . we miss the train.
   b. . . . we'll miss the train.

4. a. . . . they rent a DVD.
   b. . . . they'll go dancing.

5. a. . . . we're late for school.
   b. . . . we'll have to walk to work.

6. a. . . . you miss the test.
   b. . . . you'll miss the exam.

7. a. . . . the teacher is boring.
   b. . . . the teacher will be bored.

8. a. . . . it isn't too expensive.
   b. . . . it won't cost as much.

9. a. . . . he complains to his boss.
   b. . . . he'll quit his job.

10. a. . . . you'll decide to visit me.
    b. . . . you want to go jogging.

11. a. . . . she has time.
    b. . . . she won't be too busy.

12. a. . . . I take them to the doctor.
    b. . . . I'll call the nurse.

13. a. . . . we have too much work.
    b. . . . we'll be too busy.

14. a. . . . she doesn't study.
    b. . . . she won't work harder.

Listen. Then clap and practice.

If it rains,   I'll take   a taxi.
If it snows,   I'll take   the train.
If it's sunny,   I'll ride my   brand new   bike,
The one   that was made in Spain.

If it's hot,   they'll wear   their sandals.
If it's cold,   they'll wear   their boots.
If the weather is   nice,   they'll go   to the beach.
And swim   in their bathing   suits.

If the party   starts   at seven   o'clock,
We'll plan   to arrive   at eight.
If we're tired, we'll come home   early.
If we aren't,   we'll get home   late.

If I'm hungry,   I'll have   a midnight   snack.
If I'm sleepy,   I'll go to   bed.
If I'm wide   awake,   I'll stay up   late
With a book   I haven't   read.

THEY MIGHT

1. Remember, if you plan to have your wedding outside, it _____ .
   a. might rain
   b. rains

2. If we take the children to visit their grandparents, they _____ sore throats.
   a. might give
   b. might give them

3. If Marvin breaks up with Susan, he _____ trouble finding another girlfriend.
   a. might have
   b. might be

4. If you go to bed too late, _____ have trouble getting up on time for work.
   a. you might
   b. you'll might

5. If you don't take that job, you _____ it for the rest of your life.
   a. regret
   b. might regret

6. If you have trouble seeing well, _____ rejected by the army.
   a. I might be
   b. you might be

7. If our teacher tries to break up that fight, _____ .
   a. he might get hurt
   b. he might hurt

8. If we take the children to see the skeletons at the museum, they _____ .
   a. might scare
   b. might be scared

G **YOU DECIDE:** *What Might Happen?*

| if _____ might _____ |

1. A. I still have a cold, and I feel terrible.

   B. That's too bad. Why don't you drink tea with honey?

   If _____you drink_____ tea with honey, _____you might_____

   _____ feel better soon _____ .

2. A. Should I put more pepper in the casserole?

   B. I'm not sure. If _____ more pepper in

   the casserole, _____

   _____ .

3. A. It's the boss's birthday tomorrow. Why don't we send her flowers?

B. I'm not sure. If _____

her flowers, _____

_____.

4. A. I'm thinking of skipping English class today.

B. I don't think you should. If _____

English class, _____

_____.

5. A. Mrs. Wong, I really enjoy taking violin lessons with you. I'm going to practice every day.

B. I'm happy to hear that. If _____

every day, _____

_____.

6. A. Good-bye!

B. Please don't stay away too long! If _____

away for a long time, _____

_____.

7. A. Danny, I don't think you should go hiking in the woods by yourself.

B. Why not?

A. If _____ by yourself, _____

_____.

8. A. You've known each other for only a few weeks. I don't think you should get married so soon.

B. Why not?

A. If _____ so soon, _____

_____.

YOU DECIDE: *What Might Happen?*

if _____ might _____

1. A. I don't think I'll ever learn to speak English well.

   B. Why don't you _____?

   If _____,

   _____ *you might learn* _____ to speak English better.

2. A. I feel exhausted.

   B. Why don't you _____?

   If _____,

   _____ more energetic.

3. A. I can't fall asleep.

   B. Maybe you should _____.

   If _____,

   _____ more easily.

4. A. I've been feeling depressed lately.

   B. I think you should _____.

   If _____,

   _____ a lot better.

5. A. My girlfriend and I had a terrible argument. She won't go out with me anymore.

   B. Why don't you _____?

   If _____,

   _____ with you again.

I WHAT'S THE POLITE ANSWER?

1. I like to play tennis every day.
   I hope it _____ tomorrow.
   a. rains
   b. doesn't rain

2. My daughter sometimes rides her bicycle too fast.
   I hope she _____ hurt.
   a. gets
   b. doesn't get

3. I'm going to a party this Saturday night.
   I hope you _____ a good time.
   a. have
   b. don't have

4. My daughter's wedding is next week.
   I hope the weather _____ bad.
   a. is
   b. isn't

5. I love my new flowerpot.
   I hope it _____ and break.
   a. falls
   b. doesn't fall

6. I'm going to refuse to marry Jonathan.
   I hope you _____ it later.
   a. don't regret
   b. regret

7. My poodle loves to splash in puddles.
   I hope she _____ dirty.
   a. gets
   b. doesn't get

J LISTENING

Listen and choose the polite response.

1. a. I hope so.
   b. I hope not.

2. a. I hope so.
   b. I hope not.

3. a. I hope so.
   b. I hope not.

4. a. I hope so.
   b. I hope not.

5. a. I hope so.
   b. I hope not.

6. a. I hope so.
   b. I hope not.

7. a. I hope so.
   b. I hope not.

8. a. I hope so.
   b. I hope not.

9. a. I hope so.
   b. I hope not.

10. a. I hope so.
    b. I hope not.

11. a. I hope so.
    b. I hope not.

12. a. I hope so.
    b. I hope not.

1. A. Do you think it will rain tomorrow?

B. I hope not. If _____it rains_____ tomorrow, we'll have to cancel our picnic.

And if ___we have to cancel___ the picnic, everybody will be disappointed.

A. You're right. I hope _____it doesn't rain_____ tomorrow.

2. A. Do you think it'll be cold tonight?

B. I hope not. If _____ tonight, our car won't start in the morning.

And if our car _____ in the morning, we'll have to walk to work.

A. You're right. I hope _____ tonight.

3. A. Do you think it'll be a hot summer?

B. I hope not. If _____ a hot summer, the office will be very warm.

And if the office _____ very warm, it'll be impossible to work.

A. You're right. I hope _____ a hot summer.

4. A. Do you think our TV will be at the repair shop for a long time?

B. I hope not. If our TV _____ at the repair shop for a long time, we won't have anything to do in the evening.

And if _____ anything to do in the evening, we'll go crazy.

A. You're right. I hope _____ at the repair shop for a long time.

1. A. I've gotten up early every day this semester, and I haven't missed anything important.

    B. That's great! I hope get up early again tomorrow.

        It's the last class and the last exam.

    A. I know. [I / I'll] definitely get up early tomorrow.

2. A. Do you think tomorrow's exam will be difficult?

    B. I hope not. If [it will be / it's] difficult, I'll probably do poorly.

        And if [I do / I'll do] poorly, my parents [are / will be] disappointed.

3. A. What happened? You overslept and missed the exam!

    B. I have a terrible cold. I'm going to call my professor now.

        I hope she [isn't / doesn't be] angry. If she [will be / is] angry, [she / she'll]

        give me a bad grade.

4. A. What did your professor say?

    B. She said she hopes [I / I'll] feel better soon. If [I / I'll]

        feel better tomorrow, [I / I'll] take the exam at 2 o'clock.

        If [I'll be / I'm] still sick tomorrow, [I / I'll] take the exam on

        Wednesday morning.

M WHAT IF?

1. If my apartment _____ bigger, I would be more comfortable.
   a. was
   b. were *(circled)*

2. If you _____ more, you'd be stronger.
   a. exercised
   b. exercise

3. If it were a nice day today, _____ to the park.
   a. we'll go
   b. we'd go

4. If I _____ more, I'd be happy working here.
   a. got paid
   b. get paid

5. If I were going to be here this weekend, _____ a movie with you.
   a. I'll see
   b. I'd see

6. If _____ more friends in our apartment building, we'd be much happier living there.
   a. we had
   b. we have

7. If you _____ up your engine more often, you'd get better gas mileage.
   a. tune
   b. tuned

8. If _____ more, you'd feel more energetic.
   a. you sleep
   b. you slept

9. If she were more careful, _____ a better driver.
   a. she'd be
   b. she'll

10. If you _____ older, we'd let you stay up later.
    a. were
    b. are

11. If Rick and Rita had more in common, I'm sure _____ get along better with each other.
    a. they'd
    b. they

12. If the president _____ more concerned about the environment, he'd do something about it.
    a. is
    b. were

N LISTENING

Listen and choose the correct answer based on what you hear.

1. a. George probably feels energetic.
   b. George probably feels tired. *(circled)*

2. a. The musicians aren't very talented.
   b. The musicians are talented.

3. a. He's very aggressive.
   b. He isn't aggressive enough.

4. a. Bob's car needs to be tuned up.
   b. Bob's car doesn't need to be tuned up.

5. a. They have a lot in common.
   b. They don't have a lot in common.

6. a. She cares a lot about her students.
   b. She isn't a very good teacher.

7. a. Their school needs more computers.
   b. Their school has enough computers.

8. a. The cookies aren't sweet enough.
   b. The cookies are sweet enough.

1. A. Mr. Montero, why doesn't my daughter Lisa get better grades in English?

B. She doesn't ___*do her homework carefully*___ ,

she doesn't _____ ,

she doesn't _____ ,

and she doesn't _____ .

If she ___*did her homework carefully*___ ,

if she _____ ,

if she _____ ,

and if she _____ ,

_____ much better grades. She's a very intelligent girl.

2. A. What's wrong with me, Dr. Green? Why don't I feel energetic anymore? I'm only thirty years old, and I feel exhausted all the time.

B. You don't _____ ,

you don't _____ ,

you don't _____ ,

and you _____ .

If you _____ ,

if you _____ ,

if you _____ ,

and if you _____ less,

_____ much more energetic.

(continued)

3. A. How do you like your new car?

B. It's better than my old one, but I really don't like it very much.

A. That's too bad. Why not?

B. It doesn't _____,

it doesn't _____,

I'm not _____,

and my husband _____.

If _____,

if _____,

if _____,

and if _____,

_____ my car a lot more. I guess all cars have their problems.

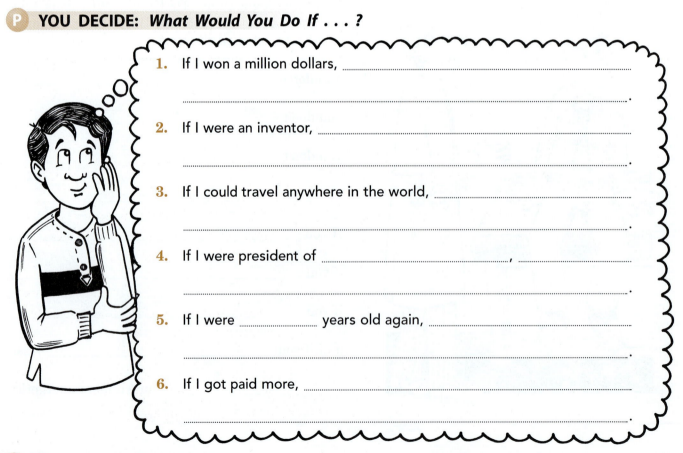

P YOU DECIDE: *What Would You Do If . . . ?*

1. If I won a million dollars, _____
_____.

2. If I were an inventor, _____
_____.

3. If I could travel anywhere in the world, _____
_____.

4. If I were president of _____, _____
_____.

5. If I were _____ years old again, _____
_____.

6. If I got paid more, _____
_____.

MATCHING

_d_ **1.** If this party weren't so boring,

_____ **2.** If I didn't hate working here,

_____ **3.** If I didn't have a big exam tomorrow,

_____ **4.** If I weren't such a careless driver,

_____ **5.** If I weren't a vegetarian,

_____ **6.** If I weren't always late,

_____ **7.** If I weren't allergic to cats,

_____ **8.** If they weren't in love,

_____ **9.** If I didn't like the outdoors so much,

_____ **10.** If your car weren't so old,

_____ **11.** If we didn't make so much noise,

a. I wouldn't have so many accidents.

b. I wouldn't be sneezing so much.

c. you wouldn't have so many problems with it.

d. we wouldn't want to leave so early.

e. people wouldn't have to wait for me.

f. I wouldn't go hiking every weekend.

g. I wouldn't be so nervous.

h. I wouldn't always order vegetables.

i. the neighbors wouldn't be complaining.

j. I wouldn't be looking for another job.

k. they wouldn't hold hands all the time.

R **YOU DECIDE:** *What Are They Saying?*

1. I haven't had anything to eat all day. — You must __be very hungry__.

2. My son didn't get accepted into the college he wanted. — That's too bad. He must _____.

3. You've been driving for the past six hours. You must _____.

(continued)

4. Ted went out with Jean on Monday, with Jane on Tuesday, with Joan on Wednesday, and with Jen on Thursday.

He must _____
_____.

5. My neighbors spend every weekend at the beach. Last weekend they went water-skiing, and this weekend they're going sailing.

They must really _____
_____.

6. My daughter got the highest grade in her class.

She must _____,
and you must _____.

7. I'm going to miss something important in school tomorrow.

Really? You must _____
_____.

8. Last weekend I made three pies and four cakes. This weekend I'm going to make cookies.

No kidding! You must _____
_____.

9. My son is going to be the star of his school play this weekend.

He must _____,
and you must _____.

10. My husband has been watching a football game on TV all day, and there's a big game he's going to watch tonight.

He must really _____,
and you must _____.

11. You've been complaining about this movie since it started. You

must _____
_____.

1. Rita works overtime every night. She must want to get a raise.

   If _____*she didn't want to get*_____ a raise,

   she _____*wouldn't work overtime*_____ every night.

2. Jimmy is hiding under the bed. He must be afraid of the dark.

   If _____ of the dark,

   he _____ under the bed.

3. Stephanie runs ten miles every day. She must want to win the marathon this weekend.

   If _____ the marathon,

   she _____ ten miles every day.

4. My friend Gary wears a green shirt every day. He must love the color green.

   If _____ the color green,

   he _____ a green shirt every day.

5. My sister Karen makes a lot of mistakes on her homework. She's very careless.

   If _____,

   she _____ a lot of mistakes on her homework.

6. Gregory goes to the health club every day. He must want to lose weight.

   If _____ weight,

   he _____ to the health club every day.

(continued)

7. Andy is all dressed up. He must have a big date tonight.

If _____ a big date tonight,

he _____ all dressed up.

8. I'm driving very slowly because there's a police car behind me.

If _____ a police car behind me.

I _____ so slowly.

T **YOU DECIDE:** *Why Don't Mr. and Mrs. Miller Like Their Neighborhood?*

Mr. and Mrs. Miller don't like their neighborhood because ....,

....,

....,

....,

and ....

If _____,

if _____,

if _____,

and if _____,

_____ their neighborhood a lot more.

U GRAMMARRAP: *If I Lived Near the Sea*

Listen. Then clap and practice.

If I lived   near the sea,   I'd swim   every day.

If I had   a guitar,   I'd learn   how to play.

If I were younger   and stronger,   I'd lift   heavy weights.

If I weren't   so shy,   I'd go out   on more dates.

If Tom could speak Spanish,   he'd travel   to Spain.

If Ann had   a raincoat,   she'd walk   in the rain.

If Jack were   an actor,   he'd star   in a play.

If we weren't   so busy,   we'd go sailing   today.

V GRAMMARRAP: *If I Didn't Like Desserts*

Listen. Then clap and practice.

If I didn't like   desserts,   I wouldn't eat   cake.

If I didn't like   meat,   I wouldn't eat   steak.

If I weren't   so happy,   I wouldn't   be smiling.

If I weren't working   late,   I wouldn't be   filing.

If she didn't like   pets,   she wouldn't have   a cat.

If he didn't play   baseball,   he wouldn't have   a bat.

If they weren't   so clumsy,   they wouldn't always   fall.

If you weren't   my friend,   I wouldn't always   call.

Activity Workbook   **73**

Listen to each word and then say it.

1. <u>m</u>ight
2. <u>m</u>aybe
3. <u>m</u>ushroo<u>m</u>
4. su<u>mm</u>er
5. i<u>m</u>prove
6. re<u>m</u>e<u>m</u>ber
7. poe<u>m</u>s
8. war<u>m</u>
9. fa<u>m</u>ous

10. <u>n</u>ight
11. <u>n</u>ever
12. <u>n</u>oo<u>n</u>
13. su<u>nn</u>y
14. Su<u>n</u>day
15. i<u>n</u>crease
16. explai<u>n</u>
17. telepho<u>n</u>e
18. fa<u>n</u>tastic

X N O R <u>M</u> A <u>N</u>'S BROKEN KEYBOARD

Norman's keyboard is broken. The m's and the n's don't always work. Fill in the missing m's and n's and then read Norman's letters aloud.

1.

Dear A<u>m</u>y,

   I really e <u>n</u> joyed visiti__g you i__ your __ew apart__e__t. It's o__e of the __icest apart__e__ts I've ever see__. I liked everythi__g about it: the __oder__ kitche__ a__d bathroo__, the elega__t livi__g roo__ and di__i__g roo__, a__d the su____y bedroo__s. I ca__'t believe there's eve__ a garde__ with le__o__ and ora__ge trees i__ fro__t of the buildi__g. I thi__k you'll be very happy i__ your __ew __eighborhood. It's certai__ly very co__ve__ie__t to be so __ear a super__arket, a __ovie theater, a__d a trai__ statio__.

   I'__ looki__g forward to seei__g you agai__ a__d __eeti__g your __ew __eighbors.

                Si__cerely,

                __or__an

2.

To Who_ It _ay Co_cer_:

I a_ writi_g to reco_ _e_d _ax _iller for the job of co_puter progra_ _er at the ABC Co_puter Co_pa_y. Duri_g the _i_e years I've k_ow_ hi_, he's bee_ a_ excelle_t e_ployee a_d a ki_d a_d ho_est frie_d. He's _ever _issed a day's work at our co_pa_y, a_d he's always bee_ o_ ti_e. But _ost i_porta_t, _ax _iller really u_dersta_ds what _akes a good co_puter progra_ _er.

Si_cerely,

_or_a_ Brow_

_a_ager

XYZ Co_puter Co_pa_y

3.

Dear Bria_,

I just fi_ished readi_g your _ost rece_t poe_s, a_d i_ _y opi_io_, they're a_azi_g. The poe_ about the e_viro_ _e_t is very origi_al, but _y favorite o_es are "_issi_g _y _other" a_d "U_der _y U_brella."

Accordi_g to _y wife a_d frie_ds, you're beco_i_g fa_ous i_ _a_y foreig_ cou_tries, a_d your poe_s are bei_g tra_slated i_to Russia_, Chi_ese, Ger_a_, Spa_ish, a_d Japa_ese. I thi_k that's fa_tastic!

Have you begu_ writi_g your _ew _ovel yet? I wo_der whe_ we'll be heari_g more about it.

_or_a_

4.

Dear _ichael,

Re_e_ber whe_ you explai_ed to _e how to _ake your _other's fa_ous chicke_ a_d _ushroo_ casserole? Well, I _ade so_e for di_ _er last _ight, a_d I'_ afraid so_ethi_g _ust have go_e wro_g. I _ight have bur_t the chicke_, or _aybe I did_'t put i_ e_ough o_io_s a_d _ushroo_s. I do_'t k_ow what happe_ed, but I k_ow I _ust have _ade so_e _istakes because _obody e_joyed it very _uch. To_ and _a_cy did_'t co_plai_, but they said yours was _uch _ore delicious.

Do you thi_k you could se_d your _other's recipe to _e by e-_ail so I ca_ try it again? Whe_ you explai_ed it to _e, I should have writte_ it dow_.

_or_a_

A. Fill in the blanks.

Ex. *(What time does the plane arrive?)*

Could you please tell me _____ <u>what time the plane arrives</u> _____?

1. *(When will the next train be leaving?)*

   Can you tell me _____?

2. *(Was Michael at work yesterday?)*

   Do you know _____?

3. *(How much does this suit cost?)*

   Can you please tell me _____?

4. *(Is there a laundromat nearby?)*

   Could you tell me _____?

5. *(Why did David get up so early?)*

   Do you know _____?

6. *(Did Martha take her medicine this morning?)*

   Do you know _____?

7. *(How long have we been waiting?)*

   Do you have any idea _____?

B. Complete the sentences.

Ex. If we can afford it, ____ <u>we'll take</u> ____ a vacation next summer.

1. I'll send you an e-mail if I _____ the time.

2. If Uncle Fred were more careful, _____ a better driver.

3. If Mrs. Bell didn't enjoy classical music, _____ to concerts every weekend.

4. If I _____ a raise soon, I'll complain to my supervisor.

5. If you stay up too late tonight, _____ get a good night's sleep.

6. We're having a picnic this Sunday. I hope _____ rain.

7. Tomorrow is the most important game of the year. I hope our team _____.

8. My parents _____ extremely disappointed if I fail tomorrow's French test.

9. If you _____ your dog more often, he wouldn't be so hungry.

C. Complete the sentences.

Ex. Albert doesn't have many friends because he isn't outgoing enough.

If he ___were___ more outgoing, ___he'd have___ a lot of friends.

1. Caroline feels tired all the time because she works too hard.

   If she _____ so hard, _____ so tired all the time.

2. David doesn't get good grades in school because he doesn't study enough.

   If he _____ more, _____ better grades.

3. Allison and Paul don't get along with each other because they don't have enough in common.

   If they _____ more in common, _____ better with each other.

4. Nellie is very careless. She makes a lot of mistakes when she types.

   If she _____ so careless, _____ a lot of mistakes.

D. Listening

Listen and complete the sentences.

Ex. a. . . . I'll play tennis.
    b. . . . I'd play tennis.

1. a. . . . I'd be late for work.
   b. . . . I'll be late for work.

2. a. . . . I wouldn't make so many mistakes.
   b. . . . I won't make so many mistakes.

3. a. . . . you didn't study for the test.
   b. . . . you don't study for the test.

4. a. . . . I'd see a movie.
   b. . . . I'll see a movie.

5. a. . . . she'll go out with you.
   b. . . . she'd go out with you.

A WHAT'S THE WORD?

1. I think the children _____ scared if the lights went out.
   a. will be
   b. would be *(circled)*

2. I think your parents would be angry if you _____ school tomorrow.
   a. skipped
   b. skip

3. I think Jim would be disappointed if I _____ his party.
   a. was missing
   b. missed

4. Do you think I would be happier if I _____ rich?
   a. was
   b. were

5. I think the children would be excited if it _____.
   a. snowed
   b. snows

6. I think the neighbors _____ annoyed if I turned on my CD player now.
   a. would be
   b. are going to be

7. I think this pizza would be better if it _____ more cheese on it.
   a. have
   b. had

8. I think we would be unhappy if our teacher _____ a test today.
   a. gave
   b. gives

9. Do you think Bob _____ jealous if I got into law school?
   a. would be
   b. is going to be

10. I think my sister would be upset if I _____ her new laptop computer.
    a. use
    b. used

B IF

1. I know I would be scared if a robber *(be)* ___were___ in my house.

2. Do you think Amy would be jealous if I *(go out)* _____ with her boyfriend?

3. I'm sure I would be concerned if I *(get lost)* _____ in New York City.

4. I'm positive Johnny would be upset if he *(have)* _____ the flu on his birthday.

5. I know that my doctor would be pleased if I *(eat)* _____ healthier foods.

6. I'd be very upset if I *(lose)* _____ the keys to my car.

7. My wife would be upset if I *(quit)* _____ my job.

8. All the neighbors would be unhappy if the landlord *(sell)* _____ our apartment building.

1. A. Do you think Mom would be happy if I ....

   .... ?

   B. Of course _____ she would _____ . _____ She'd be _____
   very happy. That's a wonderful idea.

2. A. Do you think Dad would be angry if I ....

   .... ?

   B. I'm sure _____ . _____
   very angry. That's a terrible idea.

3. A. Do you think the boss would be pleased if I ....

   .... ?

   B. I'm positive _____ . _____
   very pleased.

4. A. Do you think our grandchildren would be disappointed if we

   .... ?

   B. Of course _____ . _____
   very disappointed.

5. A. Do you think our teacher would be annoyed if we ....

   .... ?

   B. I'm afraid _____ . _____
   very annoyed.

6. A. Do you think my wife would be upset if I ....

   .... ?

   B. Of course _____ . _____
   very upset.

1. If I _____ you, I wouldn't miss
   Grandma's birthday party.
   a. was
   b. were ⓑ

2. If you _____ a gallon of ice cream, you'd
   probably feel sick.
   a. ate
   b. eat

3. If you always practiced the guitar at two
   in the morning, I'm sure _____ evicted
   from your building.
   a. you'll be
   b. you'd be

4. If I were you, _____ your children to
   play a musical instrument.
   a. I encourage
   b. I'd encourage

5. If you _____ at the meeting late, you'd
   probably be embarrassed.
   a. arrived
   b. arrive

6. If I _____ the money, I would definitely
   buy a better car.
   a. have
   b. had

7. If today were Saturday, _____ until
   noon.
   a. I'd sleep
   b. I'll sleep

8. If the mayor raised taxes, people _____
   vote for him in the next election.
   a. won't
   b. wouldn't

9. If he _____ me more often, I'd be very
   pleased.
   a. visits
   b. visited

10. To tell the truth, I _____ the phone if I
    were you.
    a. wouldn't answer
    b. won't answer

11. If you said you could come home
    tomorrow, _____ very happy.
    a. we're
    b. we'd be

12. If our teacher _____ nicer, I'm sure I'd
    get better grades.
    a. was
    b. were

E LISTENING

Listen and complete the sentences.

1. a. . . . you'll look very old.
   b. . . . you'd look very old. ⓑ

2. a. . . . I'll call you.
   b. . . . I'd call you.

3. a. . . . you'll probably get carsick.
   b. . . . you'd probably get carsick.

4. a. . . . I'll clean my yard.
   b. . . . I'd clean my yard.

5. a. . . . he'll be upset.
   b. . . . he'd probably be upset.

6. a. . . . you'll be very cold.
   b. . . . you'd be very cold.

7. a. . . . I won't be very happy.
   b. . . . I'm not very happy.

8. a. . . . you'll probably regret it.
   b. . . . you'd probably regret it.

9. a. . . . you'll miss something important.
   b. . . . you miss something important.

10. a. . . . you'll probably lose your shirt.
    b. . . . you'd probably lose your shirt.

11. a. . . . I'd call the landlord.
    b. . . . I'll call the landlord.

12. a. . . . you'd be very sorry.
    b. . . . you'll be very sorry.

PERSONAL OPINIONS

1. A. I'm thinking of going skating this afternoon.

   B. I wouldn't go skating this afternoon if I were you. It's very warm. If you ____went____ skating today, ____you'd____ probably ____fall____ into the pond.

2. A. I'm thinking of tuning up my car myself.

   B. I wouldn't do that. If I were you, _____ call Charlie, the mechanic. _____ definitely _____ _____ correctly.

3. A. I'm thinking of going to the prom with Larry.

   B. You are?! I wouldn't do that if I were you. If you _____ to the prom with Larry, _____ probably _____ a terrible time.

4. A. I'm thinking of painting my house red.

   B. Really? I wouldn't paint it red if I were you. If _____ your house red, _____ look awful!

5. A. I'm thinking of driving downtown this morning.

   B. I _____ downtown if I were you. If _____ downtown, _____ probably get stuck in a lot of traffic.

6. A. I'm thinking of having a party this weekend while my parents are away.

   B. I _____ a party if I were you. If _____ _____ a party, I'm sure your parents _____ very upset.

(continued)

7. A. I'm thinking of seeing the new Julie Richards movie this weekend.

B. To tell the truth, I _____ it if I were you.

It's terrible! If _____ it, _____ probably be very bored.

8. A. I'm thinking of buying a parrot.

B. I wouldn't buy a parrot if I _____ you. If _____

_____ a parrot, _____ make a lot of noise!

9. A. I'm thinking of ....

B. I wouldn't ....

If .... ,

....

G **GrammarRap:** *If I Were You*

Listen. Then clap and practice.

A. What color do you think I should paint my house?

B. If I were you, I'd paint it blue.

A. What time do you think I should leave for the plane?

B. If I were you, I'd leave at two.

A. What food do you think I should serve my guests?

B. If I were you, I'd serve them stew.

A. Where do you think I should go with my kids?

B. If I were you, I'd go to the zoo.

H WHAT DO THEY WISH?

1. The Johnson family has a small car. They wish they _____ a larger one.
   a. have
   (b.) had

2. I work the night shift at the factory. I wish I _____ the day shift.
   a. worked
   b. work

3. I'm disappointed with my new haircut. I _____ it weren't so short.
   a. wish
   b. wished

4. Barbara has two children. She wishes she _____ three.
   a. has
   b. had

5. I always forget to check the messages on my answering machine. I wish I _____ to check them.
   a. remembered
   b. . remember

6. My boyfriend is a cook. He _____ he were a mechanic.
   a. wishes
   b. wished

7. I'm sick and tired of working. I wish I _____ on vacation.
   a. was
   b. were

8. I live in Minnesota, but I wish I _____ in Florida.
   a. live
   b. lived

9. I send e-mails to my girlfriend every day. I wish she _____ back to me.
   a. wrote
   b. writes

10. I enjoy making big holiday meals for my family. I wish I _____ washing the dishes, too.
    a. enjoy
    b. enjoyed

I LISTENING

Listen and complete the conversations.

1. a. . . . it is.
   (b.) . . . it were.

2. a. . . . you talk more.
   b. . . . you talked less.

3. a. . . . it were easier.
   b. . . . I were easier.

4. a. . . . he daydreams more.
   b. . . . he daydreamed less.

5. a. . . . they're scarier.
   b. . . . they were scarier.

6. a. . . . you sang more softly.
   b. . . . you sing softly.

7. a. . . . it has e-mail.
   b. . . . it had e-mail.

8. a. . . . I worked near my house.
   b. . . . I work near my house.

9. a. . . . I was married.
   b. . . . I were married.

10. a. . . . it were larger.
    b. . . . it was smaller.

11. a. . . . he is working.
    b. . . . he were working.

12. a. . . . you called more often.
    b. . . . you call more often.

I WISH

1. ___I wish I felt___ better today.
I really don't feel well at all.

2. _____ it _____.
When it's 5:00, I can leave work.

3. _____
as well as my sister does. She has a
magnificent voice.

4. _____ history.
Teaching history is much more interesting
than teaching driver's ed.

5. _____ our teacher _____
us less homework. She gives us a lot
of homework every day.

6. _____.
I think dogs are the best pets
in the world.

K **YOU DECIDE:** *What Does Teddy Wish?*

My friend Teddy isn't very happy.
He's never satisfied with anything.

1. Teddy lives in the suburbs. He wishes _____.

2. Teddy's father is a dentist. He wishes _____.

3. His mother teaches English at his school. He wishes _____.

4. Teddy has two older sisters. He wishes _____.

5. Teddy's father drives a used car. He wishes _____.

6. Teddy plays the trombone. _____.

7. A lot of Teddy's friends _____, but Teddy doesn't. He wishes _____

_____.

8. Also, _____. He wishes _____

_____.

LOOKING FOR A JOB

A. I wonder if you could help me. I'm looking for a job as a repairperson.

B. Most of the repair shops in town want to hire people who can repair many different kinds of things. For example, can you repair VCRs?

A. I wish ____I could___[1], but VCRs are very complicated.

B. That's too bad. If _____[2] repair VCRs, _____[3] able to find a job more easily. Hmm. *Freddy's Fix-It Shop* is looking for someone who can repair DVD players.

A. The truth is, I'm very good at repairing TVs, but I can't repair DVD players.

B. That's too bad! If _____[4], *Freddy's Fix-It Shop*

_____[5] VERY interested in you.

A. *Freddy's Fix-It Shop* is one of the best repair shops in town. I wish _____[6] repair DVD players.

B. Well, *We Fix It!* is also a repair shop, and they're looking for someone who can repair

televisions and _____[7]. They also want someone who can _____

_____[8].

A. I'm afraid I can't _____[9].

B. What a shame! If _____[10], *We Fix It!*

_____[11] interested in you. Maybe you should think about finding another kind of job. What else can you do?

A. Let's see. I used to be a waiter, but I hurt my back, so I can't do that anymore.

B. I wish you _____[12] be a waiter. If _____[13] a waiter,

_____[14] any trouble finding a job. There must be other things

you can do. For example, can you _____[15]?

A. Not really.

B. That's too bad, because if _____[16],

_____[17] send you for an interview with the _____[18] Company.

I'm sorry, but those are all the jobs I have today. I wish _____[19] help you. Come back next week. Maybe I'll have something then.

M CHOOSE

1. If the children were asleep, _____ have some peace and quiet in the house.
   a. we'd be able to
   b. we couldn't
   c. we'll

2. If I saw you more often, _____ get to know each other better.
   a. we couldn't
   b. we could
   c. we can

3. If you were more talented, _____ be in the movies.
   a. you'll
   b. you can
   c. you'd be able to

4. If the TV weren't so loud, _____ concentrate on my homework.
   a. I will
   b. I could
   c. I can't

5. If Ms. Evans weren't so busy, _____ speak with her now.
   a. you could
   b. you couldn't
   c. you wouldn't be able to

6. If he didn't live in the suburbs, _____ get to work faster.
   a. he'll
   b. he won't be able to
   c. he could

7. If you had more spare time, _____ learn to knit.
   a. you could
   b. you can
   c. you'll

8. If Ms. Jackson made more money, _____ buy a new computer.
   a. she couldn't
   b. she'd be able to
   c. she can

9. If I were more athletic, _____ play on the school basketball team.
   a. I could
   b. I can
   c. I couldn't

10. If he weren't so clumsy, _____ dance better.
    a. he will
    b. he can't
    c. he'd be able to

N LISTENING

Listen and decide what the person is talking about.

1. a. speaking a language
   b. writing a language

2. a. flowers
   b. vegetables

3. a. my driver's license
   b. a raise

4. a. the bus
   b. school

5. a. food
   b. money

6. a. preparing taxes
   b. watching TV

O YOU DECIDE WHY

A. I'm really annoyed with our neighbors upstairs.

They always _____ ,

they always _____ ,

and they're _____ .

B. I know.

I wish _____ ,

I wish _____ ,

and I wish _____ .
We should probably speak to the landlord.

P GRAMMARRAP: *I Wish*

Listen. Then clap and practice.

I wish   I had   a more interesting   job.

I wish   I made   more money.

I wish   I were sitting   and reading   a book

On a beach   where it's warm   and sunny.

I wish   we lived   on a quiet   street.

I wish   our neighbors   were nice.

I wish   our roof   weren't leaking.

I wish   we didn't   have mice.

I wish   I could be   on a sports team.

I wish   I were six feet   tall.

I wish   I knew how   to play tennis.

I wish   I could throw   a ball.

Activity Workbook   87

1. I had trouble answering the questions.
   a. The questions were confusing.
   b. The questions were amusing.
   c. I answered all the questions three times.

2. I'm positive we're having a test tomorrow.
   a. I'm afraid we might have a test.
   b. I'm sure we're having a test.
   c. I think we'll probably have a test.

3. We can't convince him to take the job.
   a. He wants to take the job.
   b. He can't take the job.
   c. He won't take the job.

4. Carl is happy he moved to the suburbs.
   a. He prefers the city.
   b. He likes taking care of his yard.
   c. He likes the noise in the city.

5. Mrs. Randall wants to teach something else.
   a. She wants to teach the same thing again.
   b. She wants to teach at a different time.
   c. She wants to teach a different subject.

6. The Super Bowl is next Sunday. I'm going to invite a friend over to watch it on TV.
   a. I'm thinking about my Super Bowl plans.
   b. I'm having a big Super Bowl party.
   c. I'm going to the Super Bowl.

7. Amy and Dan don't have enough in common.
   a. They don't get paid enough.
   b. They don't have enough clothes.
   c. They aren't interested in the same things.

8. We live in a high-rise building.
   a. Our house is in the mountains.
   b. Our building has many floors.
   c. Our building isn't very large, but the rents are high.

9. Ronald is sick and tired of his job.
   a. He's in the hospital.
   b. He's unhappy.
   c. He's taking medicine.

10. My sister Nancy is never annoyed.
    a. She's never upset.
    b. She's never in a good mood.
    c. She never enjoys anything.

11. My cousin Norman dropped out of school.
    a. He skipped a few classes.
    b. He quit school.
    c. He ran away from school very quickly.

12. Our apartment has a view of the park.
    a. We can see the park from our window.
    b. We can't see the park from our apartment.
    c. We can hear the park very well.

13. I'd like some peace and quiet around the house.
    a. Our house is very quiet.
    b. Our house is very large.
    c. Our house is very noisy.

14. Ever since I heard we were going to have an important exam next week, I've been concentrating on my work.
    a. I've been complaining more about it.
    b. I've been paying more attention to it.
    c. I've been worrying more.

15. I'm afraid your brakes are getting worse.
    a. They need to be replaced.
    b. They need to be rehearsed.
    c. They need to be tuned up.

16. My brother-in-law started a new business, and he lost his shirt.
    a. He's looked everywhere for it.
    b. It was successful.
    c. His business wasn't very successful.

Listen to each word and then say it.

bread	break

1. fell	3. eggs	5. pleasure	
2. special	4. athletic	6. many	

1. paid	3. ate	5. plays	
2. space	4. operation	6. main	

Listen and put a circle around the word that has the same sound.

1. sweater: grade ⃝gets⃝ parade
2. main: take let terrible
3. ready: away great Ted
4. operation: upset paid pepper
5. paint: rest vacation said
6. complain: then said Spain
7. spend: sprain Jane when
8. tell: friend weigh receive

Now make a sentence using all the words you circled, and read the sentence aloud.

9. _____ my _____ _____ _____ _____, he'll _____ a _____ in _____ .

10. toothpaste: best play past
11. hate: hat eight head
12. special: tennis came cat
13. lesson: late great let's
14. upset: skate made next
15. pleasure: mail Wednesday plane
16. friend: Fred wait same

Now make a sentence using all the words you circled, and read the sentence aloud.

17. _____ _____ _____ with _____ _____ _____ at _____ o'clock.

WHAT'S THE ANSWER?

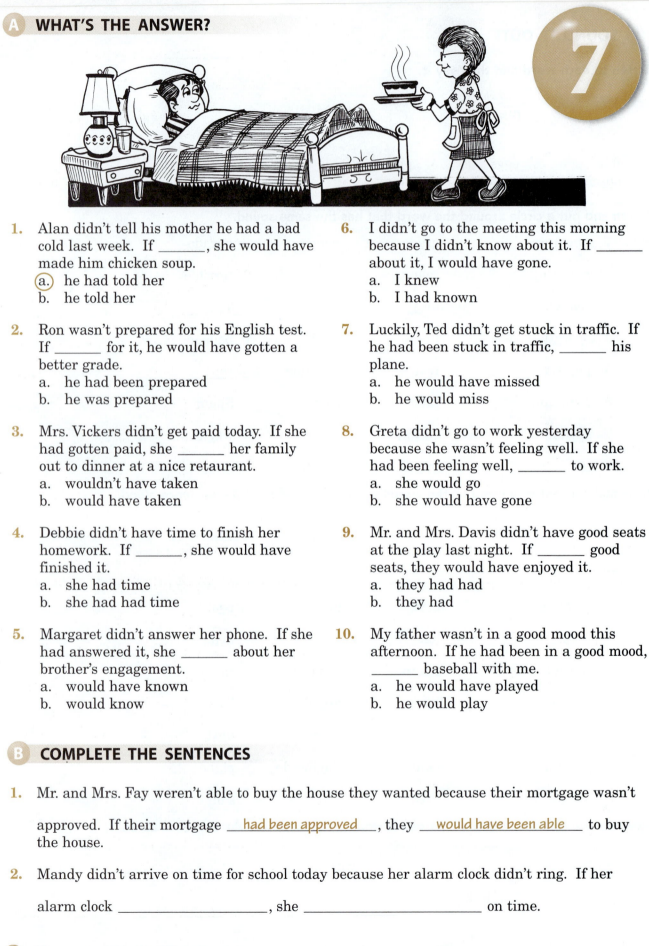

1. Alan didn't tell his mother he had a bad cold last week. If _____, she would have made him chicken soup.
   a. he had told her
   b. he told her

2. Ron wasn't prepared for his English test. If _____ for it, he would have gotten a better grade.
   a. he had been prepared
   b. he was prepared

3. Mrs. Vickers didn't get paid today. If she had gotten paid, she _____ her family out to dinner at a nice retaurant.
   a. wouldn't have taken
   b. would have taken

4. Debbie didn't have time to finish her homework. If _____, she would have finished it.
   a. she had time
   b. she had had time

5. Margaret didn't answer her phone. If she had answered it, she _____ about her brother's engagement.
   a. would have known
   b. would know

6. I didn't go to the meeting this morning because I didn't know about it. If _____ about it, I would have gone.
   a. I knew
   b. I had known

7. Luckily, Ted didn't get stuck in traffic. If he had been stuck in traffic, _____ his plane.
   a. he would have missed
   b. he would miss

8. Greta didn't go to work yesterday because she wasn't feeling well. If she had been feeling well, _____ to work.
   a. she would go
   b. she would have gone

9. Mr. and Mrs. Davis didn't have good seats at the play last night. If _____ good seats, they would have enjoyed it.
   a. they had had
   b. they had

10. My father wasn't in a good mood this afternoon. If he had been in a good mood, _____ baseball with me.
    a. he would have played
    b. he would play

COMPLETE THE SENTENCES

1. Mr. and Mrs. Fay weren't able to buy the house they wanted because their mortgage wasn't

   approved. If their mortgage ___had been approved___, they ___would have been able___ to buy the house.

2. Mandy didn't arrive on time for school today because her alarm clock didn't ring. If her

   alarm clock _____, she _____ on time.

3. Sam wasn't happy because he didn't win the tennis game.

   If he _____ the tennis game, he _____ happy.

4. My friends didn't get dressed up because they didn't know about the party. If they

   _____ about the party, they _____ dressed up.

5. My daughter didn't learn to play the piano well because she didn't practice every day.

   If she _____ every day, she _____ to play the piano well.

6. We weren't on time for the wedding because we didn't take our map with us.

   If we _____ our map with us, we _____ on time.

7. Cindy didn't stop at the traffic light because she didn't notice it.

   If she _____ it, she definitely _____ .

8. We didn't have good seats for the concert because we didn't buy our tickets early enough.

   If we _____ our tickets early enough, we _____ good seats.

C YOU DECIDE: *What Would Happen If . . . ?*

1. I had a terrible time on my vacation!

   The weather wasn't _____ warm enough _____ ,

   I didn't take _____ ,

   I wasn't able to _____ ,

   the hotel didn't have _____ ,

   _____ weren't _____ ,

   and _____ didn't write to me while I was away.

   If the weather _____ had been warmer _____ ,

   if I _____ ,

   if I _____ ,

   if the hotel _____ ,

   if _____ ,

   and if _____ while I was away,

   I'm sure I _____ would have enjoyed _____ my vacation.

(continued)

2. I had a terrible job interview yesterday at the Trans-Tel Company. I didn't get the job, and I know why.

I didn't remember to _____,

I didn't arrive _____,

I didn't _____,

I wasn't _____,

and I wasn't _____.

If I _____,

if I _____,

if I _____,

if I _____,

and if I _____,

I'm sure I _____ a better job interview.

And if I _____ a better job interview,

maybe I _____ the job.

3. I didn't enjoy myself at my cousin's birthday party last night.

The music wasn't _____,

the food wasn't _____,

the people there weren't _____,

_____ wasn't _____,

and _____ didn't _____.

If the music _____,

if the food _____,

if the people there _____,

if _____,

and if _____,

I'm sure I _____ myself at the party.

WHAT'S THE ANSWER?

1. If I hadn't expected Maria to say "yes,"
   I _____ her to marry me.
   (a.) wouldn't have asked
   b. wouldn't ask

2. If you hadn't set off the metal detector,
   you _____ searched.
   a. wouldn't get
   b. wouldn't have gotten

3. If Janet's mortgage _____ approved, she
   wouldn't have been able to buy a house.
   a. hadn't been
   b. wasn't

4. If I _____ problems with my printer
   last night, I wouldn't have turned in my
   paper late.
   a. didn't have
   b. hadn't had

5. If Timmy's report card _____ bad, his
   parents wouldn't have been upset.
   a. hadn't been
   b. wasn't

6. If we hadn't felt under the weather,
   we _____ home.
   a. didn't stay
   b. wouldn't have stayed

7. If Debbie _____ her leg, she wouldn't
   have missed the class trip.
   a. didn't sprain
   b. hadn't sprained

8. If the boss hadn't been upset, he _____
   at everybody this morning.
   a. wouldn't have yelled
   b. wouldn't yell

9. If it _____ cold last week, there
   wouldn't have been ice on the pond.
   a. wasn't
   b. hadn't been

10. If I hadn't had a bad headache, I _____
    to bed so early.
    a. wouldn't go
    b. wouldn't have gone

LISTENING

Listen and choose the statement that is true based on what you hear.

1. a. She got the job.
   (b.) She didn't speak confidently.

2. a. He got fired.
   b. He arrived on time for work every
      day.

3. a. It rained.
   b. They didn't have to cancel the picnic.

4. a. He wasn't in a hurry.
   b. He made mistakes on his homework.

5. a. She didn't call them.
   b. She remembered their phone number.

6. a. The play wasn't boring.
   b. The audience fell asleep.

7. a. They weren't in the mood to go
      swimming.
   b. They went to the beach.

8. a. He didn't get a ticket.
   b. He was speeding.

9. a. She didn't write legibly.
   b. She wrote legibly.

10. a. He remembered the meeting.
    b. He didn't go to the meeting.

F HOW I BECAME A BASKETBALL PLAYER

A. Why did you decide to become a basketball player?

B. When I was very young, my uncle took me to basketball games every weekend, my grandparents bought me a basketball, and my parents sent me to basketball camp. When I was older, I played basketball in high school and college, and I went to basketball games whenever I could.

If my uncle ___hadn't taken me___¹ to basketball games every weekend,

if my grandparents _____² a basketball,

if my parents _____³ to basketball camp,

if I _____⁴ basketball in high school and college,

and if I _____⁵ to basketball games whenever I could,

I _____wouldn't have become_____⁶ a basketball player.

G I'M REALLY GLAD

I'm really glad I went to Five-Star Business School.

If _____I hadn't gone_____¹ to Five-Star,

I _____wouldn't have_____² learned information technology.

And if I _____³ information technology,

I _____⁴ a job at the Trans-Tel Company.

And if I_____⁵ a job at Trans-Tel,

I _____⁶ sent to Vancouver on business.

And if I _____⁷ sent to Vancouver on business,

I _____⁸ met your father.

And if I _____⁹ your father,

you _____¹⁰ born!

H WHY DIDN'T YOU TELL ME?

Why didn't you tell me today's English class was canceled? If _____you had told_____ [1]

me it was canceled, I _____ [2] to school this morning. And

if I _____ [3] to school, I _____ [4] here when the

repairperson came to pick up the computer. And if _____ [5] here when the

repairperson came to pick it up, she _____ [6] able to take it to her

repair shop. And if she _____ [7] able to take it to her shop, I'm sure she

_____ [8] fixed it. And if she _____ [9] it, we would be on the

Internet right now!

Why didn't you tell me you had invited your friends for dinner last night? If you

_____ [10] me you had invited them, I definitely would have _____ [11]

more food. If I _____ [12] more food, there would have been enough for

everyone to eat. And if _____ [13] enough food for everybody to eat, we

_____ [14] to Ziggy's Restaurant for dinner. And if we _____

_____ [15] to Ziggy's for dinner, we _____ [16] sick.

And if we _____ [17] sick, we _____ [18] had to go to the hospital.

And if we _____ [19] to go to the hospital, we _____ [20]

home, and you could _____ [21] your homework. And if you _____ [22]

your homework, your teacher _____ [23] upset.

I YOU DECIDE: *Why Was Larry Late for Work?*

I'm sorry I was late for work this morning. I tried to get here on time, but everything went wrong.

First, ...

Then, ...

After that, ...

And also, ...

If _____ ,

if _____ ,

if _____ ,

and if _____ ,

I _____ so late.

J GRAMMARRAP: *If They Hadn't*

Listen. Then clap and practice.

If he hadn't   been asked   to dance   in the show,

He wouldn't have   slipped   and broken   his toe.

If she hadn't   decided   to learn   to ski,

She wouldn't have   fallen   and hurt   her knee.

If you hadn't   lost   the keys   to your car,

You wouldn't have   had   to walk   so far.

If we hadn't   left   our tickets   at home,

We wouldn't have   missed   the flight   to Rome.

WHAT'S THE ANSWER?

1. Henry didn't enjoy the lecture. He wishes
   _____ home.
   a. he stayed
   b. he had stayed ⓑ

2. I don't do my homework all the time.
   My teacher wishes _____.
   a. I did
   b. I had done

3. When I was young, I used to feel bad
   because I wasn't as athletic as the other
   students in my class. I wish _____
   athletic.
   a. I was
   b. I had been

4. When we moved into this neighborhood, we
   were invited to a big neighborhood party.
   We wish _____.
   a. we had gone
   b. we went

5. We don't know if it's a girl or a boy.
   We wish _____.
   a. we knew
   b. we had known

6. I didn't read the instructions to my VCR
   very carefully. I wish _____ them
   more carefully.
   a. I read
   b. I had read

7. My parents always worry about the
   future when they hear bad news on
   TV. I wish _____ so much.
   a. they hadn't worried
   b. they didn't worry

8. Mrs. Watson is concerned that her
   husband doesn't eat better food.
   She wishes _____ healthier things.
   a. he ate
   b. he had eaten

L **COMPLETE THE SENTENCES**

1. I'm a terrible dancer. I wish _____I had taken_____ dance lessons when I was younger.

2. Amy didn't study for her math test, and she got a bad grade. She wishes _____

   _____ for it.

3. Fred doesn't enjoy working in the Accounting Department. He wishes _____
   in the Personnel Department.

4. I love dogs. I wish _____ a dog when I was young. My mother didn't like
   dogs. She liked cats. We had five of them!

5. When my friends go skiing, I never go with them because I can't ski. I wish _____
   how to ski.

6. I'm really sorry I didn't see the new James Bond movie when it was playing downtown last

   month. I wish _____ it.

7. My wife and I are both being transferred to our company's office on the east coast, and now

   we have to sell our house. We wish _____ sell it.

These people didn't have a very good time at Patty's party last night.

1. I didn't have a very good time at Patty's party last night. I wish I
   ___**hadn't**___ ___**gone**___. There were a lot of other things I could

   have done. I wish I _____ _____ something else.

2. Patty's party was outside, and it was very cold. If it _____

   _____ so cold, I _____ _____ _____

   more comfortable.

3. I'm very sorry that Claudia Crandall was at the party. She didn't

   stop singing and playing the guitar. I CERTAINLY wish she _____

   _____ and _____ the guitar. She has the worst voice I've

   ever heard, and she plays the guitar VERY badly. If Claudia _____

   _____ and _____ the guitar at the party, I _____

   _____ _____ a headache all night!

4. I wish I _____ forget people's names all the time. Can you

   believe it? I couldn't remember Patty's sister's name. I wish I _____

   _____ it. After all, if she _____ forgotten

   MY name, I _____ _____ liked it.

5. I wish I _____ more people at the party. I didn't

   know anybody at all. If I _____ _____ more people,

   I _____ _____ _____ so lonely, and I

   _____ _____ _____ so out of place.

Listen. Then clap and practice.

I wish I hadn't skied down the mountain.

I wish I had watched TV.

If I hadn't skied down the mountain,

I wouldn't have hurt my knee.

I wish I hadn't walked to the office.

I wish I had taken the train.

If I hadn't walked to the office,

I wouldn't have gotten caught in the rain.

I wish I hadn't typed so carelessly.

I wish I had done much better.

If I hadn't typed so carelessly,

I wouldn't have had to redo this letter.

I wish I hadn't swum in the ocean.

I wish I had gone to the park.

If I hadn't swum in the ocean,

I wouldn't have gotten scared by a shark.

I wish I hadn't used so much toothpaste.

I wish I had used much less.

If I hadn't used so much toothpaste,

I wouldn't have made such a mess.

1. A. I heard that I might get a promotion. Can you tell me if it's true?

B. I wish I _____*could tell*_____ you now, but I'm not supposed to

say anything. I hope I _____*can tell*_____ you soon.

2. A. Do you like your job?

B. My job is very boring. I wish I _____ someplace
else. I'm looking for a job at an Internet company. I hope I

_____ one soon.

3. A. I wish Ricardo Palermo _____ "Loving You" last
night. He's the most fantastic singer I've ever heard.

B. I certainly hope he _____ it when I go to his concert
on Saturday night.

4. A. I'm having trouble learning to speak English. I'm afraid I'm too

old. I wish I _____ English when I was younger.

B. Don't be ridiculous! You do a lot better than many of the younger

students in our class. They all wish they _____
English as well as you.

5. A. I wish you _____ have to leave on a business trip. I'm

really going to miss you. I hope you _____ a good
time while you're away, but don't enjoy yourself TOO much!

B. You know I'm going to miss you, too. I wish you _____
going with me.

6. A. I had my yearly check-up today, and my doctor is a little concerned
about my weight.

B. What did the doctor say?

A. He wishes I _____ so heavy. He gave me a new diet
that I'm going to try. I hope I _____ a lot of weight.

P YOU DECIDE: *If*

1. I hope it doesn't rain this weekend. If it rains this weekend, _____
_____ .

2. I wish I had more free time. If I had more free time, _____
_____ .

3. I wish I didn't have to _____ . If I didn't have to
_____ , _____ .

4. I hope you can lend me _____ . If you can lend me
_____ , _____ .

5. I wish I had _____ many years ago. If I had _____
_____ , _____ .

6. I hope _____ is elected president. If _____ is elected president,
_____ .

7. I wish I knew more about _____ . If I knew more about
_____ , _____ .

8. I hope _____ in the future. If _____
_____ , _____ .

Q WISH OR HOPE?

1. They (wish   hope) they had taken their umbrellas today.

2. Timothy can't drive yet. He (wishes   hopes) he were older.

3. I (wish   hope) I find the right ingredients for the soup.

4. Mrs. Jones (wishes   hopes) her son hadn't quit the baseball team.

5. John (wishes   hopes) his shirt doesn't shrink in the washing machine.

6. I (wish   hope) I didn't have to wait so long to see if I got accepted to college.

7. Tomorrow is Saturday. I (wish   hope) I still don't feel "under the weather."

8. Mr. McDonald doesn't like his new house. He (wishes   hopes) he had bought a condominium.

9. The minister is embarrassed. He (wishes   hopes) he hadn't arrived late for the wedding.

R LISTENING

Listen and complete the sentences.

1. a. ... I wouldn't be so nervous. *(circled: a)*
   b. ... I won't be so irritable.

2. a. ... I'll be home right away.
   b. ... I wouldn't be late.

3. a. ... he'll have a lot more friends.
   b. ... he'd be a lot happier.

4. a. ... she wouldn't have gotten wet.
   b. ... she'll be dry.

5. a. ... we'd dance together.
   b. ... we'll talk to each other all evening.

6. a. ... I won't have to walk to work.
   b. ... I wouldn't have to drive everywhere.

S LISTENING: *Hopes and Wishes*

Listen and complete the sentences.

1. a. ... he isn't sick.
   b. ... he felt better. *(circled: b)*

2. a. ... tomorrow's lesson is easier.
   b. ... I understood English better.

3. a. ... she visits me more often.
   b. ... she still lived across the street.

4. a. ... she can't work someplace else.
   b. ... she can find another job.

5. a. ... I had a dog or a cat.
   b. ... I can get a pet.

6. a. ... I'm a more graceful dancer.
   b. ... I weren't so clumsy.

7. a. ... you can come.
   b. ... you could be there.

8. a. ... she were more careful.
   b. ... she finds it soon.

9. a. ... they tasted good.
   b. ... everybody likes chocolate.

10. a. ... it were healthier.
    b. ... it needs more sun.

11. a. ... you knew more about fax machines.
    b. ... you know how to fix it.

12. a. ... she owned a more reliable car.
    b. ... it starts on cold days.

13. a. ... I had some.
    b. ... we can borrow some.

14. a. ... I had a better memory.
    b. ... I can remember them.

T LISTENING

Listen to each word and then say it.

1. beg—bay

2. check—shake

3. Fred—afraid

4. men—Main

5. met—made

6. never—neighbor

7. pepper—paper

8. set—say

9. pet—paid

10. wedding—waiting

HAVE YOU HEARD?

Listen and complete the sentences.

met	made

1. a. ... all the beds.
   (b.) ... an old friend.

fell	fail

2. a. ... while they were skiing.
   b. ... whenever they take a test.

teller	tailor

3. a. ... works in a bank.
   b. ... takes in your clothes.

pepper	paper

4. a. ... in my notebook.
   b. ... in the stew.

Fred	afraid

5. a. ... you might drown?
   b. ... Smith?

met	made

6. a. ... any summer plans yet?
   b. ... their new neighbors?

men	Main

7. a. ... Street bus is leaving.
   b. ... are leaving the barber shop.

check	shake

8. a. ... hands.
   b. ... with the mechanic.

wedding	waiting

9. a. ... at the bus stop.
   b. ... was the happiest day of my life.

never	neighbor

10. a. ... just moved in yesterday.
    b. ... flown in a helicopter before.

pet	paid

11. a. ... her income tax.
    b. ... bird knows how to talk.

check	shake

12. a. ... hands with the ticket agent.
    b. ... with the ticket agent.

fell	fail

13. a. ... most of my English exams.
    b. ... asleep very late last night.

wedding	waiting

14. a. ... for us.
    b. ... is at 11:00.

never	neighbor

15. a. ... is very noisy.
    b. ... been to Hawaii.

Fred	afraid

16. a. ... I'll get hurt.
    b. ... Jones. What's your name?

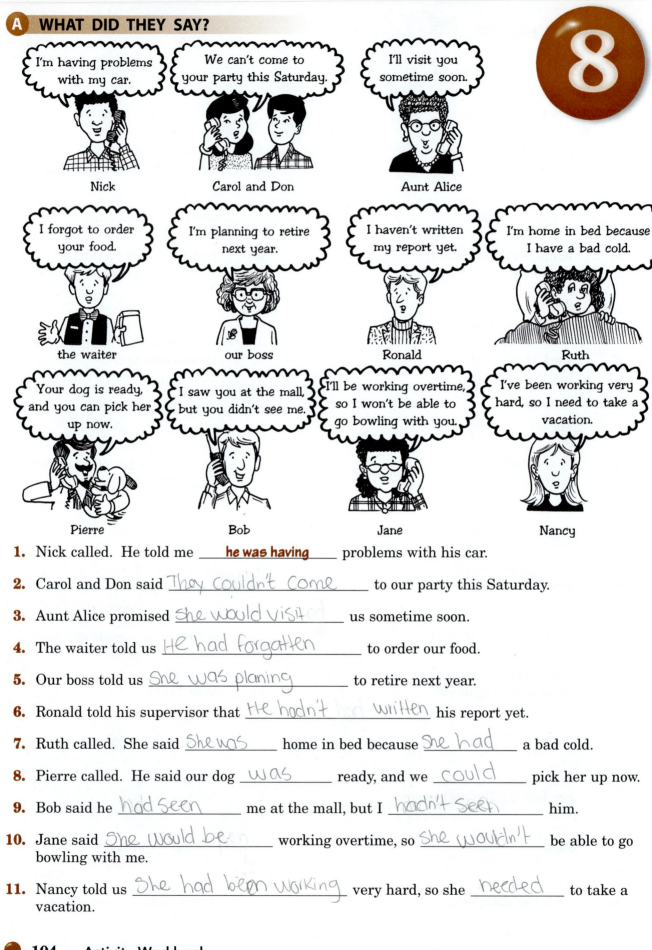

I'm having problems with my car.

Nick

We can't come to your party this Saturday.

Carol and Don

I'll visit you sometime soon.

Aunt Alice

I forgot to order your food.

the waiter

I'm planning to retire next year.

our boss

I haven't written my report yet.

Ronald

I'm home in bed because I have a bad cold.

Ruth

Your dog is ready, and you can pick her up now.

Pierre

I saw you at the mall, but you didn't see me.

Bob

I'll be working overtime, so I won't be able to go bowling with you.

Jane

I've been working very hard, so I need to take a vacation.

Nancy

1. Nick called. He told me ____**he was having**____ problems with his car.

2. Carol and Don said _They couldn't come_ to our party this Saturday.

3. Aunt Alice promised _She would visited_ us sometime soon.

4. The waiter told us _He had forgotten_ to order our food.

5. Our boss told us _She was planing_ to retire next year.

6. Ronald told his supervisor that _He hadn't had written_ his report yet.

7. Ruth called. She said _She was_ home in bed because _she had_ a bad cold.

8. Pierre called. He said our dog _was_ ready, and we _could_ pick her up now.

9. Bob said he _had seen_ me at the mall, but I _hadn't seen_ him.

10. Jane said _She would been_ working overtime, so _she wouldn't_ be able to go bowling with me.

11. Nancy told us _She had been working_ very hard, so she _needed_ to take a vacation.

1.

Dear Mother,

I got an "A" on my biology test.

                              Love,
                              Amy

A. I just got an e-mail from my daughter in college.

B. Really? What did she say?

A. She said _____ *she had gotten an "A"* _____

_____ *on her biology test* _____ .

2. A. I received a note from Uncle Ralph today.

B. Oh, that's nice. What did he say?

A. He said _____

_____ .

Dear Gloria,

I'm home from the hospital and I'm feeling much better.

                              Uncle Ralph

3.

Dear Sue and Mike,

We saw the Colosseum, but we haven't gone to the Vatican yet.

                The Wilsons

A. The Wilsons sent us a postcard from Rome.

B. Oh, really? What did they say?

A. They said _____

_____ .

4. A. I got an e-mail from my friend Richard today.

B. He hasn't written in a while. What did he say?

A. He said _____

_____ .

Kathy,

I hope you can visit me when you come to Japan this summer.

                              Richard

5.

Dear Mr. Watson,

I'm sorry, but you aren't the right person for the job.

Sincerely,
Roberta Bennett

A. I received an e-mail from Ms. Bennett at the Apex Company.

B. Oh. You've been expecting her to write. What did she say?

A. She said _____

_____ .

(continued)

6. A. Charlie, the plumber, left us a note.

B. Oh. What did he say?

A. He said _____

_____ .

> Dear Mr. and Mrs. Blake,
>
> I'm very busy, and I can't repair your dishwasher this week.
>
> Charlie

7.

> Hi everyone!
>
> We love Hawaii, and we're thinking of buying a condominium.
>
> Love,
> Grandma & Grandpa

A. We received a postcard from Grandma and Grandpa in Hawaii.

B. That's nice. Are they enjoying their vacation there?

A. Yes. They said _____

_____ .

8. A. I received an e-mail from my father last night.

B. What did he say?

A. He said _____

_____

_____ .

> Dear Brian,
>
> I was hoping to send you more money for college, but I won't be able to because I'm having financial problems.
>
> Dad

9.

> Dear Ann and Tom,
>
> I'll be arriving ....
>
> and I plan to ....
>
> ....

A. We received a note from Cousin George.

B. Oh. What did he say?

A. He said _____

_____ .

10. A. We got a letter from Aunt Clara today.

B. That's nice. What did she say?

A. She said _____

_____ .

> Dear .... ,
>
> I have some good news.
>
> I'm finally going to ....
>
> ....
>
> ....

11.

Dear ....,

You won't believe it, but ....

....

....

A. I received an e-mail from my friend Larry.

B. He hasn't written in a long time. What did he say?

A. He said _____

_____

_____ .

C **GRAMMARRAP:** *What Did They Say?*

Listen. Then clap and practice.

A.   What did he   say?

B.   He said he was   mad.

A.   What did she   say?

B.   She said she was   sad.

A.   What did she   say?

B.   She said she was   busy.

A.   What did he   say?

B.   He said he was   dizzy.

A.   What did she   say?

B.   She said she'd been   hired.

A.   What did he   say?

B.   He said he'd been   fired.

A.   What did they   say?

B.   They said they'd be   late.

A.   What did you   say?

B.   We said we would   wait.

D WHAT'S THE ANSWER?

1. A. We can't fish here.
   B. Really? I was sure _____ fish here.
   a. we can
   b. we could *(circled)*

2. A. My husband wants to sell our house.
   B. Oh. I didn't know _____ to sell it.
   a. he wanted
   b. he had wanted

3. A. Has the meeting been canceled?
   B. I thought everybody knew it _____.
   a. was canceled
   b. had been canceled

4. A. Susan got a big promotion.
   B. That's nice. I didn't know _____ a promotion.
   a. she had gotten
   b. she got

5. A. My parents have moved to Miami.
   B. Yes. I knew _____ there.
   a. they moved
   b. they had moved

6. A. Our big sale starts tomorrow.
   B. Really? I didn't know _____ tomorrow.
   a. it starts
   b. it started

7. A. Do we have to work overtime today?
   B. I thought everybody knew _____.
   a. we had to work overtime
   b. we have to work overtime

8. A. The school picnic is going to be canceled.
   B. You're kidding! I didn't know the school picnic _____ to be canceled.
   a. was going
   b. is going

E LISTENING

What did they say? Listen and choose the correct answer.

1. a. He said he had fixed their car last week.
   b. He said he could fix their car next week. *(circled)*

2. a. She said her daughter was going to have a baby in July.
   b. She said her daughter had had a baby in July.

3. a. He said that the meeting had been canceled.
   b. He said the meeting was important.

4. a. He said his wife was going to be promoted.
   b. He said his wife had been promoted.

5. a. She said she didn't believe the bus drivers were going on strike.
   b. She said she didn't know the bus drivers.

6. a. He said they had loved each other.
   b. He said they loved each other.

7. a. She said the monkeys had escaped from the zoo.
   b. She said she hadn't believed the monkeys would escape from the zoo.

8. a. He said he was nervous about his interview.
   b. He said he had been nervous about his interview.

9. a. She said her parents had sold their condominium and moved into a house.
   b. She said that her parents had sold their house.

10. a. She said she was going to quit her job.
    b. She said she had moved to Hollywood.

Paula Wilson just returned home after working in Australia for two years. She's talking to her old friend Steve.

A. Welcome home, Paula! I'm glad you're back. How have you been?

B. Fine. Tell me, what's happened since I've been away?

A. Well, your cousin Frank got married last month.

B. He did? I didn't know _____ *he had gotten married* _____ ¹ last month. I wonder why he didn't write me.

A. He probably thought you knew. Have you heard about Aunt Martha? She's in the hospital.

B. Really? I had no idea _____ ². What happened? Did she have an accident?

A. No. Actually, she had a third heart attack last week.

B. That's terrible! I knew _____ ³ having problems with her heart for

the past several years, but I didn't know she _____ ⁴ another heart attack. I hope she's okay. Tell me, how's your sister Eileen?

A. You probably haven't heard. She's going to become the president of her company next month.

B. That's wonderful! I knew she _____ ⁵ promoted many times, but I didn't know

she _____ ⁶ the president of her company! That's very exciting news. And how are your children?

A. They've been doing very well. My son _____ ⁷,

and my daughter _____ ⁸.

B. That's fantastic! I didn't know that your son _____ ⁹

and your daughter _____ ¹⁰.

A. By the way, have you heard about Nancy and Tom? They _____

_____ ¹¹.

B. Really? I had no idea _____ ¹².
A lot sure has happened recently!

YOU WON'T BELIEVE IT!

Do you like being old?

1. My daughter asked me _____!
   a. do I like being old
   b. if I liked being old

2. My students asked me _____.
   a. why the test had been difficult
   b. why was the test so difficult

3. My dentist asked me _____.
   a. whether I ever brushed my teeth
   b. if do I ever brush my teeth

4. My boss asked me what time _____.
   a. did I go to bed last night
   b. I had gone to bed last night

5. My neighbor asked me _____.
   a. if I would sell him my car
   b. if will I sell him my car

6. The job interviewer asked me _____.
   a. where I had learned to spell
   b. where did I learn to spell

7. The salesperson in the store asked me _____!
   a. how old are you
   b. how old I was

8. My girlfriend asked me _____.
   a. if we could get married next month
   b. whether could we get married next month

9. My employees asked me _____.
   a. when was I going to give them raises
   b. when I was going to give them raises

10. My daughter's boyfriend asked me _____.
    a. if I dyed my hair
    b. do I dye my hair

H **LISTENING**

Listen and choose the correct answer.

1. Patty's father asked her _____.
   a. did she break up with Gary
   b. if she had broken up with Gary
   c. whether she had broken up with Larry

2. She asked them _____.
   a. how long they had been swimming there
   b. how long had they been sitting there
   c. how long they had been sitting there

3. He asked her _____.
   a. if was she eating when they called
   b. whether she was eating when they called
   c. if she had been reading when they called

4. She asked him _____.
   a. when was he going to repaint it
   b. when he was going to repaint it
   c. if he was going to repair it

5. He asked her _____.
   a. whether she was still sad
   b. if was she still mad
   c. if she was still mad

6. She asked him _____.
   a. when he was going to take a bath
   b. when he was going to study math
   c. if he had studied math

7. He asked me _____.
   a. were they too tall
   b. if they were too tall
   c. whether they were too small

8. She asked him _____.
   a. who had fixed the kitchen floor
   b. who had fixed the kitchen door
   c. who was going to fix the kitchen floor

I WHAT DID THEY ASK?

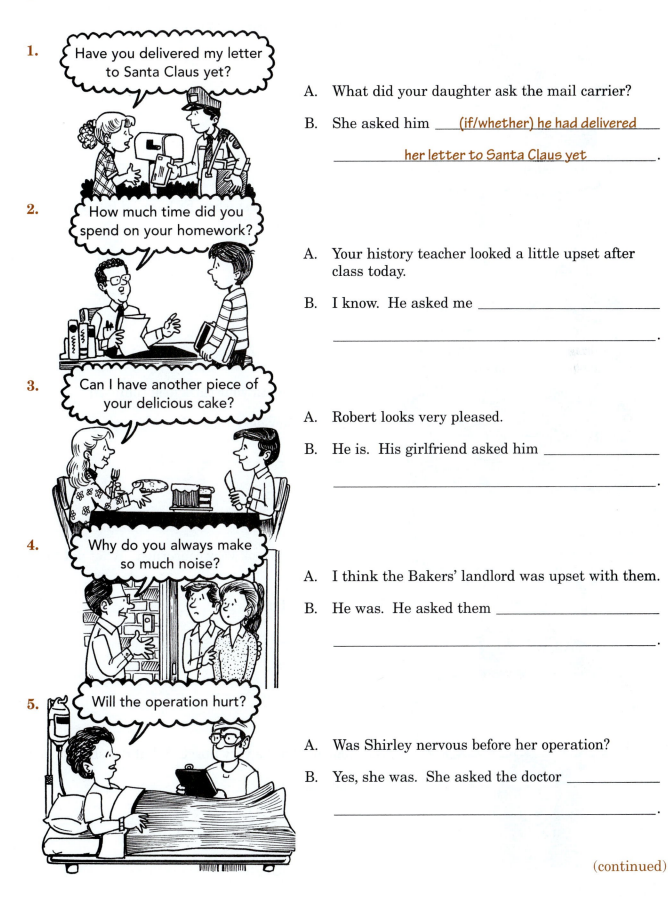

1.

Have you delivered my letter to Santa Claus yet?

A. What did your daughter ask the mail carrier?

B. She asked him (if/whether) he had delivered her letter to Santa Claus yet.

2.

How much time did you spend on your homework?

A. Your history teacher looked a little upset after class today.

B. I know. He asked me ______________________________ ______________________________.

3.

Can I have another piece of your delicious cake?

A. Robert looks very pleased.

B. He is. His girlfriend asked him ______________________________ ______________________________.

4.

Why do you always make so much noise?

A. I think the Bakers' landlord was upset with them.

B. He was. He asked them ______________________________ ______________________________.

5.

Will the operation hurt?

A. Was Shirley nervous before her operation?

B. Yes, she was. She asked the doctor ______________________________ ______________________________.

(continued)

6.

> When is the lecture going to end?

A. George looks bored. What did he just ask his wife?

B. He asked her _____

_____.

7.

> Do you still love me?

A. How did Alan feel when he bumped into his former girlfriend?

B. He was VERY surprised. She asked him _____

_____.

8.

> Why are there so many grammar rules in English?

A. The students in your class look confused.

B. I know. They asked me _____

_____.

9.

> _____
> _____

A. Your parents look very concerned. What did they ask you?

B. They asked me _____

_____.

10.

> _____
> _____

A. Your boss looks very upset. What did she ask you?

B. She asked me _____

_____.

Listen. Then clap and practice.

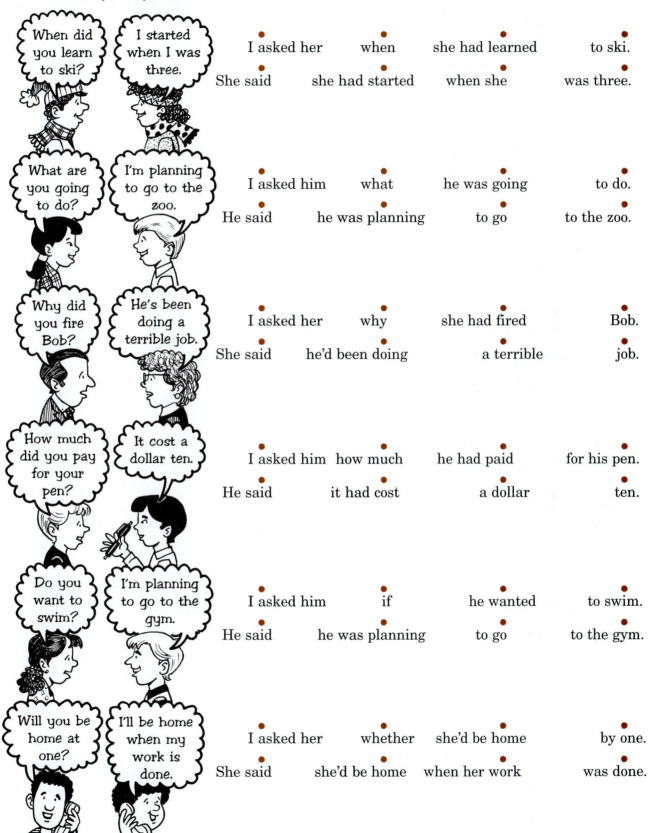

When did you learn to ski?

I started when I was three.

I asked her   when   she had learned   to ski.
She said   she had started   when she   was three.

What are you going to do?

I'm planning to go to the zoo.

I asked him   what   he was going   to do.
He said   he was planning   to go   to the zoo.

Why did you fire Bob?

He's been doing a terrible job.

I asked her   why   she had fired   Bob.
She said   he'd been doing   a terrible   job.

How much did you pay for your pen?

It cost a dollar ten.

I asked him   how much   he had paid   for his pen.
He said   it had cost   a dollar   ten.

Do you want to swim?

I'm planning to go to the gym.

I asked him   if   he wanted   to swim.
He said   he was planning   to go   to the gym.

Will you be home at one?

I'll be home when my work is done.

I asked her   whether   she'd be home   by one.
She said   she'd be home   when her work   was done.

K WHAT DID THEY TELL YOU?

1. *Speak confidently!*

   My teacher told me _____ to speak confidently _____.

2. *Don't drive too fast!*

   My parents told me _____.

3. *Work quickly!*

   My boss told me _____.

4. *Don't eat too much candy!*

   My doctor told me _____.

5. *Don't play loud music!*

   My neighbors told me _____.

L WHAT'S THE ANSWER?

1. We're getting worried about our son. We told him _____ by 11:00 P.M.
   a. to be home
   b. be home

2. Howard looks exhausted. I told him _____ so hard.
   a. not to work
   b. don't work

3. My doctor told me _____ exercising every day.
   a. start
   b. to start

4. The food at this restaurant is terrible! Now I know why my friends told me _____ here.
   a. not to eat
   b. don't eat

5. My supervisor told me _____ the report over because I had made a lot of mistakes.
   a. do
   b. to do

6. I'm really upset. My girlfriend told me _____ her anymore.
   a. to not call
   b. not to call

7. The teacher told us _____ Chapter 5, but I read Chapter 4.
   a. to read
   b. read

8. I'm in trouble! My father told me _____ his new car, but I did. And I got into an accident!
   a. not to drive
   b. to not drive

I'm tired of being told what to do. All day yesterday everybody told me what to do.

1. Hurry! Your breakfast is getting cold.

As soon as I woke up, my mother told me ___to hurry___ .

She said _____my breakfast was getting cold_____ .

2. Don't forget your umbrella! It's going to rain later.

At breakfast my father told me _____

_____ .

He said _____ .

3. Don't walk so slowly! We'll be late for school.

On the way to school, my friend Jimmy told me _____

_____ .

He said _____ .

4. Be quiet! You're disturbing the class!

At school, Ms. Johnson told me _____

_____ .

She said _____ .

5. ....

When we were walking home from school, the police

officer on the corner told me _____ .

He said _____ .

(continued)

6.

[speech bubble - empty]

When I went to soccer practice, my coach told me

_____ .

He said _____ .

7.

[speech bubble - empty]

At my music lesson, my violin teacher told me

_____ .

She said _____ .

8.

[speech bubble - empty]

When I was helping my family wash the dinner dishes,

my mother told me _____ .

She said _____ .

9.

[speech bubble]

_____! You'll fail
your math test if you
don't study

I was hoping to watch TV after dinner, but my older

brother told me _____ .

He said _____

_____ .

10.

[speech bubble]

_____

You have to get up early for
school.

I couldn't even choose my own bedtime. My parents

told me _____ .

They said _____ .

[speech bubble]

I can't wait until I grow up!
Then I can tell everybody else
what to do!

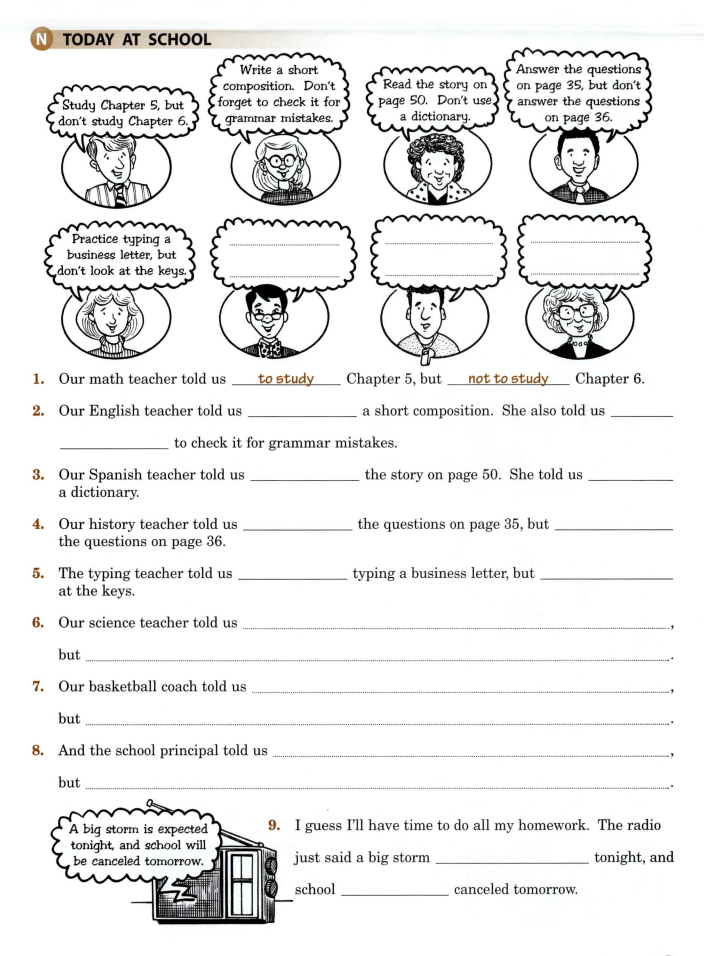

1. Our math teacher told us __to study__ Chapter 5, but __not to study__ Chapter 6.

2. Our English teacher told us _____ a short composition. She also told us _____ _____ to check it for grammar mistakes.

3. Our Spanish teacher told us _____ the story on page 50. She told us _____ a dictionary.

4. Our history teacher told us _____ the questions on page 35, but _____ the questions on page 36.

5. The typing teacher told us _____ typing a business letter, but _____ at the keys.

6. Our science teacher told us _____, but _____.

7. Our basketball coach told us _____, but _____.

8. And the school principal told us _____, but _____.

9. I guess I'll have time to do all my homework. The radio just said a big storm _____ tonight, and school _____ canceled tomorrow.

Listen. Then clap and practice.

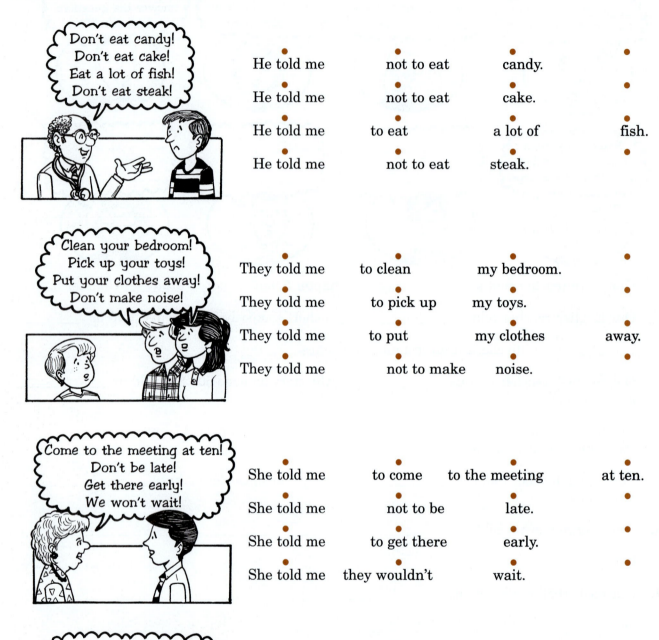

He told me	not to eat	candy.	
He told me	not to eat	cake.	
He told me	to eat	a lot of	fish.
He told me	not to eat	steak.	

They told me	to clean	my bedroom.	
They told me	to pick up	my toys.	
They told me	to put	my clothes	away.
They told me	not to make	noise.	

She told me	to come	to the meeting	at ten.
She told me	not to be	late.	
She told me	to get there	early.	
She told me	they wouldn't	wait.	

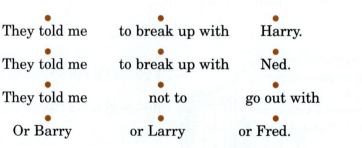

They told me	to break up with	Harry.	
They told me	to break up with	Ned.	
They told me	not to	go out with	Bob
Or Barry	or Larry	or Fred.	

P CHOOSE THE RIGHT WORD

1. Have your heard the news? A lion has (erased   (escaped)) from the zoo!

2. This (calculator   casserole) tastes delicious! Who made it?

3. What's everybody so (talking   anxious) about?

4. Please remember to (lock   look) the door when you leave tonight.

5. My niece Nancy was the most beautiful (groom   bride) I've ever seen.

6. I think I'm getting the (flu   flew). I'd better call the doctor.

7. What can we do to (present   prevent) robberies in our neighborhood?

8. I'm sorry. I don't (no   know) how to do that, but I'll ask somebody.

9. This new (puddle   poodle) is the cutest puppy I've ever seen.

10. My landlord told me not to pour (pipes   grease) down the kitchen sink.

11. We felt very (reassured   rearranged) after we spoke to the police.

12. Did you know that the president wanted to raise (taxis   taxes)?

13. We can always depend on our parents to give us good (suggest   advice).

14. I'll be (away   way) from home all next week, but you can reach me by e-mail.

15. Did you hear that all the DVD players in the store are on (sail   sale) this week?

16. My parents asked me when I was going to (brake   break) up with my boyfriend.

17. I'm so excited! I just met a wonderful girl, and I think I'm (falling   failing) in love with her.

18. Somebody broke (out of   into) the house across the street and stole a lot of jewelry.

19. I'm a little (irritable   annoyed) at my neighbors. They're noisy, and they aren't very friendly.

20. The interviewer asked me why I thought I was (qualified   willing) for the position.

21. The teacher said we weren't allowed to use (examinations   dictionaries) during the test.

22. My friend Bill asked me (whether   weather) I wanted to go sailing, and I told him it was going to rain.

23. Michael and Sue got (engaged   married) last month, and they're going to get (engaged   married) in June.

Q **LISTENING**

Listen to each word and then say it.

1. <u>st</u>and
2. <u>st</u>art
3. fanta<u>st</u>ic
4. re<u>st</u>

5. that'<u>s</u>
6. patien<u>ts</u>
7. write<u>s</u>
8. ticke<u>ts</u>

9. <u>sk</u>ate
10. a<u>sk</u>
11. <u>sc</u>are
12. di<u>sc</u>over

13. wor<u>ks</u>
14. thin<u>ks</u>
15. like<u>s</u>
16. week<u>s</u>

17. <u>sp</u>orts
18. <u>sp</u>ring
19. <u>sp</u>ecial
20. ho<u>sp</u>ital

21. sto<u>ps</u>
22. ski<u>ps</u>
23. hel<u>ps</u>
24. esca<u>pes</u>

R **WHO IS THE BEST?**

p	t	k	c

Fill in the missing letters and then read aloud.

Many pessimis _t_ s don't trus _t_ dentis _t_ s because they're s _c_ ared the wors__ will happen. However, Dr. Wes__'s patien__s are all optimis__ic. They think Dr. Wes__ is the bes__ dentis__ in Bos__on.

1. S__uart li__es Dr. Wes__.

Not only is he hones__, but he's the cheapes__ and the mos__ reliable dentis__ in Bos__on.

2. S__uar__'s sis__er also thin__s Dr. Wes__ is wonderful.

Dr. Wes__ wor__s very fas__ and never ma__es mis__a__es. He's the bes__ dentis__ on S__ate S__reet.

3. Mr. Jac__son can't s__and any other dentis__.

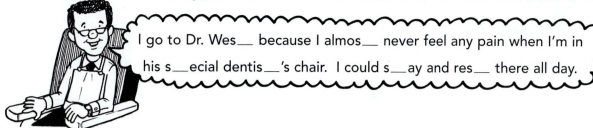

I go to Dr. Wes__ because I almos__ never feel any pain when I'm in his s__ecial dentis__'s chair. I could s__ay and res__ there all day.

4. Be__sy always tal__s about Dr. Wes__.

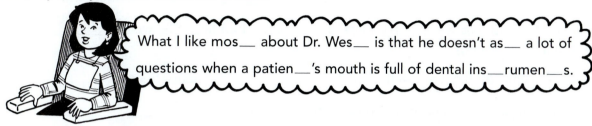

What I like mos__ about Dr. Wes__ is that he doesn't as__ a lot of questions when a patien__'s mouth is full of dental ins__rumen__s.

5. Dr. Wes__'s S__anish-s__eaking patien__s are es__ecially pleased.

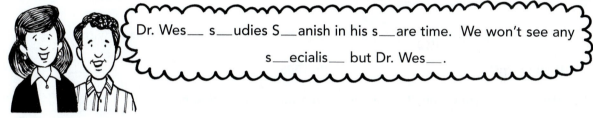

Dr. Wes__ s__udies S__anish in his s__are time. We won't see any s__ecialis__ but Dr. Wes__.

6. Margaret is very enthusias__ic about Dr. Wes__.

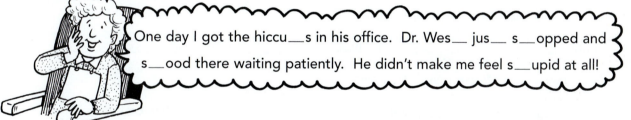

One day I got the hiccu__s in his office. Dr. Wes__ jus__ s__opped and s__ood there waiting patiently. He didn't make me feel s__upid at all!

7. Patty thin__s Dr. Wes__ is the hardes__ working dentis__ she knows.

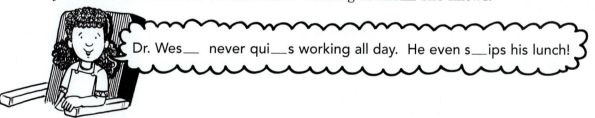

Dr. Wes__ never qui__s working all day. He even s__ips his lunch!

8. S__eve also li__es Dr. Wes__.

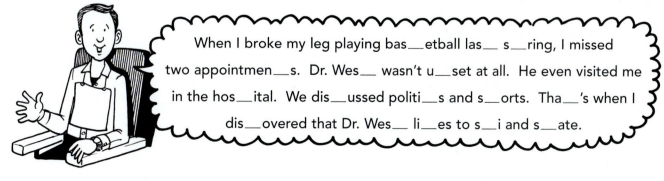

When I broke my leg playing bas__etball las__ s__ring, I missed two appointmen__s. Dr. Wes__ wasn't u__set at all. He even visited me in the hos__ital. We dis__ussed politi__s and s__orts. Tha__'s when I dis__overed that Dr. Wes__ li__es to s__i and s__ate.

A.   Fill in the blanks.

1. George doesn't enjoy being a waiter. He wishes _____ an actor.

2. Ann took violin lessons last year and didn't enjoy them. She wishes _____ guitar lessons.

3. Frank drives an old used car. He wishes _____ a more reliable car.

4. By the time Jill got to the party, most of her friends had left. She wishes _____ to the party earlier.

5. I don't speak English very well. I wish _____ more fluently.

6. You ate all the ice cream in the refrigerator! I wish _____ it all!

B.   Complete the sentences.

1. The Johnsons didn't enjoy their vacation because the weather wasn't warm.

   If the weather _____ warm, they _____ their vacation.

2. My doctor is concerned because I eat too many rich desserts.

   If I _____ so many rich desserts, my doctor _____ concerned.

3. Gloria arrived late because she missed the bus.

   If she _____ the bus, _____ late.

4. I'm frustrated because I can't type very fast.

   If _____ fast, _____ so frustrated.

5. You made a lot of mistakes because you weren't paying attention.

   If you _____ attention, you _____ so many mistakes.

6. Gary looks confused because he doesn't understand today's grammar.

   If he _____ today's grammar, he _____ so confused.

C.   Complete the sentences.

Ex. *I'm feeling fine after my operation.*

   Uncle Bill called. He said he ___was feeling___ fine after his operation.

1. *I got a big promotion.*

   My friend Betty called. She said _____ a big promotion.

2. *What's your name?*

The police officer asked me _____.

3. *Did you see me on TV last night?*

My friend Rita called. She asked me _____ on TV last night.

4. *I'm sorry I forgot your birthday.*

My sister-in-law called. She said _____ my birthday.

5. *I won't be able to visit you this weekend.*

Grandpa called. He said _____ us this weekend.

6. *Brush your teeth every day, and don't eat any candy.*

My dentist told me _____ my teeth every day, and _____
any candy.

7. *When will I be old enough to drive?*

My son asked me _____ old enough to drive.

8. *Why are you leaving so early? Are you in a hurry to get somewhere?*

Aunt Martha asked me _____ so early. She wanted to know

_____ to get somewhere.

D. Listening

Listen and complete the sentences.

Ex. **a.** I'd be able to see a movie.
  b. I had seen a movie.

1. a. I wouldn't have had to stay home in bed.
  b. I had to stay in bed.

2. a. I hadn't gotten depressed so often.
  b. I wouldn't get depressed so often.

3. a. we had forgotten to pay our rent.
  b. he'll call us back tonight.

4. a. when are we going to get married.
  b. when we were going to get married.

5. a. if I had gone to college.
  b. whether had I gone to college.

9

1. Mrs. Webber will be back soon, _____won't she_____?

2. I can park here, _____?

3. You live around the corner, _____?

4. You brought the plane tickets, _____?

5. I'm going to play today, _____?

6. We've hiked far enough, _____?

7. Santa Claus will be here soon, _____?

8. You were once a Broadway star, _____?

9. This is supposed to be a person, _____?

10. You're still in love with me, _____?

1. The fax machine is working, _____?
   a. isn't it
   b. doesn't it

2. We've eaten here before, _____?
   a. haven't we
   b. didn't we

3. I'm on time, _____?
   a. amn't I
   b. aren't I

4. He'll be in the office next week, _____?
   a. won't he
   b. isn't he

5. You finished your report, _____?
   a. don't you
   b. didn't you

6. They're going to leave soon, _____?
   a. won't they
   b. aren't they

7. She was at the meeting, _____?
   a. wasn't she
   b. isn't she

8. Timmy, this baby food tastes good, _____?
   a. isn't it
   b. doesn't it

C I THINK I KNOW YOU

A. Excuse me, but I think I know you. You're a student

at City College, _____aren't you_____ ¹?

B. Yes, _____ ².

A. That's what I thought. I was sure I had seen you there, but I've forgotten when. Now I remember! You've been

in a lot of school plays, _____ ³?

B. Yes, _____ ⁴.

A. That's what I thought. And you sang in the school chorus last year, _____ ⁵?

B. Yes, as a matter of fact, _____ ⁶.

A. I thought so. And now that I think of it, I've also seen you on Winter Street. You live **there**,

_____ ⁷?

B. Yes, _____ ⁸.

A. Isn't this ridiculous? I can remember so much about you, but I still can't remember **your name.**

Wait . . . Now I remember. Your name is Mandy, _____ ⁹?

B. No, it _____ ¹⁰.

A. It isn't?! I was sure your name was Mandy.

B. That's what everybody thinks. I'm Sandy. Mandy is my twin sister.

1. The post office hasn't closed yet, _has it_?

2. You aren't allergic to nuts, _____?

3. You don't still go out with Larry, _____?

4. I didn't hit you, _____?

5. I'm not permitted to skateboard here, _____?

6. You won't forget to call, _____?

7. We haven't run out of milk, _____?

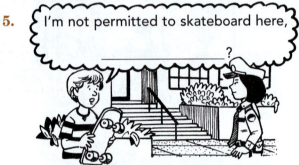

8. This apartment doesn't have cockroaches, _____?

9. Yesterday wasn't our anniversary, _____?

10. Today isn't your birthday, _____?

When I woke up yesterday morning, I knew right away it was going to be a terrible day. I knew that everything was going to go wrong all day and that I couldn't do ANYTHING about it. My problems started the minute I got up.

1.
Breakfast isn't ready yet, _____is it_____?

No, _____it isn't_____.

That's what I thought.

2.
I don't have time to take a shower, _____?

No, _____.

That's what I thought.

3.
I lost my English book. You haven't seen it anywhere, _____?

No, _____.

That's what I thought.

4.
There isn't any more orange juice, _____?

No, _____.

That's what I thought.

5.
My shirt hasn't been ironed yet, _____?

No, _____.

That's what I thought.

6.
I won't be able to finish my breakfast, _____?

No, _____.

That's what I thought.

I arrived an hour late for school. My problems continued there.

7.
School didn't start late today, _____?

No, _____.

That's what I thought.

8.
The teachers aren't all home sick today, _____?

No, _____.

That's what I thought.

(continued)

9. Today's math test wasn't canceled, _____?

No, _____.

That's what I thought.

10. I can't hand in today's history assignment next week, _____?

No, _____.

That's what I thought.

11. They aren't serving anything except "Tuna Surprise" casserole for lunch today, _____?

No, _____.

That's what I thought.

F WHAT'S THE TAG?

1. They aren't having problems, _____?
a. are they
b. aren't they

2. George was hired, _____?
a. was he
b. wasn't he

3. You didn't have to work overtime, _____?
a. did you
b. didn't you

4. You've done your homework, _____?
a. have you
b. haven't you

5. I'm not late, _____?
a. aren't I
b. am I

6. The bank will be open tomorrow, _____?
a. will it
b. won't it

7. He wants to marry you, _____?
a. doesn't he
b. is he

8. Your mother isn't upset, _____?
a. isn't she
b. is she

9. I can skate on this pond, _____?
a. can I
b. can't I

10. You received my letter, _____?
a. didn't you
b. did you

11. There wasn't a big storm, _____?
a. was there
b. wasn't there

12. I'm going to be promoted, _____?
a. am I
b. aren't I

13. Your son has been here before, _____?
a. hasn't he
b. has he

14. You won't be upset if I'm late, _____?
a. won't you
b. will you

Listen and complete the sentences.

1. a. do you?
    b. don't you? *(b circled)*

2. a. aren't you?
    b. are you?

3. a. do we?
    b. don't we?

4. a. did you?
    b. didn't you?

5. a. does she?
    b. doesn't he?

6. a. haven't you?
    b. have you?

7. a. was she?
    b. wasn't she?

8. a. hasn't he?
    b. has he?

9. a. won't we?
    b. will we?

10. a. can we?
    b. can't we?

11. a. is it?
    b. isn't it?

12. a. didn't I?
    b. did I?

H **YOU DECIDE:** *A Good Father*

I can't understand why I've been having so many problems with my son, Timmy. After all,

I'm a good father, _____aren't I_____ [1]? I usually try to be patient, _____ [2]?

I'm not very strict, _____ [3]? And I'm always nice to his friends, _____ [4]?

Also, I've always _____ [5], _____ [6]?

I didn't _____ [7], _____ [8]?

When he was little, I _____ [9], _____ [10]?

And now that he's older, I _____ [11], _____ [12]?

I'm not _____ [13], _____ [14]?

I don't _____ [15], _____ [16]?

And I'm always there when he needs me, _____ [17]? So what could have gone
wrong?

1 GRAMMARRAP: *She Drives to Work, Doesn't She?*

Listen. Then clap and practice.

She drives   to work,   doesn't she?
She was   late,   wasn't she?

He doesn't   type well,   does he?
He wasn't   hired,   was he?

I work   very hard,   don't I?
I'll get   a raise,   won't I?

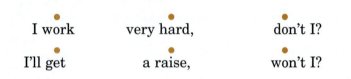

I shouldn't   buy it,   should I?
I wouldn't be   sorry,   would I?

You know them   well,   don't you?
You'll intro   duce me,   won't you?

We should   see it,   shouldn't we?
We'd   enjoy it,   wouldn't we?

You love to   dance,   don't you?
You'll come to   the party,   won't you?

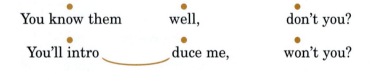

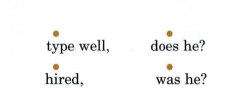

1. A. You haven't been standing in the rain long, ___have you___?

B. I'm afraid ___I have___.

A. ___You have___?! I'm really sorry. I had no idea it was so late.

2. A. Barbara is going to law school next year, _____?

B. No, _____.

A. _____?! I thought she wanted to be a lawyer like her mother.

3. A. Alan won't be graduating from college this year, _____?

B. Yes, _____.

A. _____?! I can't believe the time has gone by so fast.

4. A. Our spring vacation begins tomorrow, _____?

B. No, _____.

A. _____?! I'm really surprised. I've been looking forward to tomorrow all month.

5. A. It's time to eat. You brought the sandwiches, _____?

B. Sandwiches?! No, _____.

A. _____?! How could you have forgotten? I was sure you were going to bring them.

6. A. Ricky doesn't drive yet, _____?

B. I know it's hard to believe, but _____.

A. _____?! I can remember when he was just learning how to walk. Children grow up so quickly.

1. A. You were expecting us, ___weren't you___?
   B. Actually, I wasn't.
   A. You weren't?! I'm really surprised! I was

   sure ___you had been expecting___ us.

2. A. You have medical insurance, _____?
   B. Actually, I don't.
   A. You don't?! That's very surprising! I was

   sure _____ medical insurance.

3. A. She's been here before, _____?
   B. Actually, she hasn't.
   A. She hasn't?! I'm surprised! I was sure

   _____ here before.

4. A. He isn't going to be transferred, _____?
   B. Actually, he is.
   A. He is?! I don't believe it! I was sure

   _____ transferred.

5. A. We can leave early today, _____?
   B. Actually, we can't.
   A. We can't?! I'm really surprised! I

   was sure _____ early.

6. A. This suit is on sale, _____?
   B. Actually, it isn't.
   A. It isn't?! I can't believe it! I was

   sure this suit _____ on sale.

7. A. I don't have to work overtime, _____?
   B. Actually, you do.
   A. I do?! I can't believe it! I was sure

   _____ have to work overtime.

8. A. You'll marry her someday, _____?
   B. Actually, I won't.
   A. You won't?! I'm surprised! I was sure

   _____ her someday.

L **LISTENING**

Listen and complete the conversations.

1. a. she had been a doctor.
   b. she was going to be a doctor.

2. a. you had sold your house.
   b. you didn't sell your house.

3. a. it had new brakes.
   b. it has new brakes.

4. a. you aren't angry with me.
   b. you weren't angry with me.

5. a. they would be arriving this weekend.
   b. they'll be arriving this weekend.

6. a. you got searched.
   b. you hadn't gotten searched.

7. a. children were allowed to see it.
   b. children weren't allowed to see it.

8. a. he still worked at the bank.
   b. he still works at the bank.

9. a. she had been hired by the Bay Company.
   b. she was hired by the Bay Company.

10. a. he can deliver babies.
    b. he could deliver babies.

Central High School Reunion

1. A. Do you ever see our old friend Susan? She was one of the nicest people in our class.

   B. As a matter of fact, I see her all the time. I married her!

   A. _____You did_____?! I don't believe it! You _____didn't_____

   really _____marry_____ Susan, _____did you_____?

   B. Yes, _____I did_____.

2. A. Do you still go canoeing every weekend?

   B. Not anymore. I'm MUCH too busy. I have three small children at home.

   A. _____?! I never would have believed it!

   You _____ really _____ three children,

   _____?

   B. Yes, _____.

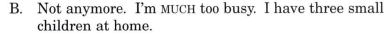

3. A. Do you still work for an insurance company?

   B. Not anymore. As a matter of fact, I'm the president of my own company.

   A. _____?! I don't believe it! You _____

   really the president of your own company,

   _____?

   B. Yes, _____.

4. A. Do you keep in touch with Julie Montero?

   B. Yes. I see her all the time. As a matter of fact, she was just chosen "Employee of the Year" at her company.

   A. _____?! That's fantastic! She _____

   really _____ "Employee of the Year," _____?

   B. Yes, _____.

(continued)

5. A. I wonder whatever happened to Margaret Wong.

B. Well, the last time I saw her she had just won a million dollars on a TV game show.

A. _____?! That's unbelievable! She _____ really _____ a million dollars, _____?

B. Yes, _____.

6. A. Have you heard? Vincent Lewis quit his job and

_____

B. _____?! I can't believe it! He _____ really do that, _____?

A. Yes, _____.

7. A. Tell me about your son, Billy. I hear he's a very special little boy.

B. You don't really want to hear about Billy, _____?

A. Yes, of course. I'm very interested.

B. Well, Billy is only four years old, but he can _____

_____

and _____.

A. _____?! I don't believe it! He _____ really do all those things, _____?

B. Yes, _____.

8. A. How's little Patty?

B. My daughter Patty isn't so little anymore. She's going to

_____ next month.

A. _____?! I don't believe it! She _____ really going to _____ next month, _____? She was just a baby the last time I saw her.

WHAT ARE THEY SAYING?

1. A. You know . . . you've been a little "touchy" recently.

   B. I guess you're right. I _____have_____ been a little "touchy" recently, _____haven't I_____!

2. A. You know, we shouldn't be fishing here.

   B. I suppose you're right. We _____ be fishing here, _____!

3. A. I think our guests had a great time at our party.

   B. I agree. They _____ a great time, _____!

4. A. You know . . . the people in this neighborhood aren't very friendly.

   B. You're right. They _____ very friendly, _____!

5. A. Mr. Mudge is in a terrible mood today.

   B. I agree. He _____ in a terrible mood today, _____!

6. A. You know . . . this pizza tastes terrible!

   B. You're right. This pizza _____ terrible, _____!

7. A. You know, I hate to say it, but you were impolite to the boss.

   B. I guess you're right. I _____ impolite to the boss, _____!

8. A. You know . . . I think we'll have to work overtime this weekend.

   B. I'm afraid you're right. We _____ have to work overtime, _____!

9. A. You know . . . we haven't called Grandma in a long time.

   B. You're right. We _____ called her in a long time, _____!

10. A. I'm sorry to say it, but that tie looks terrible with that shirt!

    B. I guess you're right. It _____ terrible with this shirt, _____!

11. You know . . . you drove through that intersection too fast!

    You're right. I _____ through that intersection too fast, _____!

A. I'm thinking of breaking up with my boyfriend, Howard.

B. I don't believe it. Why do you want to break up with Howard? He's a wonderful person. He's kind and generous.

A. I guess he ____is__ __1__ kind and generous, ____isn't he__ __2__!

B. And he sends you flowers all the time.

A. Come to think of it, he _____ __3__ _____ __4__ me flowers all the time, _____ __5__!

B. And he's _____ __6__.

A. I guess you're right. He _____ __7__, _____ __8__!

B. And remember last month. Howard gave you _____ __9__, and you were very happy.

A. Come to think of it, he _____ __10__ _____ __11__ me _____ __12__

last month, _____ __13__! And I _____ __14__ very happy, _____ __15__!

B. Yes. But I really wasn't surprised because he's always given you a lot of presents.

A. That's true. He _____ __16__ always _____ __17__ me a lot of presents, _____ __18__!

B. Here's something else to think about. He doesn't _____ __19__.

A. You're right. He _____ __20__, _____ __21__!

B. Also, _____ __22__.

A. Come to think of it, that's true. _____ __23__,

_____ __24__!

B. And how do you think Howard would feel? He'd be very upset if you broke up with him.

A. I'm afraid you're right. He _____ __25__ be very upset, _____ __26__!
You know, I'm glad I talked to you. I guess I won't break up with Howard after all.

P LISTENING

Listen to each word and then say it.

1. boat
2. better
3. about
4. bought
5. bright

6. vote
7. vacation
8. avoid
9. oven
10. travel

11. won't
12. weather
13. away
14. window
15. worry

Q BEVERLY WILSON'S BROKEN KEYBOARD

Beverly Wilson's keyboard is broken. The b's, v's, and w's don't always work. Fill in the missing b', v's, and w's, and then read Beverly's letters aloud.

1.

Dear _B_etty,

You'_v_e pro__a__ly heard from Bo__ a__out the terri__le ro____eries __e'__e __een ha__ing in our neighborhood. (There ha__e __een se__en ro____eries in fi__e __eeks!) Of course, e__ery__ody's __een __ery __orried __ecause they still ha__en't disco__ered who the ro____ers are.

Last __ednesday, my neigh__or's __icycle __as stolen from his __asement. The next e__ening, some__ody __roke into a __uilding on __righton __oule__ard and took se__eral sil__er __racelets, a __allet, and t__o __edding rings.

Then last __eekend, __elie__e it or not, the Relia__le __ank __as ro____ed. I'll al__ays remem__er the e__ening of the ro____ery. I __as taking a __ath, and my hus__and, __ill, __as reading his fa__orite no__el in __ed __hen Ro__er __egan __arking. He must ha__e heard the ro____ers dri__ing a__ay. __y the time I got out of the __athtu__, e__ery__ody in the neigh__orhood __as talking a__out the ro____ers' escape.

__ell, e__er since the __ank ro____ery last __eekend, __e'__e all __een __ery ner__ous. Some of the neigh__ors are so __orried that they're thinking a__out mo__ing a__ay. __ill and I ha__e __een __ondering __hat __e should do.

Lo__e,

__e__erly

(continued)

2.

Dear __etsy,

__e're ha__ing a __edding anni__ersary cele__ration on __ednesday for my __rother-in-law, __arry, and his wife, Ro__erta, and __e __ould lo__e it if you and your hus__and, __alter, __ere there. It __on't __e a __ery __ig cele__ration, just a few relati__es, __illiam, __incent, Eliza__eth, Ste__e, and of course my __rothers and their __i__es.

__e've heard that your __rother's little __oy __o__ __y is __isiting you this __eek. __hy don't you __ring him along __ith you __hen you come o__er on __ednesday?

Lo__e,

__e__erly

3.

Dear Al__ert,

__e're ha__ing a __onderful time on our __acation in __oston, __ut __e __ish you and your __ife __ere here __ith us. I'm positi__e __oth you and __ar__ara __ould lo__e it here. __ar__ara __ould lo__e the __oston Pu__lic Garden and the __oats on the Charles Ri__er. And you __ould ha__e a __onderful time __isiting the uni__ersities and the __oston Pu__lic Li__rary. __e're staying __ith __ill's relati__es __hile __e're in __oston. They li__e in a __ery modern high-rise __uilding __ith a __eautiful __iew of the ri__er. __e'__e __een __ery lucky. __ill's relati__es dri__e us e__ery__here.

The __eather in __oston __as __ery __arm __hen __e arri__ed, but now it's __indy. I __ish __e had __rought __armer clothes to __ear.

__y the __ay, __ill and I __ent to a li__ely __ase__all game last __ednesday, and __e'__e __een to the __allet t__ice. __e'__e also __een __ery __usy __uying presents for e__ery__ody at home and sou__enirs for oursel__es. (Unfortunately, __e __eren't a__le to __uy the __atch your __rother __alter __anted.)

Lo__e,

__e__erly

A WHAT'S THE ANSWER?

1. I don't feel like _____ .
   a. take a walk
   b. taking a walk *(circled)*

2. I never get tired _____ .
   a. of going on picnics
   b. to go on picnics

3. I'm not going to work out today. _____ at the gym yesterday.
   a. If I had worked out
   b. I worked out

4. My friends and I usually love _____ the mall.
   a. going to
   b. going

5. Thanks. _____ to have dinner with you.
   a. I'll like
   b. I'd like

6. _____ go sailing?
   a. Would you like
   b. Would you like to

7. I'd be happy _____ you to the airport.
   a. to take
   b. take

8. _____ a movie yesterday, I'd be happy to go with you today.
   a. If I hadn't seen
   b. If I saw

9. I won't be able to go to your son's wedding. I hope _____ .
   a. you understand
   b. I understand

10. _____ you can't go bowling with us.
    a. I'd be disappointed
    b. I'm disappointed

B WHAT ARE THEY SAYING?

1. I really don't feel like ___eating___ at a restaurant with my friends tonight.

   I _____ at a restaurant last night.

2. Do you think _____ get tired of

   _____ dancing if you

   _____ dancing all the time?

3. I don't feel like _____ TV today.

   If I _____ TV all day yesterday, _____ certainly watch it today.

4. I've _____ the dishes every day this week, and I'm really tired of

   _____ them. I'd be happy

   _____ the dishes some other time, but not tonight!

see

A. Do you really want __to see__ ¹ a movie again tonight? I know

you enjoy _____ ² movies, but you've already

_____ ³ four movies this week, and you just

_____ ⁴ a movie this afternoon. Don't you EVER get

tired of _____ ⁵ movies? If I were you, I

certainly _____ ⁶ another movie tonight.

B. Maybe I'm a little crazy, but there's nothing I like more than

_____ ⁷ movies. I really DO feel like _____ ⁸

a movie with you tonight, and believe it or not, I'm planning

_____ ⁹ another movie tomorrow!

go

A. We're _____ ¹⁰ camping this weekend. Would you

like to come with us?

B. I don't really feel like _____ ¹¹ camping this

weekend. To be honest, I don't enjoy _____ ¹² camping.

A. You don't?! I thought you _____ ¹³ camping all the time!

B. I do, but that's only because everybody else in my family loves

_____ ¹⁴ camping. If you really want to know the

truth, I can't stand _____ ¹⁵ camping! Ever since I

first _____ ¹⁶ camping years ago, I've hated it! If my

family didn't enjoy _____ ¹⁷ camping so much,

I'd never _____ ¹⁸ camping at all!

A. I'm sorry you feel that way. I'll never ask you _____ ¹⁹ camping

again!

Listen. Then clap and practice.

I suppose you'd   get tired of   driving   downtown
If you drove   downtown   every day.
You would also   get tired of   driving   around
If you didn't   know   your way.

I suppose you'd   get tired of   eating   cheese
If you ate it   at every   meal.
You'd probably   get   a bad stomachache
And complain about   how   you feel.

I suppose you'd   get tired of   typing   reports
If you typed them   without   taking breaks.
If you didn't   stop   and rest   for a while,
Your reports would be   full of   mistakes.

I suppose   I'd get tired of   having   cake
If I had some   each night   for dinner.
If I had   more fruit   instead of   cake
I'd probably   be   a lot thinner.

I suppose you'd   get tired of   watching   TV
If you always   watched the same shows.
If you listened to   music   or read   a book,
You wouldn't   be bored,   I suppose.

E THEY NEVER WOULD HAVE DONE THAT!

1. Emily hit the wrong key and deleted all her files.

   If _____she hadn't hit_____ the wrong key,

   she never _____would have deleted_____ all her files.

2. Henry drove into a tree because he was daydreaming.

   If _____ daydreaming, he never

   _____ into a tree.

3. I got a terrible score on my SAT because during the test I had my mind on something else.

   If _____ my mind on something else,

   I never _____ a terrible score.

4. My wife and I were an hour late to the party because we misunderstood the directions.

   If _____ the directions,

   we never _____ an hour late to the party.

5. Albert decided to take a bath, and he forgot to take his cake out of the oven.

   If _____ to take a bath,

   he never _____ to take his cake out of the oven.

6. Alice put salt in her coffee. She thought it was sugar.

   If _____ it was sugar,

   she never _____ salt in her coffee.

7. Mr. and Mrs. Jackson accidentally mixed up their VCR tapes, and they erased the video of their wedding.

   If _____ their VCR tapes,

   they never _____ the video of their wedding.

F GRAMMARRAP: *I Must Have*

Listen. Then clap and practice.

I'm very   sorry   I took   your CD.

I must have   thought   it belonged   to me.

I'm sorry   it's midnight,   and now   you're awake.

I must have   called you   by   mistake.

The cake was   bad,   and it's all   my fault.

I must have   mixed up   the sugar   and salt.

I'm sorry   I shouted.   I know   I was rude.

I must have   been   in a very bad   mood.

G YOU DECIDE: *I'm Really Sorry*

1. You've been invited to a party. You arrive on the wrong day. Your friends are cleaning their house!

YOUR FRIENDS: What a nice surprise! As you can see, we're getting ready for tomorrow's party.

YOU: ....

YOUR FRIENDS: ....

YOU: ....

2. You've been stopped by a police officer because you went through a red light at the last intersection.

POLICE OFFICER: You just drove through a red light! Didn't you see it?

YOU: ....

POLICE OFFICER: ....

YOU: ....

1. A. My husband is out of work.

   B. What a shame! How long
      _____has he been_____ out of work?

   A. _____For_____ more than two months.

3. A. I'm having trouble concentrating on my work.

   B. That's too bad. How long _____
      _____
      concentrating on your work?

   A. _____ I moved to Hawaii.

5. A. My knees hurt!

   B. I'm sorry to hear that. How long
      _____?

   A. _____ the past few weeks.

7. A. My employees are on strike.

   B. They are? How long _____
      _____ on strike?

   A. _____ more than a month.

2. A. My house has termites!

   B. That's terrible! How long _____
      _____ termites?

   A. _____ last summer.

4. A. I've been feeling a little depressed recently.

   B. That's a shame. How long _____
      _____ depressed?

   A. _____ my girlfriend broke up with me.

6. A. My car is at the repair shop.

   B. Oh, really? How long _____
      _____ at the repair shop?

   A. _____ last Monday.

8. A. My wife wants to buy a motorcycle.

   B. She does?! How long _____
      _____ a motorcycle?

   A. _____ her fortieth birthday.

I WHAT'S WRONG?

for	since

DOCTOR: How long have you been sick, Mr. Lawson?

PATIENT: I've been sick ____*since*___ [1] last Tuesday.

DOCTOR: I see. How long have you had a pain in your chest?

PATIENT: I've had a pain in my chest _____ [2] about three days.

And I've had a backache _____ [3] last week.

DOCTOR: You have a fever, too. Do you know how long you've had a fever?

PATIENT: _____ [4] the past week. Also, I've felt dizzy _____ [5] I got the fever.

DOCTOR: Tell me, Mr. Lawson, have you been working?

PATIENT: No, I've been at home _____ [6] April 2nd. And I've been in bed _____ [7] about a week. I've been very tired.

I've been sleeping _____ [8] about 14 hours a day.

DOCTOR: I think you need to go to the hospital so we can do some tests.

How long has it been _____ [9] you had a physical examination?

PATIENT: I haven't seen a doctor _____ [10] more than a year.

DOCTOR: Well, you certainly need a complete examination. You really should take better care of yourself.

J LISTENING

Listen and complete the sentences.

1. a. last week.
   b. two days.

2. a. last weekend.
   b. three days.

3. a. Monday morning.
   b. more than a week.

4. a. a long time.
   b. I returned from my trip.

5. a. many weeks.
   b. we got married.

6. a. over a week.
   b. I started calling him.

7. a. the past few months.
   b. we discovered termites.

8. a. two or three weeks.
   b. I bought it.

9. a. at least a week.
   b. the other day.

WHAT'S THE ANSWER?

1. I can't _____ my new apartment until next week.
   - a. move into *(circled)*
   - b. move

2. My husband almost always _____ the children after school.
   - a. picks out
   - b. picks up

3. My cousin said she would come over and _____ my new curtains.
   - a. put on
   - b. put up

4. Please tell Ms. Lee I'm _____, and I'll be at the office soon.
   - a. on my way
   - b. in my way

5. My husband and I have to _____ a gift for his sister's new baby.
   - a. pick out
   - b. pick on

6. It's important to _____ the application completely.
   - a. fill
   - b. fill out

7. Our teacher wants us to _____ the math problems by ourselves.
   - a. figure
   - b. figure out

8. Can you send someone to _____ my new computer?
   - a. hook up
   - b. hook on

9. I need some help this afternoon. Can you possibly _____?
   - a. give me a hand
   - b. hand me

10. Before I can use it, I need to _____ my new cell phone.
    - a. call
    - b. program

L **COMPLETE THE SENTENCES**

1. I'm sorry I can't help you move tomorrow. I have to work.

   If I ___didn't have to___ work, I'd be glad to help you move.

2. It's a shame you're sick. If I had known you _____ sick, I wouldn't have bothered you.

3. I'm sorry you're having trouble _____ up your satellite dish. If I _____ busy all day, I'd be happy to help you.

4. I didn't realize you _____ programmed your new cell phone. That's why I couldn't reach you.

5. If I _____ on my way to an important job interview now, _____ be glad to help you hook up your new DVD player.

6. It's too bad you're having trouble _____ out the math problems. _____ come over and help you, but I've got a doctor's appointment.

7. If I _____ about _____ leave for a vacation, _____ be happy to help you move today.

8. I didn't know you _____ trouble setting up your computer. If I _____

   you _____ trouble, I _____ come over and helped you. Next time you have a problem, don't forget to call me.

Listen. Then clap and practice.

If I had known   you were packing   for your trip   to Japan,

I never would have   called you   to help me   fix my van.

If I had known that   your children   were sick   with the flu,

I never would have   offered   to take them   to the zoo.

If I had known   you were waiting for   the carpenter   to call,

I never would have   asked you   to help me   paint my hall.

If I had known that   your relatives   were visiting   from Spain,

I never would have   called you   to help me   fix my drain.

If I had known that you were planning   to give your dog   a bath,

I never would have   called you   to help me   with my math.

WHAT'S THE WORD?

about	by	in	into	of	on	out	to	up	with

1. I can't stop sneezing. I think I'm allergic ____to____ something in this room!

2. Do you _____ any chance know when the movie begins?

3. Sylvia is being sent to London _____ business next month.

4. I got confused, and I mixed _____ the sugar and flour containers.

5. Jack got _____ a terrible argument, and I had to break up the fight.

6. If you drop _____ of school, I know you'll regret it.

7. What are you worried _____? I'm sure you'll do well on the exam.

8. The elevator in our building has been out _____ order for several weeks!

9. They don't have anything _____ common. Do they get along _____ each other?

about	at	by	from	in	of	off	on	past	to	up	with

10. I'll be away for a few days. I'm sorry I won't be able to help you hook _____ your new computer.

11. Do you by any chance know who this beautiful building was designed _____?

12. I'm not sure whether your car is ready. Why don't you check _____ the mechanic?

13. I'm concerned _____ Mrs. Wong. She was taken _____ the hospital last night.

14. The Blakes love their new apartment. It has a beautiful view _____ the river.

15. You've been complaining all day. You're _____ a terrible mood, aren't you!

16. I think you just drove _____ my house. We'll have to turn around.

17. Let's meet at Dave's Diner for lunch _____ around noon.

18. I should have turned _____ the TV and gone to sleep!

19. We ate lunch at a restaurant far _____ our office.

20. Careful! Don't step _____ that wet floor!

⓪ WHAT'S THE WORD?

allergic	ingredients	quit	tie
balance	mess	rewind	tournament
delete	misunderstood	scrap	unemployed
files	move out	slipped	wallpaper
hamster	passport	suspect	wisdom

1. My father is wearing a cast on his leg. He lost his _____balance_____ and fell off a ladder.

2. Don't forget to take your _____ with you when you leave the country.

3. The painter says we need new _____ in our living room.

4. The police finally arrested the _____ in all the robberies in our neighborhood.

5. My son is growing up. Last week he learned how to _____ his shoes.

6. I'm sorry I missed your barbecue last week. It completely _____ my mind.

7. Edward couldn't finish making his cake. He ran out of _____.

8. Many people need to have their _____ teeth removed.

9. It's difficult for parents to adjust when their children grow up and _____ on their own.

10. The McDonalds had to get rid of their cat because Mr. McDonald was _____ to it.

11. It isn't a good idea to _____ your job if the economy isn't good.

12. My friends and I did our homework incorrectly. We must have _____ the directions.

13. Our _____ got out of its cage and made a big _____ in the kitchen.

14. Here. You can use this. It's just a piece of _____ paper.

15. I hope I find a job soon. I hate being _____.

16. Cindy is a talented athlete. She won the school tennis _____ again.

17. Before you use the VCR, you need to _____ the tape.

18. Be careful! Don't hit the wrong key and _____ all the _____ on your computer.

LISTENING

Read the questions. Listen to each passage. Then answer the questions.

Jeff's Problem

1. Jeff's friend advised him _____.
   a. not to talk to his boss
   b. to talk to his boss

2. Jeff told his boss _____.
   a. why he didn't like his job
   b. why he was satisfied with his work

3. Jeff's boss said _____.
   a. she complained too much
   b. she wasn't pleased with his work

4. Jeff wishes _____.
   a. he had listened to his friend
   b. he weren't unemployed

Amy and Tom

5. Amy's parents told her _____.
   a. to marry Tom
   b. not to marry Tom

6. Amy's parents thought Tom was _____.
   a. lazy
   b. successful

7. Amy is happy because _____.
   a. she followed her parents' advice
   b. Tom has been a wonderful husband

8. Amy isn't concerned because her sons _____.
   a. aren't like their father
   b. are just like her husband

Q **OUT OF PLACE**

1. cut	bite	date	hurt	destroy
2. superintendent	politician	mail carrier	snowman	librarian
3. CD	DVD	disk	mural	keyboard
4. astronomy	chemistry	apology	history	philosophy
5. lake	pond	ocean	poodle	river
6. teacher	baker	customer	professor	instructor
7. depressed	discovered	disappointed	upset	sick and tired
8. hamster	cockroach	cactus	dolphin	puppy
9. usher	prime minister	mayor	senator	governor
10. unemployed	fired	retired	promoted	out of work
11. assemble	delete	disconnect	erase	lose
12. amazing	fascinating	magnificent	aggressive	impressive
13. rewrite	register	replace	reopen	repaint
14. tires	accident	headlight	bumper	battery
15. annoyed	irritable	angry	mad	confused

Listen to each word and then say it.

1. blush—brush
2. light—right
3. long—wrong
4. vote—boat

5. chop—shop
6. she's—cheese
7. watch—wash
8. heard—hurt

9. ride—write
10. ridden—written
11. someday—Sunday
12. mice—nice

13. send—sent
14. wide—white
15. run—rung

S HAVE YOU HEARD?

Listen and complete the sentences.

watch	wash

1. a. . . . TV?
   (b.) . . . my shirt? It's dirty.

light	right

2. a. . . . I agree with you.
   b. . . . just went out. It's dark in here.

Someday	Sunday

3. a. . . . is my favorite day of the week.
   b. . . . I'll be rich and famous.

long	wrong

4. a. . . . It's more than 3 pages.
   b. . . . , but I can't find my mistake.

light	right

5. a. . . . I can lift it easily.
   b. . . . Your answer is fine.

watch	wash

6. a. . . . the dishes now.
   b. . . . my favorite TV program.

hurt	heard

7. a. . . . about Jane?
   b. . . . your arm?

chopping	shopping

8. a. . . . onions.
   b. . . . at the supermarket.

boys	voice

9. a. . . . are my nephews.
   b. . . . is better than mine.

heard	hurt

10. a. . . . my ankle.
    b. . . . from Jack recently.

ridden	written

11. a. . . . to your cousins?
    b. . . . your bicycle recently?

blushes	brushes

12. a. . . . when he makes a mistake.
    b. . . . his teeth every morning.

A. Complete the sentences.

Ex. Betty was in the office yesterday, _____wasn't she_____?

1. The plane hasn't arrived yet, _____?

2. You fed the hamster, _____?

3. There weren't any cell phones when you were young, _____?

4. We don't need a new toaster, _____?

5. Your son plays on the school baseball team, _____?

6. Your parents won't be home this afternoon, _____?

7. You didn't forget to drop off the clothes at the cleaners, _____?

8. You can come to my party this weekend, _____?

9. I'm a good husband, _____?

10. You'll be finished soon, _____?

B. Respond with an emphatic sentence.

Ex. A. Howard is a hard worker.

    B. You're right. _____He is a hard worker_____, _____isn't he_____!

1. A. Aunt Fran hasn't called in a long time.

    B. You're right. _____, _____!

2. A. That was a boring movie.

    B. I agree. _____, _____!

3. A. Carol works very hard.

    B. You're right. _____, _____!

4. A. Your son will be a fine doctor someday.

    B. I agree. _____, _____!

5. A. Those cookies taste wonderful.

    B. You're right. _____, _____!

C. Write the question.

Ex. I've decided to <u>quit my job</u>. <u>What have you decided to do</u> ?

1. We'll be staying <u>at the Ritz Hotel</u>. _____?

2. We got engaged <u>a few days ago</u>. _____?

3. We spent <u>fifty dollars</u>. _____?

4. My father has been cooking <u>all day</u>. _____?

5. She mentioned you <u>six times</u>. _____?

6. I was assembling <u>my new bookcases</u>. _____?

7. He goes to the gym <u>because he wants to lose weight</u>. _____?

D. Fill in the blanks.

see

I don't really feel like _____ [1] a movie again tonight. I usually enjoy _____ [2] movies, but I've already _____ [3] three movies this week, and I just _____ [4] a very boring movie last night. If I _____ [5] so many movies this week, I'd be happy _____ [6] a movie with you tonight.

E. Listening

Listen and complete the sentences.

Ex. a. I never drive past your house.
   (b.) I never would have driven past your house.

1. a. I'd be happy to take a walk with you today.
   b. I'll be happy to take a walk with you today.

2. a. I wouldn't delete all my files.
   b. I wouldn't have deleted all my files.

3. a. if you go dancing all the time.
   b. if you went dancing all the time.

4. a. I wouldn't have called you.
   b. I won't call you.

5. a. I'll be glad to help you put in your air conditioner.
   b. I'd be glad to help you put in your air conditioner.

ACHIEVEMENT TESTS

Name _____

Date _____ **Class** _____

Example:

Sam has to _____ his son at school.
- Ⓐ worry
- Ⓑ volunteer
- ● pick up
- Ⓓ pay attention

1. He's gotten behind in class because he was _____ for three days.
- Ⓐ absent
- Ⓑ appointment
- Ⓒ absence
- Ⓓ afraid

2. Parents should _____ the teacher about bullying.
- Ⓐ discuss
- Ⓑ tease
- Ⓒ compliment
- Ⓓ speak with

3. Parents have to sign _____ form for the class trip.
- Ⓐ a concern
- Ⓑ an absence
- Ⓒ a permission
- Ⓓ an appointment

4. If you are worried about your child's progress in school, it's a good idea to _____.
- Ⓐ apologize to the teacher
- Ⓑ contact the teacher
- Ⓒ call the school nurse
- Ⓓ excuse the teacher

5. Talking with children about what they are learning at school shows that you _____ their education.
- Ⓐ pay attention
- Ⓑ succeed
- Ⓒ value
- Ⓓ don't care about

6. Children should _____ while doing their homework.
- Ⓐ watch TV
- Ⓑ talk to friends online
- Ⓒ talk to friends on the telephone
- Ⓓ study in a quiet place

7. Pay attention to any social problems your child talks about, such as _____.
- Ⓐ fights or teasing
- Ⓑ parties or games
- Ⓒ grades or tests
- Ⓓ lunches or snacks

8. A breakfast that is _____ will give students energy for the school day.
- Ⓐ quick and strong
- Ⓑ high in sugar
- Ⓒ low in protein
- Ⓓ nutritious

9. A _____ is a good way to find out about your child's progress in school.
- Ⓐ school health meeting
- Ⓑ parent-teacher conference
- Ⓒ school volunteer meeting
- Ⓓ class field trip

1 Ⓐ Ⓑ Ⓒ Ⓓ   4 Ⓐ Ⓑ Ⓒ Ⓓ   7 Ⓐ Ⓑ Ⓒ Ⓓ

2 Ⓐ Ⓑ Ⓒ Ⓓ   5 Ⓐ Ⓑ Ⓒ Ⓓ   8 Ⓐ Ⓑ Ⓒ Ⓓ

3 Ⓐ Ⓑ Ⓒ Ⓓ   6 Ⓐ Ⓑ Ⓒ Ⓓ   9 Ⓐ Ⓑ Ⓒ Ⓓ

Go to the next page ⟩

Example:

Grant School. How _____ help you?
- Ⓐ I can
- Ⓑ may
- Ⓒ I may
- ⬤ may I

10. This is Mary Chan. My son Tim _____ very sick. He won't be at school today. His teacher is Ms. Clark.
- Ⓐ will be
- Ⓑ has been
- Ⓒ been
- Ⓓ isn't

11. Okay. I'll let Ms. Clark know that Tim _____ today.
- Ⓐ absence
- Ⓑ absent
- Ⓒ will be absent
- Ⓓ reports his absence

12. Thank you. I think _____ better tomorrow.
- Ⓐ he'll
- Ⓑ he was
- Ⓒ he'll be
- Ⓓ he's been

13. I'm your daughter's teacher. I'm calling because I'm _____ her progress at school.
- Ⓐ worried about
- Ⓑ afraid of
- Ⓒ helpful
- Ⓓ pleased to meet

$12 \div 2 =$
$15 \div 3 =$

14. Oh, really? _____ problems lately?
- Ⓐ Does she have
- Ⓑ Will she be having
- Ⓒ Did she used to have
- Ⓓ Has she been having

15. Yes. She seems very tired, and _____ trouble concentrating in class.
- Ⓐ she had
- Ⓑ she's having
- Ⓒ she'll have
- Ⓓ she's going to have

16. Thanks for telling me. She usually _____ to bed at midnight.
- Ⓐ goes
- Ⓑ going
- Ⓒ had gone
- Ⓓ will have gone

17. That's very late. I think she needs _____.
- Ⓐ she's sleeping
- Ⓑ help her sleep
- Ⓒ a good night's sleep
- Ⓓ good night

18. I understand. I'll make sure _____.
- Ⓐ she gets up earlier
- Ⓑ she goes to bed earlier
- Ⓒ she is awake in the morning
- Ⓓ she has breakfast

10 Ⓐ Ⓑ Ⓒ Ⓓ   13 Ⓐ Ⓑ Ⓒ Ⓓ   15 Ⓐ Ⓑ Ⓒ Ⓓ   17 Ⓐ Ⓑ Ⓒ Ⓓ

11 Ⓐ Ⓑ Ⓒ Ⓓ   14 Ⓐ Ⓑ Ⓒ Ⓓ   16 Ⓐ Ⓑ Ⓒ Ⓓ   18 Ⓐ Ⓑ Ⓒ Ⓓ

12 Ⓐ Ⓑ Ⓒ Ⓓ

Name _____ **Date** _____

Look at this school announcement. Then do Numbers 19 through 24.

Mark your calendar!

BACK-TO-SCHOOL NIGHT
GRANT MIDDLE SCHOOL
TUES., SEPT. 15, 7:00 PM – 9:30 PM

Save the date!

Parents: *You're invited to our first school event of the year. Come meet your child's teachers, the school staff, and the principal!*

Schedule
7:00 – 7:10 **Principal Sandra Lopez** (Greeting and opening message)
Auditorium

7:15 – 7:25 **Homeroom visits** (Visit the homeroom class where your child begins the day. This is Period 1.)

7:30 – 8:40 **Subject classroom visits** (Follow your child's schedule.)
7:30–7:40 Period 2   8:00–8:10 Period 4   8:30–8:40 Period 6
7:45–7:55 Period 3   8:15–8:25 Period 5

8:45 – 9:00 **Talk with subject teachers** (Talk with your child's subject teachers and sign up for October Parent-Teacher Conferences.)
Gym

9:00 – 9:30 **Visit information tables** (Learn more about the Parent-Teacher Association, After-school programs, Sports, Counseling, and Volunteer opportunities.)
Library

19. The homeroom is _____.
   Ⓐ where students register
   Ⓑ where students do homework
   Ⓒ where students have their first class
   Ⓓ where students have all of their classes

20. To find out about athletic programs, parents should go to _____.
   Ⓐ the gym
   Ⓑ the library
   Ⓒ the auditorium
   Ⓓ the homeroom

21. Parent-Teacher conferences are held in _____.
   Ⓐ the gym
   Ⓑ the library
   Ⓒ September
   Ⓓ October

22. Each subject classroom visit lasts for _____ minutes.
   Ⓐ 5
   Ⓑ 10
   Ⓒ 30
   Ⓓ 60

23. The first place parents should go on Back-to-School night is the _____.
   Ⓐ homeroom
   Ⓑ gym
   Ⓒ library
   Ⓓ auditorium

24. We can infer that _____ will be at the event.
   Ⓐ all of the teachers
   Ⓑ only homeroom teachers
   Ⓒ only subject teachers
   Ⓓ only parents

19 Ⓐ Ⓑ Ⓒ Ⓓ   21 Ⓐ Ⓑ Ⓒ Ⓓ   23 Ⓐ Ⓑ Ⓒ Ⓓ
20 Ⓐ Ⓑ Ⓒ Ⓓ   22 Ⓐ Ⓑ Ⓒ Ⓓ   24 Ⓐ Ⓑ Ⓒ Ⓓ

Go to the next page ➤ T3

Read the notes from parents. Then do Numbers 25 through 28.

Oct. 17, 2009

Dear Mr. Vega,

My son, Mark, will be absent from school on Friday next week. He has a dentist appointment and will not be able to return to school. He's going to have a tooth pulled. Please excuse his absence. Also, he will ask you for any assignments on Thursday.

Sincerely,
Paul Chase
379-1287

October 16, 2009

Dear Mr. Vega,

My daughter, Rachel, has been very upset about school lately. She says that other girls are teasing her during recess. They've been making fun of her clothing and her hair. Rachel has been crying every day after school.

Could you kindly call me this week to talk about this problem? The best time to call is between 6 p.m. and 9 p.m. Thank you.

Yours truly,
Roberta Smith
379-5670

Subject:	**Kim Wong**
Date:	Monday, October 17, 2009 7:59 PM
From:	Peter Wong <peter.wong@mrn.com>
To:	Daniel Vega <dvega@dps.k12.org>

Dear Mr. Vega:

I'm writing you about my daughter, Kim Wong. She's been having trouble seeing the blackboard from her seat at the back of the classroom. We have scheduled an appointment with the eye doctor for Saturday to see if she needs glasses. In the meantime, could you please move her seat assignment to the front row so she can see the board? Thank you for your help.

Sincerely,
Peter Wong

---

25. Kim has a doctor's appointment _____.
   - Ⓐ on Saturday
   - Ⓑ on Friday
   - Ⓒ next week
   - Ⓓ on October 17

26. Ms. Smith wrote to Mr. Vega because her daughter _____.
   - Ⓐ was absent
   - Ⓑ is teasing other girls
   - Ⓒ has been upset
   - Ⓓ doesn't like her clothing

27. Currently, Kim sits _____.
   - Ⓐ in back of the blackboard
   - Ⓑ far from the blackboard
   - Ⓒ in front of the class
   - Ⓓ behind Rachel

28. Mark will be absent _____.
   - Ⓐ for a week
   - Ⓑ on Thursday
   - Ⓒ on Thursday and Friday
   - Ⓓ for one day next week

---

25 Ⓐ Ⓑ Ⓒ Ⓓ   26 Ⓐ Ⓑ Ⓒ Ⓓ   27 Ⓐ Ⓑ Ⓒ Ⓓ   28 Ⓐ Ⓑ Ⓒ Ⓓ

E CLOZE READING: A Letter from the Principal

Choose the correct answers to complete the letter.

CHAVEZ *High School*

Dear Parents,

Welcome to Chavez High School! We know you want your child to support succeed increase,
Ⓐ ● Ⓒ

so here are some homework tips questions chores ²⁹ for parents.
Ⓐ Ⓑ Ⓒ

• Make sure your child has a big quiet cheap ³⁰ place to do homework.
Ⓐ Ⓑ Ⓒ

• Be positive about homework. Your sign problem attitude ³¹ should show that
Ⓐ Ⓑ Ⓒ

you value education. Ask questions and show you are interested energetic specific ³².
Ⓐ Ⓑ Ⓒ

• Many students need help to manage and organize research behave ³³ their study time.
Ⓐ Ⓑ Ⓒ

Help your child show schedule cancel ³⁴ a daily time for homework.
Ⓐ Ⓑ Ⓒ

• Make sure your child understands each test attention assignment ³⁵. If something is not
Ⓐ Ⓑ Ⓒ

clear, your child can call a classmate or contact come up limit ³⁶ the teacher by e-mail.
Ⓐ Ⓑ Ⓒ

• If you have any questions or examples opportunities concerns³⁷, get in touch with your
Ⓐ Ⓑ Ⓒ

child's teacher by phone or e-mail.

Sincerely,

Janet Morris

Janet Morris, Principal

F LISTENING ASSESSMENT: Reporting an Absence

Read and listen to the questions. Then listen to the parent's message and answer the questions.

38. Who is leaving a message?
Ⓐ The student.
Ⓑ The mother.
Ⓒ The secretary.
Ⓓ The principal.

39. What grade is the student in?
Ⓐ Ninth.
Ⓑ Tenth.
Ⓒ Eleventh.
Ⓓ Twelfth.

40. Why is the student absent?
Ⓐ He has a baseball game.
Ⓑ He is sick.
Ⓒ He broke his leg.
Ⓓ He hurt his ankle.

29 Ⓐ Ⓑ Ⓒ Ⓓ 32 Ⓐ Ⓑ Ⓒ Ⓓ 35 Ⓐ Ⓑ Ⓒ Ⓓ 38 Ⓐ Ⓑ Ⓒ Ⓓ
30 Ⓐ Ⓑ Ⓒ Ⓓ 33 Ⓐ Ⓑ Ⓒ Ⓓ 36 Ⓐ Ⓑ Ⓒ Ⓓ 39 Ⓐ Ⓑ Ⓒ Ⓓ
31 Ⓐ Ⓑ Ⓒ Ⓓ 34 Ⓐ Ⓑ Ⓒ Ⓓ 37 Ⓐ Ⓑ Ⓒ Ⓓ 40 Ⓐ Ⓑ Ⓒ Ⓓ

Go to the next page  **T5**

Duc Vu needs to write a note to Mrs. Roke, his son's teacher. His son's name is Tom Vu. Tom was absent on Wednesday and Thursday because he was sick. He had a bad stomachache and a fever. Today is Friday, May 1. Tom is at school today. He needs the assignments from Wednesday and Thursday. On Monday morning, May 4, Tom has a doctor's appointment. He will arrive at school after the appointment at about 11:00 A.M. Write a letter to the teacher.

_____
(today's date)

_____
(salutation)

_____

_____

_____

_____

_____

_____

_____

_____

_____

_____

_____

_____
(closing)

_____
(signature)

H SPEAKING ASSESSMENT

I can ask and answer these questions:

Ask Answer
- ☐ ☐ How long have you lived here?
- ☐ ☐ Where did you live before?
- ☐ ☐ How long did you live there?
- ☐ ☐ How long have you been going to this school?

Ask Answer
- ☐ ☐ Have you ever been absent from class? When? Why?
- ☐ ☐ Where do you usually do your homework?
- ☐ ☐ How can parents help children succeed in school?

STOP

Name _____

Date _____ Class _____

2

A DRIVING RULES; DIRECTIONS

Example:

The police officer _____ the speeding car.
- Ⓐ pulled on
- ● pulled over
- Ⓒ passed over
- Ⓓ pulled

1. Be sure to _____ in a school zone.
   - Ⓐ go through
   - Ⓑ stop
   - Ⓒ slow down
   - Ⓓ slow up

2. If you are stopped, an officer will ask for your _____.
   - Ⓐ social security card
   - Ⓑ registration and license
   - Ⓒ license and social security card
   - Ⓓ address

3. Rashid got a ticket for driving _____ on a one-way street.
   - Ⓐ the wrong way
   - Ⓑ the right way
   - Ⓒ the left way
   - Ⓓ the legal way

4. Could you tell me _____ the post office?
   - Ⓐ how going to
   - Ⓑ to get to
   - Ⓒ how get to
   - Ⓓ how to get to

5. You can cause _____ if you drive through a red light.
   - Ⓐ an accident
   - Ⓑ a ticket
   - Ⓒ a crime
   - Ⓓ a violation

6. The train *departs at 10:05* means it _____ at 10:05.
   - Ⓐ arrives
   - Ⓑ leaves
   - Ⓒ delays
   - Ⓓ returns

7. You should _____ if you are pulled over by an officer.
   - Ⓐ get out of your car
   - Ⓑ stay in your car
   - Ⓒ put your hands up
   - Ⓓ open your car door

8. Making an illegal left turn is a traffic _____.
   - Ⓐ zone
   - Ⓑ report
   - Ⓒ ticket
   - Ⓓ violation

9. Always answer a police officer's questions _____.
   - Ⓐ intelligently
   - Ⓑ quickly
   - Ⓒ politely
   - Ⓓ loudly

1 Ⓐ Ⓑ Ⓒ Ⓓ   4 Ⓐ Ⓑ Ⓒ Ⓓ   7 Ⓐ Ⓑ Ⓒ Ⓓ

2 Ⓐ Ⓑ Ⓒ Ⓓ   5 Ⓐ Ⓑ Ⓒ Ⓓ   8 Ⓐ Ⓑ Ⓒ Ⓓ

3 Ⓐ Ⓑ Ⓒ Ⓓ   6 Ⓐ Ⓑ Ⓒ Ⓓ   9 Ⓐ Ⓑ Ⓒ Ⓓ

Go to the next page

Example:

_____ your license and registration. Do you know what you did wrong?
- Ⓐ You see
- Ⓑ I see
- Ⓒ Let you see
- ● Let me see

10. Yes. I _____ made a left turn at the corner.
- Ⓐ shouldn't
- Ⓑ shouldn't have
- Ⓒ didn't
- Ⓓ drove

11. That's right. You _____ caused an accident.
- Ⓐ might
- Ⓑ could
- Ⓒ could have
- Ⓓ had

12. I'm sorry. I _____ see the sign.
- Ⓐ didn't
- Ⓑ must
- Ⓒ must have
- Ⓓ may have

13. Excuse me. _____ me how to get to the library?
- Ⓐ Could tell
- Ⓑ Can't you tell
- Ⓒ Can you tell
- Ⓓ Have you told

14. Sure. _____ one block and _____ on Oak Street.
- Ⓐ Go straight . . . turn left
- Ⓑ Turn . . . straight
- Ⓒ Go . . . make right
- Ⓓ Down . . . make turn

15. Where's your sister? She _____ home an hour ago.
- Ⓐ should
- Ⓑ could
- Ⓒ could arrive
- Ⓓ should have arrived

16. She _____ missed the 5:30 train.
- Ⓐ might
- Ⓑ might have
- Ⓒ may
- Ⓓ could

17. Or, she _____ had to work late at the office.
- Ⓐ could
- Ⓑ have
- Ⓒ may
- Ⓓ may have

18. Maybe we _____ call her.
- Ⓐ might
- Ⓑ must have
- Ⓒ should
- Ⓓ should have

10 Ⓐ Ⓑ Ⓒ Ⓓ   13 Ⓐ Ⓑ Ⓒ Ⓓ   15 Ⓐ Ⓑ Ⓒ Ⓓ   17 Ⓐ Ⓑ Ⓒ Ⓓ

11 Ⓐ Ⓑ Ⓒ Ⓓ   14 Ⓐ Ⓑ Ⓒ Ⓓ   16 Ⓐ Ⓑ Ⓒ Ⓓ   18 Ⓐ Ⓑ Ⓒ Ⓓ

12 Ⓐ Ⓑ Ⓒ Ⓓ

Go to the next page ⟹

Look at the bus and train schedules. Then do Numbers 19 through 22.

Greyhound Bus		Bus 1431
Location	**Arrives**	**Departs**
Seattle, WA		1:35 PM
Tacoma, WA	2:20 PM	2:25 PM
Olympia, WA	3:05 PM	3:10 PM
Longview, WA	4:35 PM	4:35 PM
Vancouver, WA	5:25 PM	5:25 PM
Portland, OR	5:50 PM	6:55 PM
Salem, OR	7:55 PM	8:05 PM
Eugene, OR	9:25 PM	9:40 PM
Grants Pass, OR	12:15 AM	12:20 AM
Medford, OR	1:20 AM	1:30 AM
Redding, CA	4:30 AM	4:50 AM
Sacramento, CA	7:30 AM	

Greyhound Bus		Bus 1436
Location	**Arrives**	**Departs**
Sacramento, CA		6:00 PM
Chico, CA	8:15 PM	8:20 PM
Red Bluff, CA	9:10 PM	9:10 PM
Redding, CA	9:50 PM	10:20 PM
Medford, OR	1:20 AM	1:35 AM
Eugene, OR	4:35 AM	4:45 AM
Salem, OR	6:05 AM	6:10 AM
Portland, OR	7:10 AM	8:00 AM
Olympia, WA	10:00 AM	10:05 AM
Tacoma, WA	10:45 AM	10:55 AM
Seattle, WA	11:40 AM	

COAST STARLIGHT

Seattle • Vancouver • Portland • Eugene Redding • Chico • Sacramento

11		Train Number		11
Daily		Days of Operation		Daily
Read Down				Read Up
9 45A	Dp	Seattle, WA	Ar	8 45P
10 31A		Tacoma, WA		7 11P
11 21A		Olympia-Lacey, WA		6 22P
12 29P		Kelso-Longview, WA		5 14P
1 08P		Vancouver, WA		4 36P
1 50P	Ar	Portland, OR	Dp	4 20P
2 25P	Dp		Ar	3 40P
3 37P		Salem, OR		2 03P
4 10P		Albany, OR		1 30P
5 10P		Eugene-Springfield, OR		12 44P
8 05P		Chemult, OR		9 40A
10 00P		Klamath Falls, OR		8 25A
12 35A		Dunsmuir, CA		5 04A
2 21A		Redding, CA		3 14A
3 50A		Chico, CA		1 55A
6 35A	Ar	Sacramento, CA	Dp	11 59P

19. How long does it take to go by bus from Tacoma, WA, to Sacramento, CA?
- Ⓐ 13 hours
- Ⓑ 13 hours and 15 minutes
- Ⓒ 17 hours
- Ⓓ 17 hours and 5 minutes

20. How long does Bus 1436 stop in Portland, OR?
- Ⓐ 10 minutes
- Ⓑ 15 minutes
- Ⓒ 50 minutes
- Ⓓ 1 hour and 5 minutes

21. What time does the train depart Vancouver, WA, for Seattle, WA?
- Ⓐ 9:45 AM
- Ⓑ 1:08 PM
- Ⓒ 4:36 PM
- Ⓓ 8:45 PM

22. On Train 14, how long does it take to travel from Chico, CA, to Portland, OR?
- Ⓐ 13 hours and 15 minutes
- Ⓑ 13 hours and 45 minutes
- Ⓒ 14 hours
- Ⓓ 14 hours and 35 minutes

19 Ⓐ Ⓑ Ⓒ Ⓓ   20 Ⓐ Ⓑ Ⓒ Ⓓ   21 Ⓐ Ⓑ Ⓒ Ⓓ   22 Ⓐ Ⓑ Ⓒ Ⓓ

Go to the next page ⟶

Read the flyer. Then do Numbers 23 though 28.

Neighborhood Watch

What is Neighborhood Watch?

The NEIGHBORHOOD WATCH program works to bring communities together with the police to achieve the common goal of preventing crime. NEIGHBORHOOD WATCH informs residents about how to discourage and prevent crimes such as burglary, auto theft, and car break-ins. Issues such as vandalism, graffiti, drug dealing, and gang activity are also discussed when necessary.

How can a meeting be arranged?

To request a NEIGHBORHOOD WATCH, call Crime Prevention at (321) 223-4567. The Crime Specialist will work with you to schedule the meeting date. Invitation notices will be sent to you to distribute to your neighbors.

NEIGHBORHOOD WATCH meetings are held on Monday, Tuesday, Wednesday, or Thursday evenings at 7:00 P.M. and last approximately two hours. At least TEN homes must be represented in order for the meeting to take place. Most meetings are held in your home or at a neighborhood center.

What happens at the meeting?

At a NEIGHBORHOOD WATCH meeting, you will meet a representative of your police department and discuss how to solve problems in your community or to keep the problems from starting in the first place!

Through this program, you will learn facts about:
- Police districts
- Duties of local officers
- Crime trends in your area
- How to react to suspicious or criminal activity
- How our city's 911 system works
- How to make your home safer with special locks, alarms, and lighting

Residents at the meeting will receive a NEIGHBORHOOD WATCH window sign and other materials.

If at least 80% of the homes on your block come to the meeting, metal NEIGHBORHOOD WATCH signs will be installed on the streetlight poles on your block.

> YOUR CITY'S POLICE DEPARTMENT wants to work with you to reduce crime!

---

23. The goal of a Neighborhood Watch program is to help residents _____.
- Ⓐ meet their neighbors
- Ⓑ have neighborhood meetings
- Ⓒ prevent crime
- Ⓓ call the police

24. To schedule a meeting, a resident _____.
- Ⓐ calls the police department
- Ⓑ calls the Crime Prevention unit
- Ⓒ calls at 7 PM
- Ⓓ writes a letter

25. At least _____ residents need to attend a meeting.
- Ⓐ ten
- Ⓑ two
- Ⓒ eighty percent of the
- Ⓓ one hundred percent of the

26. _____ would NOT be a topic of discussion at a Neighborhood Watch meeting.
- Ⓐ Gang activity
- Ⓑ Security systems
- Ⓒ Car insurance
- Ⓓ Suspicious activity

27. A Neighborhood Watch meeting usually lasts _____.
- Ⓐ one hour
- Ⓑ two hours
- Ⓒ three hours
- Ⓓ four hours

28. All residents who attend a meeting will receive _____.
- Ⓐ a certificate
- Ⓑ an alarm
- Ⓒ a street sign
- Ⓓ a window sign

---

23 Ⓐ Ⓑ Ⓒ Ⓓ   25 Ⓐ Ⓑ Ⓒ Ⓓ   27 Ⓐ Ⓑ Ⓒ Ⓓ

24 Ⓐ Ⓑ Ⓒ Ⓓ   26 Ⓐ Ⓑ Ⓒ Ⓓ   28 Ⓐ Ⓑ Ⓒ Ⓓ

Go to the next page ⇨

E CLOZE READING: Directions

Choose the correct answers to complete the e-mail.

From: Ted Pran
To: Felipe Santos
Date: Tuesday, November 15, 11:45 AM
Subject: Your visit

Hi, Felipe. Here are the [instructions (A)] [directions (●)] [maps (C)] to my apartment. If you're driving from

the school, go [straight (A)] [direct (B)] [down (C)] 29 on Hamilton Avenue. Then drive five [block (A)] [blocks (B)] [stops (C)] 30.

Don't [speed (A)] [drive (B)] [run (C)] 31 because that part of the street is in a school [exit (A)] [entrance (B)] [zone (C)] 32.

At the second stop [street (A)] [sign (B)] [vehicle (C)] 33, turn left on Williams Street. Then [make (A)] [turn (B)] [get (C)] 34

your second left. That's Rose Street. It's a [one-way (A)] [only-way (B)] [three-way (C)] 35 Street. My address is

217 Rose Street, Apartment 3C. By bus, take Bus number 39 on Hamilton Avenue.

Get [on (A)] [off (B)] [in (C)] 36 at Williams Street. Walk [illegal (A)] [straight (B)] [fast (C)] 37 on Williams and take

the second left. That's Rose Street. My apartment is on the left.
See you soon!
Ted

F LISTENING ASSESSMENT: Recorded Directions to a Place

Read and listen to the questions. Then listen to the recording and answer the questions.

38. Why did the person call?
- Ⓐ To ask questions about an account.
- Ⓑ To get directions to the store.
- Ⓒ To talk with the customer service department.
- Ⓓ To find out store hours.

39. Which directions does the recording give?
- Ⓐ Only walking.
- Ⓑ By car and walking.
- Ⓒ By car and by bus.
- Ⓓ Only by car.

40. Which buses stop at the mall?
- Ⓐ 880 and 17.
- Ⓑ 19 and Stevens Avenue.
- Ⓒ 9 and 21.
- Ⓓ 19 and 21.

29 Ⓐ Ⓑ Ⓒ Ⓓ   32 Ⓐ Ⓑ Ⓒ Ⓓ   35 Ⓐ Ⓑ Ⓒ Ⓓ   38 Ⓐ Ⓑ Ⓒ Ⓓ

30 Ⓐ Ⓑ Ⓒ Ⓓ   33 Ⓐ Ⓑ Ⓒ Ⓓ   36 Ⓐ Ⓑ Ⓒ Ⓓ   39 Ⓐ Ⓑ Ⓒ Ⓓ

31 Ⓐ Ⓑ Ⓒ Ⓓ   34 Ⓐ Ⓑ Ⓒ Ⓓ   37 Ⓐ Ⓑ Ⓒ Ⓓ   40 Ⓐ Ⓑ Ⓒ Ⓓ

Go to the next page

G WRITING ASSESSMENT: A Personal Letter with Directions

A classmate is going to visit you at your home. Write a personal letter with directions from the school to your home. You can give the directions for public transportation, walking, or driving. Number each part of the directions.

_____
(today's date)

_____
(salutation)

_____

_____

_____

_____

_____

_____

_____

_____

_____

_____

_____
(closing)

_____
(signature)

H SPEAKING ASSESSMENT

I can ask and answer these questions:

Ask Answer
☐ ☐ Can you tell me how to get to the nearest supermarket?
☐ ☐ Can you tell me how to get to the nearest police station?
☐ ☐ If a bus is late, what might have happened?
☐ ☐ Have you ever been pulled over for a traffic violation? What happened? What should you have done differently?
☐ ☐ Have you apologized to someone recently? Why? What should you have done differently?
☐ ☐ How can residents work with the police department to improve their city?

STOP

T12

A   UNITED STATES HISTORY

Example:

The United Nations was formed to _____ between countries.
- Ⓐ promote war
- Ⓑ increase trade
- ⬤ keep peace
- Ⓓ develop communication

1. The United Nations provides economic _____ to many countries.
- Ⓐ protests
- Ⓑ forces
- Ⓒ aid
- Ⓓ welfare

2. During the _____, many banks and businesses closed.
- Ⓐ Depression
- Ⓑ economy
- Ⓒ stock market
- Ⓓ history

3. The stock market _____ on October 29, 1929.
- Ⓐ controlled
- Ⓑ gained
- Ⓒ collapsed
- Ⓓ lasted

4. The Social Security system was _____ during the New Deal.
- Ⓐ established
- Ⓑ revised
- Ⓒ unemployed
- Ⓓ invested

5. During World War II, Germany, _____, and Japan fought against the Allies.
- Ⓐ Spain
- Ⓑ Italy
- Ⓒ China
- Ⓓ Russia

6. The United States dropped the first atomic _____ during World War II.
- Ⓐ attack
- Ⓑ plane
- Ⓒ collapse
- Ⓓ bomb

7. On September 11, 2001, terrorists _____ four planes.
- Ⓐ bombed
- Ⓑ hijacked
- Ⓒ bought
- Ⓓ conquered

8. During the Cold War, the U.S. fought against _____ forces.
- Ⓐ Communist
- Ⓑ democratic
- Ⓒ Allied
- Ⓓ United Nations

9. Reverend Martin Luther King, Jr., was a leader of the _____ movement.
- Ⓐ civics
- Ⓑ civil rights
- Ⓒ holiday
- Ⓓ discrimination

1 Ⓐ Ⓑ Ⓒ Ⓓ   4 Ⓐ Ⓑ Ⓒ Ⓓ   7 Ⓐ Ⓑ Ⓒ Ⓓ

2 Ⓐ Ⓑ Ⓒ Ⓓ   5 Ⓐ Ⓑ Ⓒ Ⓓ   8 Ⓐ Ⓑ Ⓒ Ⓓ

3 Ⓐ Ⓑ Ⓒ Ⓓ   6 Ⓐ Ⓑ Ⓒ Ⓓ   9 Ⓐ Ⓑ Ⓒ Ⓓ

Go to the next page ⟩   **T13**

Example:

Do you _____ any questions about today's history lesson?
- Ⓐ had
- ● have
- Ⓒ having
- Ⓓ have had

10. Yes. I have a question. What _____ the Great Depression?
- Ⓐ caused
- Ⓑ did cause
- Ⓒ has caused
- Ⓓ should cause

11. Who knows the answer? _____ did the Depression happen?
- Ⓐ Which
- Ⓑ When
- Ⓒ Why
- Ⓓ What

12. I know. Americans _____ money and invested in companies, and then the value of the companies _____ suddenly.
- Ⓐ borrow . . . fell
- Ⓑ borrowed . . . fell
- Ⓒ borrow . . . fall
- Ⓓ borrowed . . . fall

13. Which president _____ laws that helped the economy?
- Ⓐ introduce
- Ⓑ introducing
- Ⓒ introduced
- Ⓓ was introduced

14. Franklin D. Roosevelt. His plan _____ the New Deal.
- Ⓐ called
- Ⓑ has called
- Ⓒ calling
- Ⓓ was called

15. What important event _____ in 1939?
- Ⓐ should occur
- Ⓑ occurred
- Ⓒ what happened
- Ⓓ didn't happen

16. World War II _____. The Allies _____ against Germany, Italy, and Japan.
- Ⓐ has begun . . . fight
- Ⓑ began . . . fight
- Ⓒ begins . . . fought
- Ⓓ began . . . fought

17. When did the U.S. _____ World War II?
- Ⓐ enter
- Ⓑ entered
- Ⓒ was entered
- Ⓓ should have entered

18. In 1941. Pearl Harbor _____ by Japan, and then the U.S. _____ war.
- Ⓐ attacked . . . declared
- Ⓑ attacked . . . was declared
- Ⓒ was attacked . . . declared
- Ⓓ was attacked . . . was declared

10 Ⓐ Ⓑ Ⓒ Ⓓ	13 Ⓐ Ⓑ Ⓒ Ⓓ	16 Ⓐ Ⓑ Ⓒ Ⓓ
11 Ⓐ Ⓑ Ⓒ Ⓓ	14 Ⓐ Ⓑ Ⓒ Ⓓ	17 Ⓐ Ⓑ Ⓒ Ⓓ
12 Ⓐ Ⓑ Ⓒ Ⓓ	15 Ⓐ Ⓑ Ⓒ Ⓓ	18 Ⓐ Ⓑ Ⓒ Ⓓ

Go to the next page →

Read the civics textbook lesson. Then do Numbers 19 through 24.

GEORGE H.W. BUSH 1989-1993

George Bush had been the vice president during the presidency of Ronald Reagan. During Bush's term, the Cold War came to an end. In 1989, the Berlin Wall was destroyed. It had separated West Berlin from communist East Germany. In 1990, Iraqi leader Saddam Hussein invaded Kuwait. Bush sent military troops into Iraq in 1991 for a short and successful war. This was called the Gulf War. During Bush's four years in office, the economy slowed more and more.

WILLIAM J. (BILL) CLINTON 1993–2001

Clinton worked to improve the economy. He increased taxes, cut government spending, and increased federal money for schools and police departments. Under Clinton, the North American Free Trade Agreement (NAFTA) was signed in 1994. NAFTA removed restrictions on commerce and investment with Mexico and Canada.

Clinton worked to keep peace in the Middle East, Eastern Europe, and Africa. Clinton was accused of an improper relationship with a female employee. The House of Representatives tried to remove him from office, but the Senate did not approve. Clinton was president for eight years.

GEORGE W. BUSH 2001–2009

George W. Bush is the son of the former President Bush. On September 11, 2001, international terrorists crashed planes into the World Trade Center in New York City, the Pentagon in Washington, D.C., and in Pennsylvania. Bush ordered attacks on terrorists in Afghanistan. In 2003, he ordered troops into Iraq to destroy the government of the dictator Saddam Hussein. Under Bush, the economy in the U.S. became very weak.

---

19. _____ was president before George H.W. Bush.
- Ⓐ William J. Clinton
- Ⓑ George W. Bush
- Ⓒ Ronald Reagan
- Ⓓ Barack Obama

20. The _____ took place during the early 1990s.
- Ⓐ Gulf War
- Ⓑ Cold War
- Ⓒ Iraq War
- Ⓓ Afghanistan War

21. Clinton and George W. Bush both _____.
- Ⓐ sent troops to Iraq
- Ⓑ tried to bring peace to the Middle East
- Ⓒ were sons of presidents
- Ⓓ were in office for 8 years

22. You can infer that _____ was an important part of the end of the Cold War.
- Ⓐ George Bush
- Ⓑ the fall of the Berlin Wall
- Ⓒ the year 1990
- Ⓓ East Germany

23. George W. Bush ordered troops into Afghanistan after _____.
- Ⓐ the attacks on September 11, 2001
- Ⓑ sending troops to Iraq
- Ⓒ NAFTA
- Ⓓ they fought in Kuwait

24. You can infer that the economy got better under _____.
- Ⓐ Ronald Reagan
- Ⓑ George H.W. Bush
- Ⓒ George W. Bush
- Ⓓ William J. Clinton

---

19 Ⓐ Ⓑ Ⓒ Ⓓ   21 Ⓐ Ⓑ Ⓒ Ⓓ   23 Ⓐ Ⓑ Ⓒ Ⓓ

20 Ⓐ Ⓑ Ⓒ Ⓓ   22 Ⓐ Ⓑ Ⓒ Ⓓ   24 Ⓐ Ⓑ Ⓒ Ⓓ

Read the civics textbook lesson. Then do Numbers 25 though 28.

Dr. Martin Luther King, Jr.

Martin Luther King, Jr., was born on January 15, 1929 in Atlanta, Georgia. His father was the minister of a church. His mother and father taught him to respect all people, but King saw that black people were not respected. In many states, discrimination against blacks was legal.

He married Coretta Scott in 1953, and the next year they moved to Montgomery, Alabama, where he was the minister of a church.

King became active in the civil rights movement in Montgomery. By state law, African-Americans had to sit in the back of the bus. In December of 1955, the African-American community organized an action against the city bus company in Montgomery. No African-Americans rode the bus for almost 11 months. Finally, the United States Supreme Court said that the laws were illegal.

Dr. King became one of the most famous leaders of the civil rights movement. He traveled to many cities and towns in the southern U.S., giving speeches and helping to organize efforts to end discrimination.

In 1960, Dr. King returned to Atlanta, Georgia, and became a minister in his father's church. Dr. King became more and more active in the growing civil rights movement. There were many demonstrations and confrontations with the police. The civil rights movement was growing stronger, but many people were against it. In 1963, King led the March on Washington with 200,000 demonstrators.

In 1964, President Johnson signed into law the Civil Rights Act. That same year, King won the Nobel Peace Prize. He continued working for the civil rights of all Americans. In addition, he protested the Vietnam War. On April 4, 1968, he was assassinated.

Martin Luther King, Jr., was one of the most important leaders of the American civil rights movement of the 1950s and 1960s. Although he died more than 40 years ago, his life influences and educates people all over the world.

25. The civil rights movement in the U.S. started in _____.
   Ⓐ 1963
   Ⓑ 1964
   Ⓒ the 1950s
   Ⓓ the 1960s

26. King was _____ years old when he was assassinated.
   Ⓐ 29
   Ⓑ 39
   Ⓒ 40
   Ⓓ 49

27. King was _____ the Vietnam War.
   Ⓐ a soldier in
   Ⓑ jobless during
   Ⓒ a supplier for
   Ⓓ against

28. You can infer that African-Americans protested the bus laws in Montgomery because _____.
   Ⓐ they weren't allowed on the buses
   Ⓑ there was discrimination on the buses
   Ⓒ buses didn't go to their neighborhoods
   Ⓓ bus tickets were too expensive

25 Ⓐ Ⓑ Ⓒ Ⓓ   27 Ⓐ Ⓑ Ⓒ Ⓓ

26 Ⓐ Ⓑ Ⓒ Ⓓ   28 Ⓐ Ⓑ Ⓒ Ⓓ

Go to the next page ⟶

E CLOZE READING: A History Textbook Lesson

Choose the correct answers to complete the reading.

Immigration in the United States

Immigrants are people who come to a country to live. The United States is often called "a nation border city of immigrants." Except for Native Americans, all

Americans come from families of immigrants. In the late 1800s and early 1900s, thousands of immigrants came to the U.S. Between 1880 and 1930, over 27 million people

left entered completed [29] the U.S. The doors to the U.S. were wide open to

immigrants.

However, after the start of World War I World War II the Cold War [30] in 1914,

new laws controlled the number of immigrants coming into the U.S. In addition,

during the stock market health program Great Depression [31] of the early 1930s, the

effort economy democracy [32] was very weak so fewer people came to the U.S.

to work.

During World War II (1939–1945), the U.S. adjusted offered permitted [33]

fewer immigrants, and many Europeans were turned away. In 1948 the Displaced Persons Act was passed. Hundreds of thousands of Europeans came to the U.S. However, many people from other parts of the world were replaced reopened rejected [34].

In 1965, a new law allowed offered stopped [35] immigrants from any country.

There was a great example increase fight [36] in immigrants from

Asian European German [37] countries such as China, Korea, Vietnam, and Thailand.

The future of the United States is stronger and brighter because of the immigrants who come here.

---

29 Ⓐ Ⓑ Ⓒ Ⓓ   32 Ⓐ Ⓑ Ⓒ Ⓓ   35 Ⓐ Ⓑ Ⓒ Ⓓ

30 Ⓐ Ⓑ Ⓒ Ⓓ   33 Ⓐ Ⓑ Ⓒ Ⓓ   36 Ⓐ Ⓑ Ⓒ Ⓓ

31 Ⓐ Ⓑ Ⓒ Ⓓ   34 Ⓐ Ⓑ Ⓒ Ⓓ   37 Ⓐ Ⓑ Ⓒ Ⓓ

F LISTENING ASSESSMENT: Classroom Discussion

Read and listen to the questions. Then listen to the conversation and answer the questions.

38. What subject WON'T be on the test?

    Ⓐ World War I
    Ⓑ World War II
    Ⓒ The Great Depression
    Ⓓ The war between the U.S. and England

39. When did the United States enter World War I?

    Ⓐ 1907.
    Ⓑ 1917.
    Ⓒ 1918.
    Ⓓ 1929.

40. Who did the Allies fight against?

    Ⓐ England, France, and Russia.
    Ⓑ Germany.
    Ⓒ Germany and Austria-Hungary.
    Ⓓ The United States.

G WRITING ASSESSMENT: A Personal Timeline

Draw a personal timeline like the one below. Start with the year you were born. Include important events and dates in your life. Include as many details as possible.

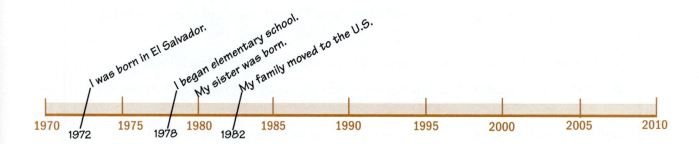

H SPEAKING ASSESSMENT

I can ask and answer these questions:

Ask Answer

☐ ☐ What is the name of the war that happened from 1914 to 1918?
☐ ☐ What happened during the Great Depression?
☐ ☐ How did the New Deal help the U.S. after the Great Depression?
☐ ☐ What three countries did the Allies fight against during World War II?
☐ ☐ What is the purpose of the United Nations?
☐ ☐ What two political systems were in conflict during the Cold War?
☐ ☐ Who was the most famous leader of the Civil Rights Movement?
☐ ☐ What happened on September 11, 2001?

38 Ⓐ Ⓑ Ⓒ Ⓓ   39 Ⓐ Ⓑ Ⓒ Ⓓ   40 Ⓐ Ⓑ Ⓒ Ⓓ

A **CONSUMER COMPLAINTS AND WARRANTIES**

Example:

I need to return this because it is
_____.

Ⓐ breaking
Ⓑ breaks
⬤ broken
Ⓓ break

1. Would you like to _____ this iron for a new one?
   Ⓐ return
   Ⓑ exchange
   Ⓒ repair
   Ⓓ receipt

2. The warranty doesn't _____ water damage.
   Ⓐ insist
   Ⓑ deduct
   Ⓒ obtain
   Ⓓ cover

3. The store _____ is to accept returns that are made within 30 days.
   Ⓐ privacy
   Ⓑ policy
   Ⓒ exchange
   Ⓓ refund

4. Unfortunately, the warranty on my computer _____ last month.
   Ⓐ expired
   Ⓑ broke
   Ⓒ dropped
   Ⓓ started

5. Sam wrote a letter of _____ to the company.
   Ⓐ consumer
   Ⓑ complaining
   Ⓒ complaint
   Ⓓ exchange

6. To get a refund, you have to mail in your proof of _____.
   Ⓐ receipt
   Ⓑ refund
   Ⓒ defect
   Ⓓ purchase

7. The manager _____ my defective air conditioner with one that works.
   Ⓐ replaced
   Ⓑ refunded
   Ⓒ repaired
   Ⓓ returned

8. The _____ is good for 90 days.
   Ⓐ bill of sale
   Ⓑ warranty
   Ⓒ refund
   Ⓓ receipt

9. The new faucet must have a _____ because it is leaking.
   Ⓐ defect
   Ⓑ dispute
   Ⓒ return
   Ⓓ exchange

1 Ⓐ Ⓑ Ⓒ Ⓓ   4 Ⓐ Ⓑ Ⓒ Ⓓ   7 Ⓐ Ⓑ Ⓒ Ⓓ

2 Ⓐ Ⓑ Ⓒ Ⓓ   5 Ⓐ Ⓑ Ⓒ Ⓓ   8 Ⓐ Ⓑ Ⓒ Ⓓ

3 Ⓐ Ⓑ Ⓒ Ⓓ   6 Ⓐ Ⓑ Ⓒ Ⓓ   9 Ⓐ Ⓑ Ⓒ Ⓓ

Go to the next page ⇨

Example:
I'd like _____ this printer.
- Ⓐ to returning
- Ⓑ returning
- Ⓒ return
- ⬤ to return

10. What _____ the problem?
- Ⓐ are
- Ⓑ seem to be
- Ⓒ seems to be
- Ⓓ is the matter

11. The paper _____ every time I use the machine. Here's my receipt.
- Ⓐ jam
- Ⓑ jammed
- Ⓒ jams
- Ⓓ was jammed

12. It's still under warranty. You _____ and get a new one.
- Ⓐ will exchange me
- Ⓑ can exchange it
- Ⓒ could have exchanged
- Ⓓ exchanged it

13. I bought this coffee machine here, and _____ broken.
- Ⓐ I
- Ⓑ I'm
- Ⓒ it
- Ⓓ it's

14. Can you tell me what the problem _____?
- Ⓐ is
- Ⓑ be
- Ⓒ are
- Ⓓ will be

15. The water _____.
- Ⓐ leak
- Ⓑ leaking out
- Ⓒ leak out
- Ⓓ leaks out

16. _____ your receipt?
- Ⓐ Does it have
- Ⓑ Do you have
- Ⓒ Would you
- Ⓓ Will there be

Yes. Here you are.

17. Could you tell me _____ there will be a charge for this repair?
- Ⓐ where
- Ⓑ what
- Ⓒ whether
- Ⓓ when

18. Yes, there will. The warranty _____.
- Ⓐ has expired
- Ⓑ have expired
- Ⓒ expire
- Ⓓ expires

10 Ⓐ Ⓑ Ⓒ Ⓓ   13 Ⓐ Ⓑ Ⓒ Ⓓ   16 Ⓐ Ⓑ Ⓒ Ⓓ

11 Ⓐ Ⓑ Ⓒ Ⓓ   14 Ⓐ Ⓑ Ⓒ Ⓓ   17 Ⓐ Ⓑ Ⓒ Ⓓ

12 Ⓐ Ⓑ Ⓒ Ⓓ   15 Ⓐ Ⓑ Ⓒ Ⓓ   18 Ⓐ Ⓑ Ⓒ Ⓓ

Go to the next page ⇨

C READING: A Web Page with Consumer Protection Information

Read the web page with consumer information. Then do Numbers 19 through 22.

Is the new car you just bought a "lemon?" Is it having many problems? Every state has a **"lemon law"** that protects consumers against problems with new products they purchase. The lemon law usually covers new cars, but in some states the law also covers used cars. The coverage considers the number of repair attempts (times the customer tried to repair the car) and how many days the car is out of service (days when the car cannot be used).

Here are some examples of lemon law coverage for cars. For more information, check with your state consumer affairs office.

Lemon Law Coverage

State	Car	Repair attempts	Lemon Law Coverage
Arizona	New and used cars	4 repair attempts or 30 days out of service	Manufacturer's warranty period, 2 years, or 24,000 miles
California	New cars only	4 repair attempts or 30 days out of service	18 months or 18,000 miles
Florida	New cars only	3 repair attempts or 30 days out of service	2 years
Illinois	New cars only	4 repair attempts or 30 days out of service	1 year or 12,000 miles
New Jersey	New and used cars	3 repair attempts or 30 days out of service	2 years or 18,000 miles
New Mexico	New and used cars	4 repair attempts or 30 days out of service	Manufacturer's warranty period or 1 year
New York	New cars only	4 repair attempts or 20 days out of service	2 years or 24,000 miles
Texas	New cars only	4 repair attempts or 30 days out of service	Manufacturer's warranty period or 1 year

19. Which states have lemon laws to cover used cars?
- Ⓐ Arizona, Florida, and New Jersey.
- Ⓑ New Jersey, New York, and New Mexico.
- Ⓒ Arizona, New Jersey, and New Mexico.
- Ⓓ Arizona, New York, and New Mexico.

20. How many states have coverage for more than 20,000 miles?
- Ⓐ One.
- Ⓑ Two.
- Ⓒ Three.
- Ⓓ Four.

21. What is the number of repair attempts required before using the lemon law in most of these states?
- Ⓐ One.
- Ⓑ Two.
- Ⓒ Three.
- Ⓓ Four.

22. Which state has the best coverage for consumers?
- Ⓐ Arizona.
- Ⓑ California.
- Ⓒ Texas.
- Ⓓ Illinois.

Go to the next page ⟩ **T21** ●

D READING: A Consumer Action Newspaper Advice Column

Look at the newspaper advice column. Then do Numbers 23 through 28.

CONSUMER ACTION MAILBAG—SEND US YOUR QUESTIONS

Dear Consumer Action,

I bought a sofa from Sofas & More. In the store, I checked the sofa that I bought, and it looked fine. The sofa was delivered 3 days later. It was wrapped in plastic for protection. It looked like the right sofa, so I signed the receipt saying that I had received the sofa in good condition. Later, when I took off the plastic, I saw that the sofa color was wrong. I called the store, and the salesperson said it was the last one so I couldn't exchange it. I had signed the delivery receipt, so I can't get a refund. The store is going out of business in one week. What can I do?

Sorry in San Jose

Dear Sorry in San Jose,

You took the first step to take care of your problem—you called the store. However, you didn't take the next step—you needed to talk with the manager. If you have a problem, always ask to speak with the manager or supervisor. I called the manager at Sofas & More, and he apologized for the problems. The manager said that he would refund the amount you paid to your credit card when the sofa is returned. Please call him to schedule a pick-up!

Consumer Action

Dear Consumer Action,

I have a serious problem with the person I hired to paint my house. I thought I was hiring a company, A-1 Painters. I discovered that this is not a real company, just a man with a business card. I hired this man because he gave me a low price and because he seemed very experienced. When we agreed on the job, he asked me for $300.00 in cash to buy the paint. I gave him the money. That was two weeks ago. He doesn't return my phone calls and the phone number for his company doesn't work. Help!

Paintless in Piedmont

Dear Paintless in Piedmont,

I'm sorry to tell you that you have lost $300.00, but you have learned an important lesson: Always find out about a company, and never pay in cash. I called the Better Business Bureau (BBB). They said that they have received many complaints about this company. Unfortunately, the BBB said that it would be hard to get your money back since you paid in cash. However, if you write to the BBB and explain your problem, they will try to help you.

Consumer Action

23. The person who bought the sofa _____.
- Ⓐ will get the sofa she wanted
- Ⓑ will get a cash refund
- Ⓒ will keep the sofa that was delivered
- Ⓓ will get a refund to her credit card

24. Sorry in San Jose should have _____.
- Ⓐ paid by check
- Ⓑ spoken with the truck driver
- Ⓒ checked the sofa before accepting it
- Ⓓ called the salesperson again

25. The manager of Sofas & More _____.
- Ⓐ apologized
- Ⓑ offered to give a cash refund
- Ⓒ refused to take back the sofa
- Ⓓ offered to exchange the sofa

26. Paintless in Piedmont _____.
- Ⓐ paid $300 by check
- Ⓑ paid $300 in cash
- Ⓒ didn't pay for the paint
- Ⓓ received $300 in cash

27. Paintless in Piedmont _____.
- Ⓐ probably won't get the money back
- Ⓑ will get a cash refund
- Ⓒ probably had the wrong phone number
- Ⓓ should have paid $300

28. The Better Business Bureau _____.
- Ⓐ collects money for consumers
- Ⓑ can help consumers with problems
- Ⓒ had never heard of A-1 Painters
- Ⓓ only helps businesses

23 Ⓐ Ⓑ Ⓒ Ⓓ 25 Ⓐ Ⓑ Ⓒ Ⓓ 27 Ⓐ Ⓑ Ⓒ Ⓓ
24 Ⓐ Ⓑ Ⓒ Ⓓ 26 Ⓐ Ⓑ Ⓒ Ⓓ 28 Ⓐ Ⓑ Ⓒ Ⓓ

Go to the next page ⟹

E CLOZE READING: A Product Complaint Letter

Choose the correct answers to complete the letter.

Camera Warehouse, Inc.
598 South St.
Danville, NY 10019

Dear Sir or Madam:

I [replaced (A) | ordered (●) | returned (C)] a camera from your company on December 10, 2009,

and I [received (A) | resolved (B) | requested (C)] 29 the shipment on December 17. When I opened the

package, I saw that the camera was [arrived (A) | disputed (B) | damaged (C)] 30. I called your

[salesperson (A) | customer (B) | refund (C)] 31 service department, and the manager told me to return the

camera to you. I mailed it back with a note and the [receipt (A) | return (B) | proof (C)] 32 of purchase.

Two weeks later, I called your company. The person said that they had not received the package.

He said it must have gotten [found (A) | lost (B) | exchanged (C)] 33. However, the post office said that it

was [received (A) | delivered (B) | disputed (C)] 34 to you on December 27. I have called many times, but

the clerk says that they are still [investigating (A) | complaining (B) | insisting (C)] 35 the problem. Could

you please help me with this problem? How can I [expire (A) | result (B) | obtain (C)] 36 a replacement?

Please [call (A) | come by (B) | bill (C)] 37 me at 432-923-4567.

Sincerely,

Ben Vuong

Ben Vuong

F LISTENING ASSESSMENT: Calling a Store about a Problem

Read and listen to the questions. Then listen to the conversation and answer the questions.

38. Why is the customer calling the store?
  (A) She wants to buy a refrigerator.
  (B) She doesn't have a warranty.
  (C) She wants to exchange her refrigerator.
  (D) The refrigerator light doesn't work.

39. How long has she had the refrigerator?
  (A) Two months.
  (B) Two weeks.
  (C) Three months.
  (D) Three weeks.

40. What does the salesman offer to do?
  (A) Exchange the refrigerator.
  (B) Send a repairperson.
  (C) Explain how to fix it.
  (D) Give her a warranty.

29 (A) (B) (C) (D)   32 (A) (B) (C) (D)   35 (A) (B) (C) (D)   38 (A) (B) (C) (D)

30 (A) (B) (C) (D)   33 (A) (B) (C) (D)   36 (A) (B) (C) (D)   39 (A) (B) (C) (D)

31 (A) (B) (C) (D)   34 (A) (B) (C) (D)   37 (A) (B) (C) (D)   40 (A) (B) (C) (D)

Go to the next page

You bought a new flat-screen TV (Model XY79) this year on November 3 at Big Buy Appliance Store. The serial number of the TV is AJ-128739-CX. Fill in the form below.

SonoVision *2-Year Warranty Registration Form*

Receive a 2-Year Warranty with the purchase of our flat-screen television models XY76, XY79, and XY83.

Please print clearly and complete all information. (No P.O. Box numbers will be accepted.)

Name _____

Address (No P.O. boxes) _____

City _____ State _____ Zip _____

Phone Number _____ E-mail Address (optional) _____

Where did you buy it? (Name of store) _____

Model Number _____ Serial Number _____

Date of Purchase _____

Signature _____ Today's Date _____

Mail your completed warranty form to: *SonoVision* 2-Year Warranty
P. O. Box 599
Memphis, TN 38101

I can ask and answer these questions:

Ask Answer
☐ ☐ What is a warranty?
☐ ☐ Are any of your appliances covered by warranties? Which ones?
☐ ☐ Have you ever returned something you purchased? What was it? Why did you return it?
☐ ☐ What is the best way to take care of a complaint in a store?
☐ ☐ Have you ever written a letter of complaint? What was the situation?
☐ ☐ What is a consumer hotline?
☐ ☐ What should you do if you receive a damaged product in the mail?

STOP

A   HOME FIRE SAFETY AND EMERGENCY PROCEDURES

Example:
  Every family should have and should
  _____ an emergency route.
  (A) replace
  ● practice
  (C) lock up
  (D) shut off

1. The _____ in smoke detectors should be
replaced every six months.
  (A) batteries
  (B) electricity
  (C) fire extinguishers
  (D) utilities

2. Newspapers, clothing, and furniture are
all _____ materials.
  (A) soft
  (B) resistant
  (C) inflammable
  (D) flammable

3. Space heaters should be at least _____
away from walls and furniture.
  (A) one inch
  (B) three inches
  (C) three feet
  (D) three yards

4. Your family should have _____ in case of
a fire in your home.
  (A) an inside meeting place
  (B) an outside meeting place
  (C) a special door
  (D) a neighbor's phone number

5. Don't put a _____ in the kitchen. Install
a _____ instead.
  (A) fire extinguisher . . . smoke detector
  (B) smoke detector . . . heat detector
  (C) fire extinguisher . . . utility shutoff
  (D) smoke detector . . . first-aid kit

6. Smoke detectors should be installed
outside each _____.
  (A) sleeping area
  (B) bathroom
  (C) hallway
  (D) house

7. If a person is _____, you must act very
quickly.
  (A) breathing
  (B) coughing
  (C) blocking
  (D) choking

8. If a person's airway is blocked, the
person can die _____.
  (A) slowly
  (B) in a few seconds
  (C) in a few minutes
  (D) in several hours

9. For the Heimlich maneuver, stand _____
the person, make a fist, and use your
arms to thrust.
  (A) next to
  (B) over
  (C) in front of
  (D) behind

1 (A) (B) (C) (D)   4 (A) (B) (C) (D)   7 (A) (B) (C) (D)

2 (A) (B) (C) (D)   5 (A) (B) (C) (D)   8 (A) (B) (C) (D)

3 (A) (B) (C) (D)   6 (A) (B) (C) (D)   9 (A) (B) (C) (D)

Go to the next page ⟹

Example:

What _____ you buy at the hardware store?
- (A) are
- (●) did
- (C) was
- (D) does

10. I _____ three new smoke detectors.
- (A) buy
- (B) was buying
- (C) bought
- (D) would buy

11. Why? We _____ two detectors last year.
- (A) install
- (B) installed
- (C) installing
- (D) have installed

12. Yes, but we should _____ a detector outside each bedroom, too.
- (A) had
- (B) to have
- (C) have
- (D) will have

13. You're right. If there were a fire at night, we probably _____ the detector in the hallway.
- (A) will hear
- (B) won't hear
- (C) didn't hear
- (D) wouldn't hear

14. I hope we don't ever _____ a fire in the house.
- (A) have
- (B) had
- (C) having
- (D) would have

15. Emergency Operator. _____ your emergency?
- (A) What is
- (B) How is
- (C) What was
- (D) Why is

16. My grandfather _____ and suddenly he fell from his chair.
- (A) eat
- (B) eating
- (C) is eating
- (D) was eating

17. Is he _____?
- (A) breathe
- (B) breathing
- (C) breathed
- (D) breathes

18. Yes. And his eyes _____ open.
- (A) is
- (B) are
- (C) will be
- (D) weren't

I'll send an ambulance right away.

10 (A) (B) (C) (D)
11 (A) (B) (C) (D)
12 (A) (B) (C) (D)
13 (A) (B) (C) (D)
14 (A) (B) (C) (D)
15 (A) (B) (C) (D)
16 (A) (B) (C) (D)
17 (A) (B) (C) (D)
18 (A) (B) (C) (D)

Go to the next page

Read the news article. Then do Numbers 19 though 22.

Boy saves mother's life with Heimlich maneuver

HARWOOD – A Harwood boy is being called an amazing nine-year-old for saving his mother's life after she choked on a grape. Jason Clark performed the Heimlich maneuver on his mother, Terry Clark, at their home on Wednesday afternoon.

Terry Clark said she choked on a grape while she was eating. She started hitting the kitchen table to get the attention of her son, who was in the living room.

"All of a sudden, he came behind me, grabbed me, and then he started squeezing me hard. He did several thrusts. At first it didn't work," she said Thursday.

"Then he grabbed me again, gave a big thrust, and suddenly the grape flew out of my mouth."

When the mother could breathe, she told her son that he had saved her life.

Where did Jason learn the Heimlich maneuver? The boy said he saw a safety demonstration at school. Later, he looked up the procedure on the Internet and

9-year-old Jason Clark performed the Heimlich maneuver on his mother.

learned it on his own.

After the emergency, Jason said, "I'm so happy that I knew how to do the Heimlich maneuver. She might have died."

On Friday night, the Clark family enjoyed a special dinner at a local restaurant.

---

19. The mother was _____.
   Ⓐ breathing hard
   Ⓑ swallowing a grape
   Ⓒ choking on a grape
   Ⓓ calling her son

20. Jason learned the Heimlich maneuver _____.
   Ⓐ from the Internet
   Ⓑ in a safety class
   Ⓒ from his mother
   Ⓓ at a local restaurant

21. When the boy did the Heimlich maneuver, the grape came out _____.
   Ⓐ after one thrust
   Ⓑ after several thrusts
   Ⓒ after three minutes
   Ⓓ after he hit the kitchen table

22. Jason's mother must be very _____ him.
   Ⓐ exhausted by
   Ⓑ concerned about
   Ⓒ afraid of
   Ⓓ proud of

19 Ⓐ Ⓑ Ⓒ Ⓓ   20 Ⓐ Ⓑ Ⓒ Ⓓ   21 Ⓐ Ⓑ Ⓒ Ⓓ   22 Ⓐ Ⓑ Ⓒ Ⓓ

Go to the next page **T27**

Read the announcement. Then do Numbers 23 though 28.

WESTVIEW APARTMENTS

TO: All Residents of Westview Apartments
FROM: Ron Manning, Building Manager
RE: Smoke Detectors and Fire Safety

> **Change your clocks!**
> **Change your batteries!**

This Sunday, we change our clocks to Standard Time. Please remember to **replace** the batteries in your smoke detectors. Please also review our fire safety procedures below. All residents should have a fire emergency plan and map. Practice your escape route. If you have any questions, please call me at 499-1222.

Fire Safety Procedures

If the fire alarm sounds, all residents must immediately leave the building. Follow these instructions:

1. Put on a coat and hard-soled shoes.
2. Take a towel with you so that you don't breathe smoke.
3. Close windows.
4. Check your doorknob and door. If they are hot, do *not* open your door. Exit through a window (if you are on the first floor) or wait for help.
5. Stay low to the floor.
6. Leave the building through the nearest exit. Always know an additional emergency exit in case your first exit is blocked.
7. *Never* use the elevators! Use the stairways to leave the building.
8. Go to the emergency meeting area 100 feet away from the building.
9. Do not re-enter the building.

Important! If you can't get out because of smoke or fire in the hallway, call 9-1-1 to report your exact location. Wait in a room with a window. Close the door and seal it with tape or towels. Stay by the window and signal to firefighters with a flashlight or cloth. *Sometimes the safest thing you can do in a tall building fire is to stay in your apartment and wait for the firefighters.*

---

23. This announcement tells residents to change smoke detector batteries and to _____.
- Ⓐ review fire safety procedures
- Ⓑ check their heat detectors
- Ⓒ participate in a fire drill
- Ⓓ listen for the fire alarm

24. All residents should practice their _____ routes.
- Ⓐ fire
- Ⓑ escape
- Ⓒ building
- Ⓓ stairway

28. To not breathe smoke, residents should _____.
- Ⓐ drink water
- Ⓑ open a window
- Ⓒ take a towel
- Ⓓ use the stairway

26. If the apartment door is very hot, _____.
- Ⓐ throw water on it
- Ⓑ you should not use the elevator
- Ⓒ you should not open the door
- Ⓓ open the door slowly

27. In a tall apartment building, if you can't get out, _____.
- Ⓐ stay in a room with a window
- Ⓑ climb out a window
- Ⓒ take the elevator
- Ⓓ call the building manager

28. You can *infer* from the notice that the apartment building _____.
- Ⓐ doesn't have elevators
- Ⓑ has many floors
- Ⓒ has one floor
- Ⓓ has many older residents

. . . .

23 Ⓐ Ⓑ Ⓒ Ⓓ   25 Ⓐ Ⓑ Ⓒ Ⓓ   27 Ⓐ Ⓑ Ⓒ Ⓓ
24 Ⓐ Ⓑ Ⓒ Ⓓ   26 Ⓐ Ⓑ Ⓒ Ⓓ   28 Ⓐ Ⓑ Ⓒ Ⓓ

Go to the next page ⟶

E CLOZE READING: A Workplace Fire Safety Memo

Choose the correct answers to complete the memo.

To: All Employees
From: Sam Thomas, Human Resources Manager
Date: December 1
Subject: Emergency Preparedness

> PRECISION
> ACCOUNTING
> COMPANY

Next Tuesday, December 7, we will   practice   prevent   escape   our company safety
            (●)   (B)   (C)

detectors   procedures   kits   29. When the fire alarm sounds, the fire department will come and
  (A)   (B)   (C)

watch as we leave the building. They will tell us how to improve our fire escape plans. Please remember:

1. When the alarm sounds, all employees must   enter   return   leave   30 the building quickly.
                                                  (A)   (B)   (C)

2. Do not use the elevators. During a fire   choking   emergency   airway   31, you must use the
                                                (A)   (B)   (C)

   storage room   elevators   stairways   32.
       (A)   (B)   (C)

3. Know the   first-aid   escape   test   33 route for your office area.
                 (A)   (B)   (C)

4. If an exit is   blocked   open   free   34, use a different exit.
                     (A)   (B)   (C)

5. When you leave the building, go to the emergency   life   inside   meeting   35 place.
                                                        (A)   (B)   (C)

6. Follow the   instructions   flames   plans   36 of the fire department.
                    (A)   (B)   (C)

Before December 7, please review these fire   detector   extinguisher   safety   37 procedures
                                                (A)   (B)   (C)

with other employees in your department.

F LISTENING ASSESSMENT: Reporting an Emergency

Read and listen to the questions. Then listen to the conversation and answer the questions.

38. Why is the person calling 9-1-1?
- (A) For a fire emergency.
- (B) For a weather emergency.
- (C) For a car accident.
- (D) For a medical emergency.

39. What happened to the caller's husband?
- (A) He cut his arm.
- (B) He broke his ankle.
- (C) He cut his thumb.
- (D) He was choking.

40. What does the operator tell the caller to do?
- (A) Call an ambulance.
- (B) Press on the cut with a towel.
- (C) Wash the arm.
- (D) Put medicine on it.

29 (A) (B) (C) (D)   32 (A) (B) (C) (D)   35 (A) (B) (C) (D)   38 (A) (B) (C) (D)
30 (A) (B) (C) (D)   33 (A) (B) (C) (D)   36 (A) (B) (C) (D)   39 (A) (B) (C) (D)
31 (A) (B) (C) (D)   34 (A) (B) (C) (D)   37 (A) (B) (C) (D)   40 (A) (B) (C) (D)

> Go to the next page ⟹   T29 ●

G WRITING ASSESSMENT: A Fire Escape Plan

Draw an escape plan for your classroom. Show the classroom and the floor it is on in your school building. Show the emergency exits and the escape route. Include labels such as *window, door, stairway,* and *hallway.* Then write the instructions students should follow to use the escape route if there is a fire or other emergency. (Number the instructions.)

Classroom Escape Plan and Map

Map

Escape Route Instructions

_____

_____

_____

_____

_____

_____

_____

H SPEAKING ASSESSMENT

I can ask and answer these questions:

Ask Answer

☐ ☐ Have you ever had an emergency at home? What happened? What did you do?
☐ ☐ Who would you call to report an emergency at home?
☐ ☐ How many smoke detectors are there in your home?
☐ ☐ Do you have any fire extinguishers in your home? Where are they?
☐ ☐ How can you improve fire safety in your home?
☐ ☐ If there were a fire in your living room, how would you escape?
☐ ☐ Do you have an escape plan for your family?
☐ ☐ Do you know how to perform CPR? the Heimlich maneuver?

A BANK SERVICES; BUDGET PLANNING

Example:

I'd like to open a _____ account.
- Ⓐ saving
- ⬤ savings
- Ⓒ saved
- Ⓓ save

1. My checking account balance is low.
   I need to make a _____ soon.
   - Ⓐ paycheck
   - Ⓑ withdrawal
   - Ⓒ deposit
   - Ⓓ check

2. My bank charges a high monthly _____
   for a checking account.
   - Ⓐ fee
   - Ⓑ fine
   - Ⓒ rent
   - Ⓓ penalty

3. Most banks require a _____ deposit to
   open an account.
   - Ⓐ maximum
   - Ⓑ minimum
   - Ⓒ typical
   - Ⓓ monthly

4. It's convenient to use a _____ account
   to pay your bills.
   - Ⓐ savings
   - Ⓑ deposit
   - Ⓒ checking
   - Ⓓ money market

5. With a higher _____ rate, you will earn
   more money on your savings account.
   - Ⓐ interest
   - Ⓑ fee
   - Ⓒ withdrawal
   - Ⓓ penalty

6. Some ATM machines charge a $2.00 fee
   to _____ cash.
   - Ⓐ deposit
   - Ⓑ save
   - Ⓒ check on
   - Ⓓ withdraw

7. With _____, your paycheck is
   automatically put into your account.
   - Ⓐ monthly savings
   - Ⓑ variable deposit
   - Ⓒ direct withdrawal
   - Ⓓ direct deposit

8. A monthly _____ will help you keep track
   of your spending.
   - Ⓐ budget
   - Ⓑ deposit
   - Ⓒ financial
   - Ⓓ appointment

9. You can usually reduce your _____
   expenses, such as food and gas.
   - Ⓐ fixed
   - Ⓑ variable
   - Ⓒ online
   - Ⓓ bargain

1 Ⓐ Ⓑ Ⓒ Ⓓ   4 Ⓐ Ⓑ Ⓒ Ⓓ   7 Ⓐ Ⓑ Ⓒ Ⓓ

2 Ⓐ Ⓑ Ⓒ Ⓓ   5 Ⓐ Ⓑ Ⓒ Ⓓ   8 Ⓐ Ⓑ Ⓒ Ⓓ

3 Ⓐ Ⓑ Ⓒ Ⓓ   6 Ⓐ Ⓑ Ⓒ Ⓓ   9 Ⓐ Ⓑ Ⓒ Ⓓ

Go to the next page ⟩ **T31**

Example:

_____ order more checks.
- Ⓐ I'll like
- ● I'd like to
- Ⓒ I would
- Ⓓ I like

10. Okay. Please _____ this form.
- Ⓐ report
- Ⓑ write
- Ⓒ fill out
- Ⓓ cut out

11. How long _____ to get new checks?
- Ⓐ did it take
- Ⓑ would take
- Ⓒ taking
- Ⓓ will it take

12. If you order them today, you _____ them in 10 days.
- Ⓐ will get
- Ⓑ getting
- Ⓒ got
- Ⓓ have gotten

13. I'd like _____ a checking account, please.
- Ⓐ open
- Ⓑ to open
- Ⓒ opening
- Ⓓ opened

14. Certainly. The minimum opening deposit _____ $50.00.
- Ⓐ has been
- Ⓑ was
- Ⓒ will
- Ⓓ is

15. I wish we _____ keep to our monthly budget.
- Ⓐ can
- Ⓑ could
- Ⓒ do
- Ⓓ did

16. I know. We have enough money for our fixed expenses, but it's difficult to _____ our variable expenses.
- Ⓐ keep
- Ⓑ keep track
- Ⓒ keep track of
- Ⓓ keep a record

17. If you ask me, we've _____ too much money at fast-food restaurants.
- Ⓐ spend
- Ⓑ have spent
- Ⓒ spending
- Ⓓ been spending

18. I agree. If we ate at home more, we _____ about $200 a month.
- Ⓐ save
- Ⓑ saved
- Ⓒ would save
- Ⓓ will save

··

10	Ⓐ Ⓑ Ⓒ Ⓓ	13	Ⓐ Ⓑ Ⓒ Ⓓ	16	Ⓐ Ⓑ Ⓒ Ⓓ
11	Ⓐ Ⓑ Ⓒ Ⓓ	14	Ⓐ Ⓑ Ⓒ Ⓓ	17	Ⓐ Ⓑ Ⓒ Ⓓ
12	Ⓐ Ⓑ Ⓒ Ⓓ	15	Ⓐ Ⓑ Ⓒ Ⓓ	18	Ⓐ Ⓑ Ⓒ Ⓓ

Go to the next page ⇨

C READING: Comparing Checking Accounts

Look at the chart comparing checking accounts at three banks. Then do Numbers 19 through 22.

	Bank A	Bank B	Bank C
Minimum Opening Deposit	$10	$500	$1000
Monthly Fee	$20	$9	$20
No Monthly Fee	No fee when you have a minimum balance of $1,000	No fee when you have a minimum balance of $5,000	No fee when you have a minimum balance of $10,000
Check Writing	$0.15 per check	$0.15 per check	Unlimited check writing
Interest Rate	1%	3%	1%
Other Features	• First order of checks is free • No-fee ATM card • No fee for traveler's checks or money orders • Free online banking • No fee for safe deposit box	• Free checks including reorders • No-fee ATM card • No fee for traveler's checks • Free online banking	• Free checks including reorders • No-fee ATM card • No fee for traveler's checks or cashier's checks • Free online banking • 50% discount on safe deposit box

19. An interest rate of 3% is available at _____.
- Ⓐ Bank A
- Ⓑ Bank B
- Ⓒ Bank C
- Ⓓ Banks A and C

20. At all three banks, there is no monthly fee if you _____.
- Ⓐ have a minimum amount in your account
- Ⓑ budget your account
- Ⓒ pay $20
- Ⓓ don't write any checks

21. Bank C has _____ for a safe deposit box.
- Ⓐ no fee
- Ⓑ a $50 fee
- Ⓒ a half-price fee
- Ⓓ a percentage

22. If you can maintain a minimum balance of $8,000 and you rarely write checks, the best bank for you is _____.
- Ⓐ Bank A
- Ⓑ Bank B
- Ⓒ Bank C
- Ⓓ Bank A or C

Read the bank statement. Then do Numbers 23 through 28.

STATEMENT PERIOD
4/16/09 THROUGH 5/14/09

CENTRAL BANK ◎

CHECKING ACCOUNT NUMBER **024-00543**
MARTA GONZALEZ

DEPOSITS				
DATE	**AMOUNT**			
04/17/09	$1643.00	ELECTRONIC DEP	UNIX CORP.	PAYROLL
05/01/09	$1643.00	ELECTRONIC DEP	UNIX CORP.	PAYROLL

WITHDRAWALS		
DATE	**AMOUNT**	
04/17/09	$200.00	CASH WD ATM
05/01/09	$150.00	CASH WD ATM

CHECKS		
DATE	**AMOUNT**	**NUMBER**
04/19/09	123.55	1515
04/29/09	87.62	1516
05/01/09	583.00	1517

BEGINNING BALANCE	1520.33	**AVERAGE DAILY BALANCE**	3193.77
DEPOSITS	3286.00		
WITHDRAWALS	350.00		
CHECKS	794.17		
ENDING BALANCE	3662.16		

*MONTHLY SERVICE CHARGE OF 15.00 WAS WAIVED DUE TO AVERAGE DAILY BALANCE OVER 1000.00

---

23. The bank statement is for _____.
- Ⓐ April
- Ⓑ May
- Ⓒ two weeks
- Ⓓ four weeks

24. Unix is the name of _____.
- Ⓐ Marta's bank
- Ⓑ Marta's boss
- Ⓒ the company where Marta works
- Ⓓ the building where Marta lives

25. Marta is paid _____.
- Ⓐ once a week
- Ⓑ every two weeks
- Ⓒ twice a week
- Ⓓ once a month

26. The total amount of her ATM withdrawals during this statement period was _____.
- Ⓐ $150
- Ⓑ $200
- Ⓒ $300
- Ⓓ $350

27. The total amount of money Marta spent from this account was _____.
- Ⓐ $350.00
- Ⓑ $1,796.17
- Ⓒ $1,144.17
- Ⓓ $3,286.00

28. During this statement period, Marta _____.
- Ⓐ saved more than she spent
- Ⓑ spent more than she saved
- Ⓒ paid a monthly service charge
- Ⓓ made two ATM deposits

···

23 Ⓐ Ⓑ Ⓒ Ⓓ   25 Ⓐ Ⓑ Ⓒ Ⓓ   27 Ⓐ Ⓑ Ⓒ Ⓓ

24 Ⓐ Ⓑ Ⓒ Ⓓ   26 Ⓐ Ⓑ Ⓒ Ⓓ   28 Ⓐ Ⓑ Ⓒ Ⓓ

Go to the next page ⟶

E CLOZE READING: A News Article

Choose the correct answers to complete the article.

Do you | want (A) | like (B) | wish (●) | you could manage your | finances (A) | balances (B) | averages (C) | [29]

better? It's a good idea to make a | monthly fee (A) | budget (B) | passbook (C) | [30]. If you don't

| plan (A) | trim (B) | take (C) | [31] control of your spending, you will not be able to pay your bills or

| save (A) | spend (B) | reduce (C) | [32] for the future. A budget will help you spend

| wisely (A) | quickly (B) | frequently (C) | [33]. Here are some steps for making a personal budget.

1. Look at | daily (A) | fixed (B) | tiered (C) | [34] expenses, such as rent and car payments.

   What are your average monthly costs for these?

2. For four weeks, keep | think (A) | write (B) | track (C) | [35] of your spending for variable

   expenses, such as groceries, clothing, transportation, and entertainment.

3. What is your monthly take-home | deposit (A) | withdrawal (B) | pay (C) | [36]? Add up the monthly
   income for your family.

4. Keep an emergency | deposit box (A) | fund (B) | cost (C) | [37]. Use this for unusual expenses.

F LISTENING ASSESSMENT: Recorded Bank Account Information

Read and listen to the questions. Then listen to the phone call and answer the questions.

38. Why is this person
    calling the bank?
    (A) To make a deposit.
    (B) To make a
        withdrawal.
    (C) To get information
        about a savings
        account.
    (D) To get information
        about a checking
        account.

39. What number does the
    person give to get
    account information?
    (A) An account
        balance.
    (B) An account
        number.
    (C) A social security
        number.
    (D) A telephone
        number.

40. What account information
    does the person listen to?
    (A) The last three deposits.
    (B) The account balance.
    (C) Interest rates.
    (D) The last three
        withdrawals.

29 (A) (B) (C) (D) 32 (A) (B) (C) (D) 35 (A) (B) (C) (D) 38 (A) (B) (C) (D)
30 (A) (B) (C) (D) 33 (A) (B) (C) (D) 36 (A) (B) (C) (D) 39 (A) (B) (C) (D)
31 (A) (B) (C) (D) 34 (A) (B) (C) (D) 37 (A) (B) (C) (D) 40 (A) (B) (C) (D)

Fill in the application for a bank account.

North Bank
Bank Account Application

To open an account, simply complete this form. An asterisk (*) means the information is required. Please print clearly. As you fill out the application, please check your information carefully.

APPLICANT

Prefix: ☐ Miss: ☐ Mr. ☐ Mrs. ☐ Ms.

*First Name   Middle Initial   *Last Name

*Home phone   Cell phone   Email

CURRENT HOME ADDRESS

*Address (P.O. Box not allowed)

*City   *State   *Zip Code

*At this address for: ☐ less than 1 year   ☐ 1–3 years   ☐ 4–8 years   ☐ more than 8 years

IDENTITY INFORMATION

*Social Security Number   *Date of Birth
                                mm   dd   yyyy

*Mother's Maiden Name

*Identification: ☐ U.S. driver's license   ☐ State photo ID   ☐ Passport with photo

*Identification Number: State of Issue:

*Expiration Date:
        mm   dd   yyyy

*Employment Status: ☐ Employed   ☐ Unemployed   ☐ Retired   ☐ Student

TYPE OF ACCOUNT

☐ Checking account   ☐ Savings account   ☐ Online account

---

*Signature   *Date

I can ask and answer these questions:

Ask Answer

☐ ☐   What kind of bank account do you have?
☐ ☐   Do you use an ATM card? How often?
☐ ☐   Do you have a budget? Why or why not?
☐ ☐   What is your biggest fixed expense each month?
☐ ☐   What variable expenses can you reduce to save money?
☐ ☐   Do you sometimes shop at a wholesale store? What's the name of it? What do you buy there?
☐ ☐   Do you have an emergency fund? Why or why not?
☐ ☐   Are you saving for something special in the future? What?

STOP

Name _____

Date _____ **Class** _____

A ▎ HEALTH CARE; NUTRITION; SAFETY

Example:
Lisa called the nurse to get _____.
- Ⓐ nutrition
- Ⓑ symptoms
- ⬤ advice
- Ⓓ calories

1. At the clinic, Mark described his _____ to the doctor.
- Ⓐ causes
- Ⓑ nutrients
- Ⓒ servings
- Ⓓ symptoms

2. The doctor asked what had _____ the accident.
- Ⓐ warned
- Ⓑ exercised
- Ⓒ caused
- Ⓓ resulted

3. If you consume more _____ than you need every day, you will gain weight.
- Ⓐ minerals
- Ⓑ calories
- Ⓒ energy
- Ⓓ sodium

4. Calcium and iron are examples of _____.
- Ⓐ carbohydrates
- Ⓑ vitamins
- Ⓒ calories
- Ⓓ minerals

5. To know what is in a serving of food, read the _____ label.
- Ⓐ nutrition
- Ⓑ fiber
- Ⓒ warning
- Ⓓ medical

6. Choose your foods wisely and avoid foods that are high in _____.
- Ⓐ vitamins
- Ⓑ protein
- Ⓒ iron
- Ⓓ sodium

7. A medicine label will tell you the correct _____ for an adult and for a child.
- Ⓐ dose
- Ⓑ side effect
- Ⓒ warning
- Ⓓ number

8. Medication should be used before the _____ date printed on the bottle.
- Ⓐ end
- Ⓑ explanation
- Ⓒ expiration
- Ⓓ reservation

9. A _____ material such as gasoline can catch fire easily.
- Ⓐ flame
- Ⓑ combustible
- Ⓒ voltage
- Ⓓ explosion

....

1 Ⓐ Ⓑ Ⓒ Ⓓ   4 Ⓐ Ⓑ Ⓒ Ⓓ   7 Ⓐ Ⓑ Ⓒ Ⓓ

2 Ⓐ Ⓑ Ⓒ Ⓓ   5 Ⓐ Ⓑ Ⓒ Ⓓ   8 Ⓐ Ⓑ Ⓒ Ⓓ

3 Ⓐ Ⓑ Ⓒ Ⓓ   6 Ⓐ Ⓑ Ⓒ Ⓓ   9 Ⓐ Ⓑ Ⓒ Ⓓ

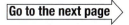

Example:

What _____ to be the problem?
- ● seems
- Ⓑ is
- Ⓒ feels
- Ⓓ was

10. I've _____ Cold-Ex for a cold, but I feel dizzy when I take it and I can't sleep at night.
- Ⓐ take
- Ⓑ took
- Ⓒ been taking
- Ⓓ taking

11. I see. _____ possible side effects of Cold-Ex.
- Ⓐ You are
- Ⓑ It is
- Ⓒ That is
- Ⓓ Those are

12. What medication _____ recommend?
- Ⓐ would
- Ⓑ would you
- Ⓒ would you have
- Ⓓ have you

13. Try using Relief. If you take it tonight, you _____ able to sleep.
- Ⓐ are
- Ⓑ would
- Ⓒ will be
- Ⓓ will

14. Thanks. I'll call back if the new medication _____.
- Ⓐ wouldn't help
- Ⓑ doesn't help
- Ⓒ don't help
- Ⓓ wouldn't have helped

15. My back _____ hurting for two weeks.
- Ⓐ is
- Ⓑ will be
- Ⓒ has been
- Ⓓ had been

16. Do you know what _____ caused this?
- Ⓐ did
- Ⓑ have
- Ⓒ might
- Ⓓ might have

17. I think I _____ a muscle while I was lifting boxes at work.
- Ⓐ was pulling
- Ⓑ pulled
- Ⓒ have been pulling
- Ⓓ had pulled

18. _____ taking a pain reliever or other over-the-counter medication?
- Ⓐ Have you been
- Ⓑ Have you
- Ⓒ Would you
- Ⓓ Did you

No, I haven't.

10 Ⓐ Ⓑ Ⓒ Ⓓ   13 Ⓐ Ⓑ Ⓒ Ⓓ   15 Ⓐ Ⓑ Ⓒ Ⓓ   17 Ⓐ Ⓑ Ⓒ Ⓓ
11 Ⓐ Ⓑ Ⓒ Ⓓ   14 Ⓐ Ⓑ Ⓒ Ⓓ   16 Ⓐ Ⓑ Ⓒ Ⓓ   18 Ⓐ Ⓑ Ⓒ Ⓓ
12 Ⓐ Ⓑ Ⓒ Ⓓ

Go to the next page ⇨

Read the food labels. Then do Numbers 19 through 22.

Low Sodium Crackers
Nutrition Facts
Serving Size 15 crackers (31g)
Servings per Container about 9

Amount per Serving	
Calories 150	Calories from Fat 50

	% Daily Value
Total Fat 6g	9%
Saturated Fat 1g	5%
Trans Fat 0g	0%
Cholesterol 0mg	0%
Sodium 80 mg	3%
Total Carbohydrate 22g	7%
Dietary Fiber 1g	4%
Sugars 4g	
Protein 2g	

Vitamin A 0%		Vitamin C	0%
Calcium 0%	•	Iron	6%

Cheese Crackers
Nutrition Facts
Serving Size 13 crackers (29g)
Servings per Container about 10

Amount per Serving	
Calories 150	Calories from Fat 72

	% Daily Value
Total Fat 8g	12%
Saturated Fat 1.5g	8%
Trans Fat 0g	0%
Cholesterol 0mg	0%
Sodium 230 mg	10%
Total Carbohydrate 16g	5%
Dietary Fiber 0g	0%
Sugars 0g	
Protein 4g	

Vitamin A 0%		Vitamin C	0%
Calcium 2%	•	Iron	6%

---

19. One serving of Low Sodium Crackers has 1 gram of _____.
Ⓐ sugar
Ⓑ total fat
Ⓒ dietary fiber
Ⓓ protein

20. One serving of Low Sodium Crackers has _____ fewer calories from fat than Cheese Crackers.
Ⓐ 22
Ⓑ 50
Ⓒ 72
Ⓓ 122

21. The Cheese Crackers have 230 _____ of sodium.
Ⓐ grams
Ⓑ milligrams
Ⓒ spoons
Ⓓ calories

22. The Cheese Crackers have more _____ than the Low Sodium Crackers.
Ⓐ iron
Ⓑ sugar
Ⓒ trans fat
Ⓓ saturated fat

- -

19 Ⓐ Ⓑ Ⓒ Ⓓ   21 Ⓐ Ⓑ Ⓒ Ⓓ

20 Ⓐ Ⓑ Ⓒ Ⓓ   22 Ⓐ Ⓑ Ⓒ Ⓓ

Go to the next page ▷

Read the medicine labels. Then do Numbers 23 through 28.

Night Time Cold Relief

Warnings: Do not use
- If you drink 3 or more alcoholic beverages every day
- If sore throat is severe and is accompanied or followed by fever, rash, or nausea
- With other medicines containing acetaminophen

Ask a doctor before use if you have
- Heart disease
- Diabetes
- High blood pressure

When using this product
- Drowsiness may occur
- Avoid alcoholic drinks
- Be careful when driving or operating machinery

Stop use and ask a doctor if
- Symptoms do not get better within 7 days
- You get nervous, dizzy, or sleepless
- Fever gets worse or lasts more than 3 days

Keep out of reach of children. In case of overdose get medical help or call a Poison Control Center right away.

Sinus Clear Allergy and Cold Medicine

Warnings: Do not use
- If you consume 3 or more alcoholic drinks every day
- With any other product containing diphenhydramine

Ask a doctor before use if you have
- High blood pressure
- Heart disease
- Diabetes
- or if you are pregnant or breastfeeding

When using this product
- avoid alcoholic drinks
- alcohol, sedatives, and tranquilizers may increase drowsiness
- excitability may occur, especially in children

Stop use and ask a doctor if
- sore throat is severe
- you get nervous, dizzy, or sleepless
- new symptoms occur
- fever gets worse or lasts more than 3 days
- sore throat lasts more than 2 days

Keep out of reach of children.
In case of overdose, get medical help or contact a Poison Control Center right away.

---

23. When using Night Time Cold Relief, you may have _____.
- Ⓐ heart disease
- Ⓑ a fever
- Ⓒ drowsiness
- Ⓓ high blood pressure

24. When you are taking Sinus Clear, you should call your doctor if _____.
- Ⓐ you have fewer symptoms
- Ⓑ you have a cough
- Ⓒ your fever gets worse
- Ⓓ you have a headache

25. Women who are _____ should check with a doctor before using Sinus Clear.
- Ⓐ pregnant
- Ⓑ coughing
- Ⓒ mothers
- Ⓓ taking acetaminophen

26. You can infer that *overdose* means _____.
- Ⓐ the dosage small children take
- Ⓑ taking much more than the recommended amount
- Ⓒ taking a small dose
- Ⓓ side effects

27. Stop taking Sinus Clear if you _____.
- Ⓐ have drowsiness
- Ⓑ feel dizzy
- Ⓒ have a headache
- Ⓓ drink an alcoholic beverage

28. You can infer that Night Time Cold Relief contains _____.
- Ⓐ alcohol
- Ⓑ poison
- Ⓒ diphenhydramine
- Ⓓ acetaminophen

---

23 Ⓐ Ⓑ Ⓒ Ⓓ   25 Ⓐ Ⓑ Ⓒ Ⓓ   27 Ⓐ Ⓑ Ⓒ Ⓓ

24 Ⓐ Ⓑ Ⓒ Ⓓ   26 Ⓐ Ⓑ Ⓒ Ⓓ   28 Ⓐ Ⓑ Ⓒ Ⓓ

Go to the next page ⟹

E CLOZE READING: A Workplace Safety Notice

Choose the correct answers to complete the notice.

To: All Manufacturing Supervisors
From: Carla Ortiz, Safety   **Manager**   Managing   Manages
                     ●   Ⓑ   Ⓒ

For our monthly **Focus on Safety** exercise, we will be having a fire safety practice. Please be sure to
review the   hazard   evacuation   explosion   ²⁹ plans and the outside meeting place with your
             Ⓐ   Ⓑ   Ⓒ
team. This is also a good time to review basic safety procedures.

1. Keep floors clean and dry. Clean up   spills   machinery   bathrooms   ³⁰ immediately.
                                    Ⓐ   Ⓑ   Ⓒ

2. When mixing powder, use a   spoon   glove   respirator   ³¹ so that you do not
                           Ⓐ   Ⓑ   Ⓒ

  inhale   exit   assemble   ³² dust.
    Ⓐ   Ⓑ   Ⓒ

3. When using machinery, make sure all machine   signs   guards   items   ³³ are in place.
                                        Ⓐ   Ⓑ   Ⓒ

4. Use required   safety   fire   poisonous   ³⁴ glasses and other protective equipment.
              Ⓐ   Ⓑ   Ⓒ

5. All   loose   machinery   combustible   ³⁵ materials should be stored away from any fire hazards.
      Ⓐ   Ⓑ   Ⓒ

6. Use caution around high   injury   safety   voltage   ³⁶ areas to avoid the risk of electric shock.
                    Ⓐ   Ⓑ   Ⓒ

7. In   place   case   contact   ³⁷ of an injury, call the safety office immediately.
      Ⓐ   Ⓑ   Ⓒ

F LISTENING ASSESSMENT: Calling for Medical Advice

Read and listen to the questions. Then listen to the phone call and answer the questions.

38. How did the woman hurt herself?
- Ⓐ She dropped a box.
- Ⓑ She lifted a box.
- Ⓒ She pulled a box.
- Ⓓ She put an ice pack on her back.

39. What DOESN'T the nurse tell her to do?
- Ⓐ Use an ice pack.
- Ⓑ Rest.
- Ⓒ Take pain reliever medication.
- Ⓓ Put a pillow on your head.

40. What should the woman do if her back isn't better in a few days?
- Ⓐ Go to the hospital.
- Ⓑ Take more medication.
- Ⓒ Make an appointment with the doctor.
- Ⓓ Stay home for a few more days.

29 Ⓐ Ⓑ Ⓒ Ⓓ   32 Ⓐ Ⓑ Ⓒ Ⓓ   35 Ⓐ Ⓑ Ⓒ Ⓓ   38 Ⓐ Ⓑ Ⓒ Ⓓ
30 Ⓐ Ⓑ Ⓒ Ⓓ   33 Ⓐ Ⓑ Ⓒ Ⓓ   36 Ⓐ Ⓑ Ⓒ Ⓓ   39 Ⓐ Ⓑ Ⓒ Ⓓ
31 Ⓐ Ⓑ Ⓒ Ⓓ   34 Ⓐ Ⓑ Ⓒ Ⓓ   37 Ⓐ Ⓑ Ⓒ Ⓓ   40 Ⓐ Ⓑ Ⓒ Ⓓ

Go to the next page ⟩

Fill out the form.

MEDICAL HISTORY FORM

Age _____ How would you rate your general health? ☐ Excellent ☐ Good ☐ Fair ☐ Poor

REVIEW OF SYMPTOMS: Please check (✓) any current symptoms that you have.

General
_____ Recent fevers
_____ Unexplained weight loss
_____ Unexplained tiredness/weakness

Eyes
_____ Change in vision

Cardiovascular
_____ Chest pains/discomfort
_____ Short of breath

Ears/Nose/Throat/Mouth
_____ Difficulty hearing
_____ Allergies
_____ Trouble swallowing

Respiratory
_____ Coughing
_____ Coughing up blood

Gastrointestinal
_____ Heartburn
_____ Nausea/vomiting
_____ Diarrhea
_____ Abdominal pain

Musculoskeletal
_____ Joint pain
_____ Back pain

Skin
_____ Rash
_____ New mole

Neurological
_____ Headaches
_____ Memory loss
_____ Fainting

Psychiatric
_____ Anxiety/stress
_____ Sleep problems

Recently, have you had little interest or pleasure in doing things, or have you felt down, depressed, or hopeless? ☐ Yes ☐ No

MEDICATIONS: List all prescription and non-prescription medicines, vitamins, etc. Note the dosage that you take.

FAMILY HISTORY

Please write family members (parent, brother, sister, grandparent, aunt, or uncle) with any of the following conditions:

Alcoholism _____   High blood pressure _____
Asthma _____   Heart disease _____
Stroke _____   Diabetes _____

H SPEAKING ASSESSMENT

I can ask and answer these questions:

Ask Answer
☐ ☐ What advice would you give someone to lose weight?
☐ ☐ What foods do you eat that are high in fat? in sodium?
☐ ☐ What foods do you like that are high in fiber?
☐ ☐ If you wanted to reduce the number of calories you consume every day, what would you do?
☐ ☐ Why is it important to read over-the-counter medicine labels carefully?
☐ ☐ To prevent injuries or fire, what safety procedures should you follow in your kitchen?
☐ ☐ Have you ever been injured at work? at home? What happened? What do you wish you had done differently?

(STOP)

A JOB INTERVIEWS; CAREER ADVANCEMENT

Example:

Be sure to arrive _____ for an interview.
- Ⓐ overtime
- ● on time
- Ⓒ timely
- Ⓓ exact

1. Before an interview, learn about the company so you are _____ with the company's work.
- Ⓐ confident
- Ⓑ dependable
- Ⓒ familiar
- Ⓓ positive

2. Be prepared for questions about your strengths and your _____.
- Ⓐ weaknesses
- Ⓑ abilities
- Ⓒ characteristics
- Ⓓ absences

3. The new job _____ was never advertised in the want ads.
- Ⓐ profession
- Ⓑ entry
- Ⓒ interviewer
- Ⓓ opening

4. You should be able to explain to the interviewer your _____ goals and your plans for the future.
- Ⓐ past
- Ⓑ long-term
- Ⓒ familiar
- Ⓓ financial

5. Most young people start their careers in _____ position.
- Ⓐ a qualified
- Ⓑ an administrative
- Ⓒ a managerial
- Ⓓ an entry-level

6. If a position is _____, it is no longer open.
- Ⓐ filled
- Ⓑ posted
- Ⓒ applied
- Ⓓ advertised

7. Employers look for applicants who are _____.
- Ⓐ annoyed
- Ⓑ enthusiastic
- Ⓒ provided
- Ⓓ supervised

8. You may want to ask if there are opportunities for _____.
- Ⓐ raises
- Ⓑ professions
- Ⓒ advancement
- Ⓓ goals

9. A positive _____ is an important ingredient for success in a job.
- Ⓐ training
- Ⓑ resume
- Ⓒ message
- Ⓓ attitude

....

1 Ⓐ Ⓑ Ⓒ Ⓓ   4 Ⓐ Ⓑ Ⓒ Ⓓ   7 Ⓐ Ⓑ Ⓒ Ⓓ

2 Ⓐ Ⓑ Ⓒ Ⓓ   5 Ⓐ Ⓑ Ⓒ Ⓓ   8 Ⓐ Ⓑ Ⓒ Ⓓ

3 Ⓐ Ⓑ Ⓒ Ⓓ   6 Ⓐ Ⓑ Ⓒ Ⓓ   9 Ⓐ Ⓑ Ⓒ Ⓓ

Go to the next page ⇨

Example:

How _____ your interview?
- ● was
- Ⓑ is
- Ⓒ has been
- Ⓓ would have been

10. Good. The interviewer said I _____ qualified for the job.
- Ⓐ will be
- Ⓑ was
- Ⓒ would have been
- Ⓓ had been

11. Did he ask you _____ your career goals were?
- Ⓐ if
- Ⓑ whether
- Ⓒ where
- Ⓓ what

12. Yes. I told him that I _____ to become a store manager.
- Ⓐ am wanting
- Ⓑ was wanting
- Ⓒ wanted
- Ⓓ had wanted

13. And did he ask you what your weaknesses _____?
- Ⓐ was
- Ⓑ were
- Ⓒ have been
- Ⓓ might have been

14. Yes. I told him that I _____ to improve my accounting skills.
- Ⓐ will
- Ⓑ would
- Ⓒ had needed
- Ⓓ needed

15. Did the interviewer _____ you any difficult questions?
- Ⓐ ask
- Ⓑ advise
- Ⓒ tell
- Ⓓ say

16. Yes. She asked whether I _____ to another city if the job required it.
- Ⓐ moved
- Ⓑ am moving
- Ⓒ had moved
- Ⓓ would move

17. What _____?
- Ⓐ do you say
- Ⓑ do you tell her
- Ⓒ did you say
- Ⓓ did you tell

18. I told her that I _____ sure and I would have to think about it carefully.
- Ⓐ wasn't
- Ⓑ was
- Ⓒ am
- Ⓓ would be

10 Ⓐ Ⓑ Ⓒ Ⓓ   13 Ⓐ Ⓑ Ⓒ Ⓓ   16 Ⓐ Ⓑ Ⓒ Ⓓ
11 Ⓐ Ⓑ Ⓒ Ⓓ   14 Ⓐ Ⓑ Ⓒ Ⓓ   17 Ⓐ Ⓑ Ⓒ Ⓓ
12 Ⓐ Ⓑ Ⓒ Ⓓ   15 Ⓐ Ⓑ Ⓒ Ⓓ   18 Ⓐ Ⓑ Ⓒ Ⓓ

Go to the next page ⟶

C READING: Help Wanted Ads

Look at the help wanted ads. Then do Numbers 19 through 22.

LANDSCAPE MANAGER for Mid-State Landscape Co. Estimate costs & time for large jobs. Supervise workers. Min. 3 yrs. exp. Strong math skills. Medical bnfts & 401(k). Fax resume to 605-423-4567 or email to admin@landscape.com.

MACHINIST Light manufacturing company. Mill & lathe work, incl. programming machinery, job setup, quality inspection. 5 year min. exp. All shifts. Call 408-572-4567.

SUMMER JOBS w/ environmental group. $10-15/hr. Stop global warming! Work w/great people! Career opportunities & bnfts. No exp. req. Call Kit at 605-423-9090.

HEAD NURSE M-F in busy downtown clinic. Great compensation & benefits. Only experienced nurses need apply. Contact ABC Health Services at 415-987-6543.

DRIVER NEEDED FOR WAREHOUSE Clean DMV record, 1 yr. exp., pass drug screening, physical exam, background check. HS dipl. or GED. Must be avail. nights and weekends. Excel. communication skills. Call 605-567-8912.

SALES Cable TV. 3 FT positions avail. Salary & commission & gas allowance. Will train. Must have HS dipl or GED. Call 408-234-5678.

ADMINISTRATIVE ASSISTANT Exp. w/Word & Excel. Gd w/ details & computers. Min. 5 yr. exp. in office. Bnfts. Fax 408-333-6789. Email: frank@A1_jobs.com.

RESTAURANT MANAGER 3-5 yrs exp. in fine dining. Excel. communication w/employees & customers; strong knowledge of restaurant business. Email resume to employment@jobs.com.

CUSTOMER SALES/SERVICE Summer work, $17.00 starting salary. All ages 17+ PT/FT, flexible hours. No exp. req. Call 800-525-4212.

DENTAL ASSISTANT FT. 3 yrs exp. req. Some nights. Front desk duties. Fax resume to 605-567-8900.

DRY CLEANER Pressers and counter clerks needed. PT or FT. Will train. 456-7890.

19. A person with no job experience could apply for the position _____.
- Ⓐ as a driver
- Ⓑ in cable TV sales
- Ⓒ as an administrative assistant
- Ⓓ as a machinist

20. The _____ position requires 5 years of experience.
- Ⓐ landscape manager
- Ⓑ dental assistant
- Ⓒ head nurse
- Ⓓ administrative assistant

21. The warehouse driver needs to be available to work _____.
- Ⓐ part time
- Ⓑ full time
- Ⓒ nights and weekends
- Ⓓ Monday through Friday

22. Rob has several years of experience with a tree service company, driving the truck and supervising workers. Previously, he was a gardener. He wants more responsibility. He could apply for the _____ position.
- Ⓐ landscape manager
- Ⓑ machinist
- Ⓒ restaurant manager
- Ⓓ warehouse driver

19 Ⓐ Ⓑ Ⓒ Ⓓ   20 Ⓐ Ⓑ Ⓒ Ⓓ   21 Ⓐ Ⓑ Ⓒ Ⓓ   22 Ⓐ Ⓑ Ⓒ Ⓓ

Go to the next page ➔

Read the resume. Then do Numbers 23 through 28.

KEN PHAN

95 California St.
San Jose, CA 95118

Cell phone: 408-555-7654
Home phone: 408-555-2793
Email: kenphan@usa.com

OBJECTIVE
A physical therapist position in a clinic

EXPERIENCE
Staff Physical Therapist — 2006–present
Valley Clinic, San Jose, CA
Treated patients of all ages. Supervised two physical therapy assistants.
Assisted in training new therapists.

Staff Physical Therapist — 2004–2006
Therapy Services, San Jose, CA
Treated patients after injuries. Assisted in training with new office software.

Staff Physical Therapist — 2000–2003
West Health Clinic, San Ramon, CA
Treated patients after injuries. Developed bilingual information brochures and exercise sheets.

EDUCATION
Bachelor of Science in Physical Therapy — 1994–1999
San Jose State University

SKILLS AND TRAINING
Certificate for Documentation Specialist (2005). Proficient in Word, Excel. Fluent in Vietnamese.

OTHER WORK EXPERIENCE
Senior Center Activities Assistant, Senior Day Center, San Jose, CA — 1994–1997

REFERENCES
Upon request

---

23. Ken has had ____ positions as a physical therapist.
(A) two
(B) three
(C) four
(D) five

24. In 2005, Ken was working at ____.
(A) Senior Day Center
(B) Therapy Services
(C) West Health Clinic
(D) Valley Clinic

25. Ken worked in San Ramon for ____ years.
(A) two
(B) three
(C) four
(D) five

26. You can infer that a physical therapist treats patients ____.
(A) who are only in the hospital
(B) who need counseling
(C) who have physical problems
(D) who are adults

27. Ken must have ____ while he was in college.
(A) been employed
(B) studied accounting
(C) received certification
(D) learned Spanish

28. Ken has ____ other employees.
(A) provided
(B) worked
(C) treated
(D) supervised

23 (A)(B)(C)(D)   25 (A)(B)(C)(D)   27 (A)(B)(C)(D)
24 (A)(B)(C)(D)   26 (A)(B)(C)(D)   28 (A)(B)(C)(D)

Go to the next page

E **CLOZE READING: A Cover Letter**

Choose the correct answers to complete the letter.

Susan Thomas

Director of Human Healthcare Candidates Resources
                   Ⓐ   Ⓑ   ●

West Health Clinic
San Ramon, CA 94583

Dear Ms. Thomas:

I am writing in response to your ad in the newspaper for a senior physical therapist. You may

remember that I worked at West Health Clinic for four years, from 2000 to 2003. Since that time,

I have been employed at clinics in San Jose. I am seeking advising preventing [29] a position at
                                                    Ⓐ   Ⓑ   Ⓒ

West Health because I would like more opportunities for associates vitals advancement [30].
                                                        Ⓐ   Ⓑ   Ⓒ

Also, I am interested in using my consultant bilingual web-based [31] language skills.
                                  Ⓐ   Ⓑ   Ⓒ

As you can see from my resume e-mail objective [32], I have learned many skills in the
                        Ⓐ   Ⓑ   Ⓒ

past years. In my present position, I cancel oversee escape [33] physical therapy assistants
                                       Ⓐ   Ⓑ   Ⓒ

and train new therapists. I am very engaged proficient willing [34] with computers and
                                     Ⓐ   Ⓑ   Ⓒ

goal field data [35] entry. I am fast-paced enthusiastic certified [36] about my profession
Ⓐ   Ⓑ   Ⓒ   Ⓐ   Ⓑ   Ⓒ

and I enjoy working with patients. I can give you references upon request update equivalent [37].
                                                                   Ⓐ   Ⓑ   Ⓒ

Thank you, and I look forward to hearing from you soon.

Sincerely,

Ken Pham

Ken Pham

---

29 Ⓐ Ⓑ Ⓒ Ⓓ   32 Ⓐ Ⓑ Ⓒ Ⓓ   35 Ⓐ Ⓑ Ⓒ Ⓓ

30 Ⓐ Ⓑ Ⓒ Ⓓ   33 Ⓐ Ⓑ Ⓒ Ⓓ   36 Ⓐ Ⓑ Ⓒ Ⓓ

31 Ⓐ Ⓑ Ⓒ Ⓓ   34 Ⓐ Ⓑ Ⓒ Ⓓ   37 Ⓐ Ⓑ Ⓒ Ⓓ

Go to the next page ⟹

F LISTENING ASSESSMENT: A Job Interview

Read and listen to the questions. Then listen to the interview and answer the questions.

38. What does the interviewer think about Ken?

- Ⓐ He thinks he has too many weaknesses.
- Ⓑ He thinks he isn't qualified.
- Ⓒ He thinks he needs more training.
- Ⓓ He thinks he is a good applicant.

39. What does Ken consider his greatest strength?

- Ⓐ He loves learning.
- Ⓑ He's qualified.
- Ⓒ He communicates well.
- Ⓓ He takes good notes.

40. How many weaknesses does Ken talk about?

- Ⓐ None.
- Ⓑ One.
- Ⓒ Two.
- Ⓓ Three.

G WRITING ASSESSMENT: A Resume

Complete these sections of a resume. List your work experience and your education history.

WORK EXPERIENCE (LIST MOST RECENT FIRST)

Dates _____

Position, Place of Employment, City, State

Description of job duties

Dates _____

Position, Place of Employment, City, State

Description of job duties

Dates _____

Position, Place of Employment, City, State

Description of job duties

EDUCATION HISTORY

Dates _____

Degree or certificate

School, City, State

Dates _____

Degree or certificate

School, City, State

H SPEAKING ASSESSMENT

I can ask and answer these questions:

Ask Answer

- ☐ ☐ Are you working now? If so, what is your position? What are your duties?
- ☐ ☐ Where would you like to work? In what position? Why?
- ☐ ☐ What skills or training do you need to advance in your career?
- ☐ ☐ What do you consider your greatest strength?
- ☐ ☐ What is your greatest weakness?
- ☐ ☐ What are your long-term goals for the future?
- ☐ ☐ Have you ever asked someone for career advice? Explain.

A **EMPLOYMENT AND BENEFITS**

Example:

Employees turn in their _____ on Friday.
- ● timesheets
- Ⓑ paychecks
- Ⓒ benefits
- Ⓓ pay stubs

1. Mario takes care of his wife, his mother, and his two children. They are his _____.
- Ⓐ independents
- Ⓑ siblings
- Ⓒ dependents
- Ⓓ offspring

2. If you are *eligible* for benefits, it means you _____.
- Ⓐ are able to receive them
- Ⓑ aren't able to receive them
- Ⓒ must pay the full price for them
- Ⓓ must apply for them

3. _____ insurance provides money to an employee's family members if the employee dies.
- Ⓐ Health
- Ⓑ Dental
- Ⓒ Tax
- Ⓓ Life

4. A 401(k) is a type of _____.
- Ⓐ retirement savings plan
- Ⓑ vacation plan
- Ⓒ bonus payment
- Ⓓ state tax

5. Employees' _____ usually include paid sick leave and vacation days.
- Ⓐ medical plans
- Ⓑ benefits
- Ⓒ taxes
- Ⓓ bonuses

6. An employee who works for the same company for many years shows _____.
- Ⓐ flexibility
- Ⓑ promotion
- Ⓒ dedication
- Ⓓ respect

7. It's easy to _____ a friendly person.
- Ⓐ get over
- Ⓑ defer
- Ⓒ carry over
- Ⓓ get along with

8. Jake has good _____ qualities. He encourages his employees to work as a **team** and motivates them to do their best.
- Ⓐ friendship
- Ⓑ leading
- Ⓒ leadership
- Ⓓ network

9. A new employee usually needs training and _____ during the first weeks.
- Ⓐ procedure
- Ⓑ feedback
- Ⓒ investment
- Ⓓ dedication

1 Ⓐ Ⓑ Ⓒ Ⓓ   4 Ⓐ Ⓑ Ⓒ Ⓓ   7 Ⓐ Ⓑ Ⓒ Ⓓ

2 Ⓐ Ⓑ Ⓒ Ⓓ   5 Ⓐ Ⓑ Ⓒ Ⓓ   8 Ⓐ Ⓑ Ⓒ Ⓓ

3 Ⓐ Ⓑ Ⓒ Ⓓ   6 Ⓐ Ⓑ Ⓒ Ⓓ   9 Ⓐ Ⓑ Ⓒ Ⓓ

Example:

Could you tell me what
_____ wrong?
- (A) am I doing
- (B) I do
- (C) do I
- ● I'm doing

10. Sure. You're supposed
_____ the original face
down.
- (A) put
- (B) to put
- (C) putting
- (D) you put

11. Oh. I _____ that.
- (A) didn't know
- (B) don't know
- (C) wouldn't know
- (D) hadn't known

12. If you put it face down, the
copier _____ correctly.
- (A) would have worked
- (B) worked
- (C) will work
- (D) has worked

13. Could you tell me
when I _____ personal
days?
- (A) use
- (B) will use
- (C) used
- (D) can use

14. Yes. They _____ for
doctor appointments and
family illness.
- (A) can use
- (B) can be used
- (C) could use
- (D) could have used

15. If I add my wife to my
health plan, what
_____ my premium be?
- (A) is
- (B) will be
- (C) will
- (D) wouldn't

16. It _____ from $160 to
$340 a month.
- (A) increase
- (B) will increase
- (C) is increasing
- (D) would have increase

17. Life insurance is free
for all employees,
_____?
- (A) it is
- (B) is it
- (C) it isn't
- (D) isn't it

18. Yes, _____. We also offer
a 401(k) plan.
- (A) it is
- (B) is it
- (C) they are
- (D) are they

10 (A) (B) (C) (D)   13 (A) (B) (C) (D)   16 (A) (B) (C) (D)
11 (A) (B) (C) (D)   14 (A) (B) (C) (D)   17 (A) (B) (C) (D)
12 (A) (B) (C) (D)   15 (A) (B) (C) (D)   18 (A) (B) (C) (D)

Go to the next page ⟹

C READING: An Employee Benefits Manual

Look at the description of employee benefits. Then do Numbers 19 through 24.

RIVERSIDE FLOORING COMPANY   **Employee Benefits at a Glance**

Full-time employees are eligible for the benefits listed below. The insurance costs are taken out of your paycheck every two weeks. The Health Maintenance Organization (HMO) has specific doctors that you must use. The Preferred Provider Organization (PPO) has a large network of doctors who give discounted prices. With the PPO, you may choose any doctor. Both plans pay for prescription drugs.

Type of Coverage	HMO	PPO	Dental
Employee	$63.82	$63.82	$ 4.25
Employee + spouse	$113.71	$115.09	$10.83
Employee + child	$113.71	$115.09	$11.30
Employee + family	$154.23	$157.40	$17.42

Benefits at no additional cost:
Life Insurance: Provides payment equal to your annual salary.
Employee Assistance Program: Provides short-term mental health counseling and career planning services.

Other Benefits:
401(k) Plan: Employees are eligible to enroll in the 401(k) plan immediately upon employment. Please see Human Resources for a complete description of the plan.
Vacation Days: Employees receive 10 days of vacation per year during the first 5 years of employment.
Personal Days: Employees are eligible for 3 personal days per year.
Sick Time: Employees receive 5 paid sick days per year. Sick days may be carried over to the next year.

19. The chart shows how much the insurance costs _____.
    Ⓐ every month
    Ⓑ every week
    Ⓒ every two weeks
    Ⓓ twice a weeks

20. If you want to have _____ when choosing your doctor, you should choose a PPO.
    Ⓐ fewer choices
    Ⓑ more choices
    Ⓒ the lowest prices
    Ⓓ the highest prices

21. If you are married with three children and you choose a PPO and dental coverage, your biweekly deduction will be _____.
    Ⓐ $154.23
    Ⓑ $157.40
    Ⓒ $164.82
    Ⓓ $174.82

22. The _____ is a good way to save money for retirement.
    Ⓐ HMO
    Ⓑ PPO
    Ⓒ 401(k) plan
    Ⓓ life insurance

23. If you don't use all of your _____, you can use them during the next year.
    Ⓐ sick time
    Ⓑ vacation days
    Ⓒ personal days
    Ⓓ holidays

24. If you have a very difficult family problem, you might use the _____ benefit.
    Ⓐ sick time
    Ⓑ dental
    Ⓒ life insurance
    Ⓓ Employee Assistance Program

19 Ⓐ Ⓑ Ⓒ Ⓓ   21 Ⓐ Ⓑ Ⓒ Ⓓ   23 Ⓐ Ⓑ Ⓒ Ⓓ

20 Ⓐ Ⓑ Ⓒ Ⓓ   22 Ⓐ Ⓑ Ⓒ Ⓓ   24 Ⓐ Ⓑ Ⓒ Ⓓ

Read the article. Then do Numbers 25 through 28.

RIVERSIDE HOSPITAL NEWS

Riverside Hospital Employees on the Move!

Selena Costa has recently been promoted to the position of head nurse on the surgery floor of the hospital. Ms. Costa has been an employee of Riverside Hospital since 2001, and most recently she was the head night nurse on the pediatric floor. Ms. Costa has shown strong leadership in her previous position and successfully led the pediatric department through the change to new software. Throughout the hospital, she is known as a problem-solver. She always meets challenges with a positive attitude. In addition, she is a very effective communicator and has worked with the Human Resources department to improve the communication procedures at nursing stations on all hospital floors.

Richard Nguyen will move up to the position of Vice President of Operations for the hospital at the end of this month. Mr. Nguyen joined our staff in 2007 as Operations Manager. He has held that position since that time, and his responsibilities have grown along with the growth of the hospital. As Operations Manager, he has overseen the day-to-day operations of the hospital, including equipment, repairs, training, and safety procedures. In his new position as Vice President of Operations, Mr. Nguyen will focus on improving hospital management and office procedures for the highest quality of patient care. He will be responsible for equipment budgets. Mr. Nguyen has great dedication to the hospital, and he has the respect of all the employees in his department.

25. We know from the article that when Selena worked on the pediatric floor, she worked _____.
   Ⓐ part time
   Ⓑ during the day
   Ⓒ at night
   Ⓓ on weekends

26. Which personal characteristic is NOT mentioned about Selena?
   Ⓐ dependability
   Ⓑ positive attitude
   Ⓒ good communicator
   Ⓓ problem-solver

27. You can infer that the hospital has _____ since 2007.
   Ⓐ become more crowded
   Ⓑ become larger
   Ⓒ lowered prices
   Ⓓ changed insurance plans

28. In his new position, Richard will NOT be responsible for _____.
   Ⓐ office procedures
   Ⓑ budgets
   Ⓒ improving management
   Ⓓ training doctors

....

25 Ⓐ Ⓑ Ⓒ Ⓓ   27 Ⓐ Ⓑ Ⓒ Ⓓ

26 Ⓐ Ⓑ Ⓒ Ⓓ   28 Ⓐ Ⓑ Ⓒ Ⓓ

Go to the next page ⇒

E CLOZE READING: A Magazine Article

Choose the correct answers to complete the article.

TIPS FOR CAREER EARNINGS ADVANCEMENT INSURANCE
(A) ● (C)

Many career counselors agree that the best time to think about your next job is when you are comfortable in your present job. Don't wait until you are sick unhappy efficient 29 in your job.
(A) (B) (C)

Plan ahead for your career advancement! Prepare for a promotion task investment 30 at
(A) (B) (C)

your present place of employment. If there are no ways to match advance defer 31 where
(A) (B) (C)

you work, you may need to look at other companies or organizations. Here are some tips for advancing.

1. Talk to your employer. Have a conversation with your boss about your future in the company.
   Explain your chain sales vision 32 for your career.
   (A) (B) (C)

   Your boss will have respect experience profits 33 for your confidence and planning.
   (A) (B) (C)

2. Show that you are interested in learning new skills. Businesses are always changing, so it is
   important to be punctual adaptable online 34.
   (A) (B) (C)

3. Improve your communication skills. Listen carefully to others. Be helpful and
   pleased famous friendly 35.
   (A) (B) (C)

4. Make Take Leave 36 friends with other people in your profession. Get to know people in
   (A) (B) (C)

   other companies—you will be more likely to hear about other jobs.

5. If you would like to be a manager, develop your marketing leadership flexibility 37 skills.
   (A) (B) (C)

   Learn how to supervise other employees.

29 (A) (B) (C) (D)   32 (A) (B) (C) (D)   35 (A) (B) (C) (D)
30 (A) (B) (C) (D)   33 (A) (B) (C) (D)   36 (A) (B) (C) (D)
31 (A) (B) (C) (D)   34 (A) (B) (C) (D)   37 (A) (B) (C) (D)

Go to the next page ➔ **T53** ●

Read and listen to the questions. Then listen to the conversation and answer the questions.

38. What procedure is the person showing the new employee?
   Ⓐ How to check out.
   Ⓑ How to lock the door.
   Ⓒ How to break into the building.
   Ⓓ How to turn on the security alarm.

39. How do you know that the security alarm is on?
   Ⓐ The top light is red.
   Ⓑ The top light is blue.
   Ⓒ All of the buttons are red.
   Ⓓ You are the last person to go home.

40. What is the last step?
   Ⓐ Ringing the alarm.
   Ⓑ Selecting the office areas.
   Ⓒ Pushing the red button.
   Ⓓ Pushing the on-off button.

G WRITING ASSESSMENT: Instructions for a Procedure

Write instructions for how to do a procedure.

_____

_____

_____

_____

_____

_____

_____

_____

H SPEAKING ASSESSMENT

I can ask and answer these questions:

Ask Answer
☐ ☐ Which of your personal qualities will be most helpful for career advancement? Why?
☐ ☐ Have you ever received a promotion? Explain the situation. Why were you promoted?
☐ ☐ If you are working now, what job would you like to be promoted to? If you aren't working now, what job would you like to have?
☐ ☐ What skills or experience do you need for this promotion or job?
☐ ☐ What is a complicated procedure that you often follow at work or at home?
☐ ☐ Do you learn procedures best by reading, by listening to an explanation, or by doing it?
☐ ☐ What benefits do you (or your family) currently receive at work?
☐ ☐ What benefit would you like to receive? Why?
☐ ☐ Who do you often give feedback to? Give an example of feedback you have given recently.
☐ ☐ Who do you receive feedback from? Is the feedback helpful? Why or why not?

Name _____

Date _____ Class _____

Example:

If a person is born in the United States, he or she is automatically _____.

Ⓐ a naturalized citizen
Ⓑ an immigrant
⬤ a legal citizen
Ⓓ a voter

1. _____ is NOT a privilege of U.S. citizenship.
Ⓐ The right to vote
Ⓑ The right to serve on a jury
Ⓒ Visiting any foreign country
Ⓓ A fair trial

2. You must _____ to become a naturalized citizen.
Ⓐ pass a citizenship test
Ⓑ be born in the U.S.
Ⓒ be a homeowner
Ⓓ serve on a jury

3. The general meaning of *citizen* is _____ who lives in a city or state.
Ⓐ a permanent resident
Ⓑ any person
Ⓒ a taxpayer
Ⓓ a registered person

4. _____ tax is based on a person's earnings.
Ⓐ Resident
Ⓑ Property
Ⓒ Service
Ⓓ Income

5. Local and state governments do NOT use tax money to pay for _____.
Ⓐ schools
Ⓑ fire and police departments
Ⓒ national defense
Ⓓ local roads

6. Citizens should read the newspaper or watch the news to stay _____ about issues.
Ⓐ informed
Ⓑ expected
Ⓒ required
Ⓓ called

7. Although hiring an attorney is expensive, most communities have free _____.
Ⓐ judges
Ⓑ legal services
Ⓒ counselors
Ⓓ trials

8. The jury observes the trial and then reaches _____.
Ⓐ an offense
Ⓑ a judge
Ⓒ innocence
Ⓓ a verdict

9. All tenants have certain _____ that are protected by the law.
Ⓐ conditions
Ⓑ buildings
Ⓒ landlords
Ⓓ rights

1 Ⓐ Ⓑ Ⓒ Ⓓ   4 Ⓐ Ⓑ Ⓒ Ⓓ   7 Ⓐ Ⓑ Ⓒ Ⓓ

2 Ⓐ Ⓑ Ⓒ Ⓓ   5 Ⓐ Ⓑ Ⓒ Ⓓ   8 Ⓐ Ⓑ Ⓒ Ⓓ

3 Ⓐ Ⓑ Ⓒ Ⓓ   6 Ⓐ Ⓑ Ⓒ Ⓓ   9 Ⓐ Ⓑ Ⓒ Ⓓ

Example:

_____ trouble understanding this letter. Could you look at it?
- (A) I would have
- ● I'm having
- (C) I am
- (D) I was having

10. This is a letter about jury duty. You _____ on a jury next month.
- (A) have served
- (B) would serve
- (C) have to serve
- (D) served

11. Can I be on a jury if I _____ a permanent resident?
- (A) was
- (B) will be
- (C) were
- (D) am

12. Yes, you can. If you are called for jury duty, you _____ to serve on a jury.
- (A) are required
- (B) were required
- (C) are requiring
- (D) require

13. _____ you _____ to vote yet?
- (A) Are . . . registering
- (B) Do . . . register
- (C) Could . . . register
- (D) Have . . . registered

14. No, I _____. I should register before next week.
- (A) have
- (B) hadn't
- (C) haven't
- (D) would have

15. Last night my landlord said she _____ me!
- (A) was going to evict
- (B) evicted
- (C) evicting
- (D) will be evicted

16. Really? But you always _____ your rent on time. How can she evict you?
- (A) are paying
- (B) will pay
- (C) pay
- (D) paying

17. I don't know. Maybe I _____ the community legal services office.
- (A) must call
- (B) should call
- (C) might call
- (D) will have called

18. Good idea. If I _____ you, I _____ right away.
- (A) am . . . will call
- (B) were . . . would call
- (C) are . . . will call
- (D) weren't . . . wouldn't call

10 (A) (B) (C) (D)   13 (A) (B) (C) (D)   15 (A) (B) (C) (D)   17 (A) (B) (C) (D)

11 (A) (B) (C) (D)   14 (A) (B) (C) (D)   16 (A) (B) (C) (D)   18 (A) (B) (C) (D)

12 (A) (B) (C) (D)

Go to the next page ⟹

Read the civics textbook lesson. Then do Numbers 19 through 24.

A LOOK AT TAXES

Who pays taxes?

Every person who works in the United States must pay federal income tax. The amount due depends on how much income is earned in a year (for example, from salary).

Federal, state, and local taxes

Federal taxes are used for the federal government, federal programs, national defense, national parks, and money that the federal government assigns to special projects in states. Federal income tax supports programs on a national level. State and local taxes support our public schools, the public health system, local hospitals, parks, streets, highways, and so on.

Tax levels

For federal, state, and local taxes, a person is not required to pay income tax if his or her income is very low. This level is called the "threshold" level. If the income is less than the "threshold" level, no income tax is due. Each year, states set their own income levels for state income taxes.

As an example, the chart below shows 2008 tax threshold levels in California. If a single mother with one child earns less than $25,145, she owes no state income tax. If a family of four with two children has an income of less than $47,715, they owe no state income tax.

Personal Income Tax Thresholds	
	Tax Threshold
Single, no children	$14,845
Married, no children	$26,690
Head of household, one child	$25,145
Head of household, two children (or more)	$32,870
Married, one child	$39,990
Married, two children (or more)	$47,715

19. Taxpayers pay local, state, and _____ taxes.
  - Ⓐ federal
  - Ⓑ income
  - Ⓒ threshold
  - Ⓓ property

20. The term *tax threshold* refers to _____.
  - Ⓐ a person's salary
  - Ⓑ the level where no income tax is due
  - Ⓒ the amount of federal tax due
  - Ⓓ the amount of state tax due

21. People with a very _____ might not have to pay taxes.
  - Ⓐ small family
  - Ⓑ high income
  - Ⓒ low income
  - Ⓓ large salary

22. In the chart, *head of household* means _____.
  - Ⓐ a single mother
  - Ⓑ a single father
  - Ⓒ a landlord
  - Ⓓ a single parent

23. According to the chart, if a husband and wife have no children and have a combined income of _____, they do not need to pay income tax.
  - Ⓐ $26,000
  - Ⓑ $27,000
  - Ⓒ $30,000
  - Ⓓ $35,000

24. For a head of household, the difference between the threshold for one child and the threshold for two children is _____.
  - Ⓐ $1,545
  - Ⓑ $2,545
  - Ⓒ $7,725
  - Ⓓ $8,725

19 Ⓐ Ⓑ Ⓒ Ⓓ   21 Ⓐ Ⓑ Ⓒ Ⓓ   23 Ⓐ Ⓑ Ⓒ Ⓓ

20 Ⓐ Ⓑ Ⓒ Ⓓ   22 Ⓐ Ⓑ Ⓒ Ⓓ   24 Ⓐ Ⓑ Ⓒ Ⓓ

Read the brochure. Then do Numbers 25 though 28.

Community Services for North County Residents

Health

Daly City Youth Health Center
Medical services for youth 6-18
623-2240

Spring Street Mental Health Association
Clinic for persons with mental illness
623-3345

Drug Abuse Recovery Services
Substance abuse prevention and treatment
623-3945

North County Health Services Agency
Medical services available to the public
623-9876

Legal Services

Legal Aid Society of North County
Legal services for tenant/landlord disputes
623-0915

North County Immigration Services
Assistance with immigration procedures
623-7654

Family Law Center
Legal counseling and referral for legal issues affecting families
623-9191

Housing

Rebuilding Together
Home repairs for low-income homeowners
623-6597

Fair Housing Program
Fair housing counseling for renters
623-6291

Human Services

Center for Domestic Violence Prevention
Services for domestic violence victims
623-0800

North County Family Counseling Agency
Mental health counseling for individuals and families
623-0555

Friends for Youth
A variety of programs for youth
623-2867

Project Read
Adult literacy tutoring
623-3871

25. Substance abuse refers to _____.
   Ⓐ housing problems
   Ⓑ immigration procedures
   Ⓒ addiction to drugs
   Ⓓ domestic violence

26. If your landlord doesn't make important repairs, call _____.
   Ⓐ the Family Law Center
   Ⓑ the Center for Domestic Violence Prevention
   Ⓒ Rebuilding Together
   Ⓓ the Legal Aid Society of North County

27. If your teenager needs a doctor, call _____.
   Ⓐ Abuse Recovery Services
   Ⓑ the Daly City Youth Health Center
   Ⓒ Friends for Youth
   Ⓓ Project Read

28. If a man and a woman want legal advice about getting a divorce, they should call _____.
   Ⓐ the Legal Aid Society of North County
   Ⓑ the Spring Street Mental Health Association
   Ⓒ the Family Law Center
   Ⓓ the North County Family Counseling Agency

25 Ⓐ Ⓑ Ⓒ Ⓓ   26 Ⓐ Ⓑ Ⓒ Ⓓ   27 Ⓐ Ⓑ Ⓒ Ⓓ   28 Ⓐ Ⓑ Ⓒ Ⓓ

Go to the next page ➡

E **CLOZE READING: A Voter Registration Information Flyer**

Choose the correct answers to complete the flyer.

Citizenship Voter Legal Registration Drive, Saturday, October 2, 10 AM–2 PM
(A)   ●   (C)

Westside Community Center

Are you registered due signed [29] to vote? Voting gives you a speech voice status [30]
(A) (B) (C)   (A) (B) (C)

in our traffic jury government [31]. You must register to vote by October 2 so that you can
(A) (B) (C)

reach participate assemble [32] in the local small neighborhood [33] and state
(A) (B) (C)   (A) (B) (C)

verdict election elected [34] on November 4. To be eligible to vote, you must be a
(A) (B) (C)

taxpayer individual citizen [35] of the United States and at least 18 years old.
(A) (B) (C)

In the upcoming election, you can vote for the following positions: members of the City

Department Council Committee [36], members of the School Jury Agency Board [37],
(A) (B) (C)   (A) (B) (C)

the mayor, your state senator, and your state representative.

Candidates' Night will be on October 10, 6:00–9:00 P.M. at City Hall

---

F **LISTENING ASSESSMENT: Recorded Community Services Information**

Read and listen to the questions. Then listen to the phone call and answer the questions.

38. What agency is the person calling?
Ⓐ City Hall.
Ⓑ Community Legal Aid.
Ⓒ Immigration.
Ⓓ Domestic Violence.

39. What number do you press for immigration?
Ⓐ 1
Ⓑ 2
Ⓒ 3
Ⓓ 4

40. Which office does the person want to reach?
Ⓐ Immigration.
Ⓑ Domestic violence.
Ⓒ Fair housing.
Ⓓ Family law.

---

29 Ⓐ Ⓑ Ⓒ Ⓓ   32 Ⓐ Ⓑ Ⓒ Ⓓ   35 Ⓐ Ⓑ Ⓒ Ⓓ   38 Ⓐ Ⓑ Ⓒ Ⓓ

30 Ⓐ Ⓑ Ⓒ Ⓓ   33 Ⓐ Ⓑ Ⓒ Ⓓ   36 Ⓐ Ⓑ Ⓒ Ⓓ   39 Ⓐ Ⓑ Ⓒ Ⓓ

31 Ⓐ Ⓑ Ⓒ Ⓓ   34 Ⓐ Ⓑ Ⓒ Ⓓ   37 Ⓐ Ⓑ Ⓒ Ⓓ   40 Ⓐ Ⓑ Ⓒ Ⓓ

WRITING ASSESSMENT: A Voter Registration Form

Fill in the voter registration application with your information.

Voter Registration Application

| Are you a citizen of the United States of America? ☐ Yes ☐ No | This space for office use only. |
| Will you be 18 years old on or before election day? ☐ Yes ☐ No | |

If you checked "No" in response to either of these questions, you are not eligible to vote.

1

(Check one) ○ ○ ○ ○
Mr. Mrs. Miss Ms.

Last Name	First Name	Middle Name(s)

(Check one) ○ ○ ○ ○ ○
Jr. Sr. II III IV

2

Home Address	Apt or Lot#	City/Town	State	Zip Code

3

Address Where You Get Your Mail If Different From Above	City/Town	State	Zip Code

4 Date of Birth _____
Month   Day   Year

5 Telephone Number (optional)

6 ID Number (Social Security or driver's license number)

7 Choice of Party (Democrat, Republican, or other)

8 Race or Ethnic Group (Optional)

9 I have reviewed my state's instructions and I swear/affirm that:
- I am a United States citizen.
- I meet the eligibility requirements of my state and subscribe to any oath required.
- The information I have provided is true to the best of my knowledge under penalty of perjury. If I have provided false information, I may be fined, imprisoned, or (if not a U.S. citizen) deported from or refused entry to the United States.

Please sign full name (or put mark) ▲

Date: _____ / _____ / _____
Month   Day   Year

SPEAKING ASSESSMENT

I can ask and answer these questions:

Ask Answer

☐ ☐ If you had legal problems with a landlord, who would you call in your community?
☐ ☐ If you had a legal question about a family matter, who would you call?
☐ ☐ If you had a legal question concerning immigration, who would you call?
☐ ☐ Do you vote in elections? Why or why not?
☐ ☐ Have you ever served on a jury? Explain.
☐ ☐ How do you keep informed about your town or city?
☐ ☐ What services and privileges do you enjoy in your community?
☐ ☐ Do you participate in your community? If so, how do you participate? If not, how *could* you participate?
☐ ☐ Do you pay taxes? If so, who prepares the forms for your tax returns?
☐ ☐ Describe something in your community that is probably paid for through *local* taxes.
☐ ☐ Describe something in your community that is probably paid for through *state* taxes.

STOP

APPENDIX

Listening Scripts

Page 3   Exercise C
Listen and decide what is being talked about.

1. A. Have they sung them yet?
   B. Yes, they have. They sang them a little while ago.
2. A. Has she written it yet?
   B. Yes, she has. She wrote it a little while ago.
3. A. I've spoken it for a long time.
   B. Oh. I didn't know that.
4. A. Have you swum there?
   B. Yes. We've swum there for a long time.
5. A. Have you ridden it yet?
   B. Yes. I rode it a little while ago.
6. A. I've drawn them for many years.
   B. I didn't know that.
7. A. Have you taken it?
   B. Yes, we have. We took it a little while ago.
8. A. Have you driven it yet?
   B. Yes. I drove it a little while ago.
9. A. She's grown them for many years.
   B. Yes. I knew that.

Page 6   Exercise G
Listen and complete the sentences.

1. A. How long have you played the violin?
   B. I've played the violin for . . .
2. A. How long has Peter known Monica?
   B. He's known her since . . .
3. A. How long have Mr. and Mrs. Johnson had that car?
   B. They've had it since . . .
4. A. How long have we been married?
   B. We've been married for . . .
5. A. How long has your sister had the flu?
   B. She's had the flu for . . .
6. A. How long have you wanted to be an actor?
   B. I've wanted to be an actor since . . .
7. A. How long has Debbie sung in the church choir?
   B. She's sung in the church choir since . . .
8. A. How long have you been a teacher?
   B. I've been a teacher for . . .
9. A. How long has Kevin had a Boston accent?
   B. He's had a Boston accent for . . .

Page 8   Exercise K
Listen and choose the correct answer.

1. I'm really frustrated. I've been having problems with my TV for the past few weeks, and I can't find anyone who can fix it.
2. I think I'll start looking for another job. I've been working here at the State Street Bank since I graduated from college.
3. We've been sitting here for more than a half hour, and no one has taken our order yet.
4. Do you think Peter and Jane will get married someday? After all, they've been going out since they were in high school.
5. We've been complaining to our landlord about the ceiling in our bedroom, but he hasn't done anything about it. We don't know what to do. It's been leaking for the past two weeks.
6. I'm exhausted. We've been riding around town all day. Let's stop somewhere and rest for a while.

Page 29   Exercise M
Listen and choose the correct answer.

1. Billy fell asleep in school today.
2. Alice called her friends at midnight and woke them up.
3. I wonder why Gary didn't come to the meeting this morning.
4. We sat at the football game in the rain all afternoon.
5. Roger was hoping to get a promotion this year, but he didn't get one.
6. The play was terrible. The actors couldn't remember their lines!
7. I called my cousin Betty all week, but she didn't answer the phone.
8. Grandpa moved the refrigerator by himself!

Page 31   Exercise P: *Have You Heard?*
Listen and complete the sentences.

1. How do you feel . . .
2. Do you still . . .
3. Does he like these . . .
4. She needed . . .
5. They live . . .
6. We're leaving . . .
7. Alan is sleeping late because he's . . .
8. I'm sorry you didn't like the salad. It . . .
9. I'll try to finish this . . .
10. This week . . .
11. Will you still want to see your old friends when you're rich . . .
12. You should fill . . .
13. They don't feed . . .
14. I'm glad you like the chocolate cake. Eat . . .
15. I don't think those boys steal . . .
16. George is very glad his . . .

Page 35   Exercise E
Listen and decide what is being talked about.

1. They've already been made.
2. It was directed by Fellini.
3. It was sent last week.
4. It was worn by her grandmother.
5. They've already been given out.
6. They've already been written.
7. It's already been sung.
8. They've already been fed.
9. It's already been set up.

Page 39   Exercise L
Listen and choose the correct answer.

1. Hello. This is Mrs. Riley. I'm calling about my VCR. Is it ready?
2. Is the meeting room ready?
3. This is a beautiful photograph of your children.
4. I can't wait to hear those songs.
5. Why is Robert so upset?
6. We've been waiting all morning for the courier from your company.
7. Have you heard the good news about Nancy's raise?
8. Why is Roberta so pleased?
9. Where are the new pictures we bought last weekend?
10. Is the birthday cake ready?
11. I'm really looking forward to hearing the Mozart sonata.
12. Why is Aunt Helen so happy?

Page 43   Exercise R
Listen and choose the correct answer.

1. This magnificent mural is being painted by students in our school.
2. Mrs. Allen, your watch has been repaired.
3. The beds will be done soon.
4. All the paychecks have been given out.

Listening scripts are not provided for the achievement tests. Complete test listening scripts are included in *Side by Side Plus* Teacher's Guide 4 and Multilevel Activity & Achievement Test Book 4 (and its accompanying CD-ROM).

5. The meeting room is ready now.
6. Mr. Winter, your car is being repaired.
7. All the cookies have been baked.
8. The babies are being fed.

Page 45   Exercise D
Listen and choose the correct answer.

Ex: It's already been painted.

1. All the photographs have been taken.
2. The holiday decorations are being hung up.
3. The beds on the third floor are ready now.
4. The report is being rewritten right now.
5. Mr. Williams, your VCR has been repaired.

Page 49   Exercise E
Listen and decide what is being talked about.

1. I'm sorry. I don't know what time it arrives. Check with the ticket agent.
2. I have no idea what this means.
3. Do you have any idea when this was taken?
4. I have no idea what the problem is with the engine. Check with the mechanic.
5. I have no idea what time it begins. You should look in the newspaper.
6. I'm sorry. I don't know how much this costs. You should ask that salesperson over there.
7. Do you know when they were sent?
8. Do you have any idea when they were fed?

Page 53   Exercise J
Listen and decide where these people are.

1. Can you tell me if surfing is allowed here?
2. Do you by any chance know whether these shirts are on sale?
3. Do you know whether the play has begun yet?
4. Do you remember if our car is on the third floor or on the fourth?
5. Do you have any idea if it'll be arriving soon?
6. Could you tell me whether there's a lot of pepper in the stew?
7. Do you know whether swimming is allowed here?
8. Could you possibly tell me if lettuce is on sale this week?
9. Do you by any chance know if the monkeys are sleeping?

Page 58   Exercise D
Listen and complete the sentences.

1. If it rains this weekend, . . .
2. I'll skip dessert if . . .
3. We'll be late for work if . . .
4. If they finish their homework soon, . . .
5. If our car doesn't start tomorrow morning, . . .
6. If you don't come to class next Monday, . . .
7. I know I'll fall asleep in class if . . .
8. I'll send your package by overnight mail if . . .
9. If Charlie doesn't get a raise soon, . . .
10. Please call me if . . .
11. Janet will pick up her husband at the airport if . . .
12. If the children don't feel any better, . . .
13. We won't go on vacation if . . .
14. She'll regret it if . . .

Page 63   Exercise J
Listen and choose the polite response.

1. Do you think it will snow soon so we can go skiing?
2. Do you think you'll lose your job?
3. Will the teacher yell at us if we make a mistake?
4. Do you think the baby will cry all night?
5. Will Jane go out with me if I ask her?
6. Am I going to regret taking this job?
7. Am I going to have trouble on my history exam?
8. Will you graduate soon?

9. Will the movie be exciting?
10. Will there be pickpockets in the crowd?
11. Do you think John will apologize to his sister?
12. Will YOUR children give their colds to MY children?

Page 66   Exercise N
Listen and choose the correct answer based on what you hear.

1. You know, George, if you took more vacations, you'd feel more energetic.
2. I would enjoy listening to the orchestra if the musicians were more talented.
3. If you were more aggressive, you'd be a much better used car salesman.
4. Bob's car would be in better condition if he tuned it up more often.
5. If they had more in common, they'd get along with each other.
6. If Mona were a good teacher, she'd care more about her students.
7. We would be able to use the Internet if our school had more computers.
8. If these cookies had more sugar, they'd be sweeter.

Page 77   Exercise D
Listen and complete the sentences.

Ex. If the weather is nice this weekend, . . .

1. If I miss the bus, . . .
2. If I were more careful, . . .
3. You'll regret it if . . .
4. If I didn't have to work overtime, . . .
5. If she weren't busy this weekend, . . .

Page 80   Exercise E
Listen and complete the sentences.

1. I wouldn't grow a beard if I were you. If you grew a beard, . . .
2. I'm not feeling well today, but if I feel better tomorrow, . . .
3. You know, I wouldn't ride in that old car if I were you. If you rode in that old car, . . .
4. If I have some time this weekend, . . .
5. I wouldn't show this political cartoon to the president. If you showed it to him, . . .
6. To be honest, I wouldn't go to Alaska in February. If you went there in February, . . .
7. If I have to spend a lot of money on car repairs this year, . . .
8. If I were you, I wouldn't buy a used computer. If you bought a used computer, . . .
9. If you skip today's meeting, I know . . .
10. To be honest with you, I wouldn't start an Internet company if I were you. If you did, . . .
11. If you keep on parking your car in my parking space, . . .
12. To tell the truth, I wouldn't marry George if I were you. If you married him, . . .

Page 83   Exercise I
Listen and complete the conversations.

1. A. Do you think the weather in London is sunny and warm at this time of year?
   B. No, I don't. But I wish . . .
2. A. Are you unhappy when I talk too much?
   B. Yes, I am. I wish . . .
3. A. Does your daughter enjoy her English class?
   B. Yes, she does. But she wishes . . .
4. A. Do you think Michael daydreams too much in class?
   B. Yes, I do. I wish . . .
5. A. Do you like scary movies?
   B. Yes. As a matter of fact, I usually wish . . .

Activity Workbook

6. A. Are you annoyed when I sing loudly in the shower?
   B. The truth is, I wish . . .
7. A. Do you like your cell phone?
   B. Yes, I do. But I wish . . .
8. A. Are you tired of getting stuck in traffic?
   B. Of course, I am. I wish . . .
9. A. Do you like being single?
   B. It's okay. But the truth is, I wish . . .
10. A. Are you enjoying living in your new apartment?
    B. It's fine, but it's a little too small. I wish . . .
11. A. Is Harry upset about being laid off?
    B. He certainly is. He wishes . . .
12. A. Are you worried when I don't call you?
    B. Yes, I am. I wish . . .

Page 86   Exercise N
Listen and decide what the person is talking about.

1. If your pronunciation were better, I'd be able to understand you.
2. If I planted them now, I could eat them in three months.
3. If I took driver's ed, I could get it soon.
4. If I skipped it, my mother would be angry.
5. If I saved enough, I'd probably be able to visit you.
6. If I didn't concentrate, I could make a mistake.

Page 93   Exercise E
Listen and choose the statement that is true based on what you hear.

1. If she had spoken more confidently at her job interview, she would have gotten the job.
2. If he hadn't been late for work every day, he wouldn't have gotten fired.
3. If it had rained, we would have had to cancel the picnic.
4. If you hadn't been in a hurry, you wouldn't have made so many careless mistakes on your homework.
5. If I had remembered their phone number, I would have called them.
6. If the play hadn't been so boring, the audience wouldn't have fallen asleep.
7. If we had been in the mood to go swimming, we would have gone to the beach with you.
8. If he hadn't been speeding, he wouldn't have gotten a ticket.
9. If I had written legibly, they would have been able to read my letter.
10. If I hadn't forgotten about the meeting, I definitely would have been there.

Page 102   Exercise R
Listen and complete the sentences.

1. I wish I didn't have an exam tomorrow. If I didn't have an exam, . . .
2. I hope we're having spaghetti for dinner tonight. If we're having spaghetti for dinner, . . .
3. I wish my brother weren't in a bad mood all the time. If he weren't in a bad mood all the time, . . .
4. I wish my daughter had taken her umbrella to school. If she had taken her umbrella, . . .
5. I hope Jim is at the party Saturday night. If he's at the party, . . .
6. I wish I lived near a bus stop. If I lived near a bus stop, . . .

Page 102   Exercise S: *Hopes and Wishes*
Listen and complete the sentences.

1. My son isn't feeling very well. I wish . . .
2. I was confused about yesterday's English lesson. I hope . . .
3. My best friend just moved away. I wish . . .

4. Alice hates working at Paul's Pizza Shop. She hopes . . .
5. I sometimes feel lonely. I wish . . .
6. I'll try not to step on your feet. I wish . . .
7. The school play is this weekend. We hope . . .
8. My daughter lost her notebook. I wish . . .
9. I'm making chocolate chip cookies for dessert. I hope . . .
10. This cactus looks terrible. I wish . . .
11. Our fax machine is broken. I hope . . .
12. Vicky's used car has been giving her a lot of trouble. She wishes . . .
13. I don't have any eggs. I hope . . .
14. I sometimes forget people's names. I wish . . .

Page 103   Exercise U: *Have You Heard?*
Listen and complete the sentences.

1. This morning I met . . .
2. They fell . . .
3. A tailor . . .
4. There isn't enough pepper . . .
5. Are you afraid . . .
6. Have they made . . .
7. The men . . .
8. We're going to shake . . .
9. My daughter's wedding . . .
10. Nancy's neighbor . . .
11. Barbara paid . . .
12. I'll check . . .
13. I don't want to go to school because I fail . . .
14. We have to hurry because Tom's waiting . . .
15. Roger's never . . .
16. I'm Fred . . .

Page 108   Exercise E
What did they say? Listen and choose the correct answer.

1. I have some good news. I can fix your car next week.
2. My daughter is going to have a baby in July.
3. I have an important announcement. Tomorrow's meeting has been canceled.
4. My wife was just promoted to manager of her department.
5. I don't believe it! The bus drivers are going on strike!
6. I love Melanie, and she loves me!
7. You won't believe it! The monkeys have escaped from the zoo!
8. I'm nervous about my interview tomorrow.
9. My parents sold their house and moved into a condominium.
10. I'm going to do something I've always want to do. I'm going to quit my job and move to Hollywood!

Page 110   Exercise H
Listen and choose the correct answer.

1. Patty, did you break up with Gary?
2. How long have you been sitting here?
3. Were you reading when they called?
4. When are you going to repaint it?
5. Are you still mad?
6. When are you going to study math?
7. Are they too small?
8. Who fixed the kitchen floor?

Page 123   Exercise D
Listen and complete the sentences.

Ex: I wish I didn't have to study tonight. If I didn't have to study tonight, . . .

1. I wish I hadn't been sick last weekend. If I hadn't been sick, . . .
2. I wish I were an optimist. If I were an optimist, . . .
3. The landlord called this morning. He said . . .

4. You won't believe what my girlfriend asked me! She asked me . . .
5. You won't believe what one of my students asked me! He asked me . . .

Page 129　Exercise G
Listen and complete the sentences.

1. You live at the corner of Broadway and Main, . . .
2. You aren't thinking of quitting, . . .
3. We don't need any more onions, . . .
4. You returned your library books, . . .
5. Nancy doesn't go out with Peter any more, . . .
6. You've done your assignment, . . .
7. Your sister was invited to the wedding, . . .
8. He's been a good employee, . . .
9. We won't we leaving soon, . . .
10. My brother and I can swim at this beach, . . .
11. This isn't your parking space, . . .
12. I didn't forget to call my mother last weekend, . . .

Page 132　Exercise L
Listen and complete the conversations.

1. A. Ruth is going to be a doctor, isn't she?
   B. Actually, she isn't.
   A. She isn't?! That's surprising! I was sure . . .
2. A. You sold your house, didn't you?
   B. Actually, I didn't.
   A. You didn't?! I'm surprised. I was sure . . .
3. A. This car has new brakes, doesn't it?
   B. No, it doesn't.
   A. It doesn't?! I was sure . . .
4. A. You aren't angry with me, are you?
   B. Actually, I am.
   A. You are?! I'm disappointed. I was sure . . .
5. A. Your cousins from Chicago will be arriving this weekend, won't they?
   B. Actually, they won't be arriving until next month.
   A. Oh. I was sure . . .
6. A. You didn't get searched at the airport, did you?
   B. Actually, I did.
   A. You did?! I'm surprised. I was sure . . .
7. A. Children aren't allowed to see this movie, are they?
   B. Actually, they are.
   A. They are?! That's very surprising! I was sure . . .
8. A. Albert still works at the bank, doesn't he?
   B. Actually, he doesn't.
   A. He doesn't?! I didn't know that. I was sure . . .
9. A. Cynthia was hired by the Bay Company, wasn't she?
   B. Actually, she wasn't.
   A. She wasn't?! That's too bad. I was sure . . .
10. A. Dr. Miller can deliver babies, can't he?
    B. Actually, he can't. He's a dentist.
    A. Oh. I didn't know that. I was sure . . .

Page 145　Exercise J
Listen and complete the sentences.

1. My fax machine has been broken since . . .
2. My son has had chicken pox for . . .
3. Our elevator has been out of order since . . .
4. My passport has been missing since . . .
5. We've been having trouble communicating for . . .
6. He's refused to fix our shower for . . .
7. We've wanted to sell our house since . . .
8. I've been having problems with my VCR for . . .
9. My wisdom teeth have hurt since . . .

Page 150　Exercise P
Read the questions. Listen to each passage. Then answer the questions.

Jeff's Problem

When I was unhappy with my job last month, my friend told me not to complain to him. He said I should tell my boss how I felt. So I decided to take my friend's advice. I made an appointment with my boss and told her why I didn't like my job. My boss listened quietly for a while, and then she told me why she wasn't satisfied with my work. She said I worked much too slowly, I made too many mistakes, and I complained too much. She told me she thought we'd both be happier if I worked someplace else. I'm very sorry I listened to my friend's advice. If I hadn't listened to his advice, I wouldn't have been fired and I wouldn't be out of work right now.

Amy and Tom

I started going out with Tom when I was a teenager. We fell in love with each other when we were in high school. When I was 25 years old, Tom asked me to marry him, and I accepted. My parents urged me not to marry Tom. They told me if I married Tom, I'd always regret it. They said he didn't work hard enough, he wasn't serious enough, and he would never be successful. Well, I'm glad I didn't follow my parents' advice, and so are they. Tom and I have been married for 20 years, and we've been very happy. Tom has a good job, and he's a wonderful husband and father. Our sons are teenagers now, and my parents are a little concerned about them because they aren't serious enough. But I'm not worried about my sons at all. They're just like their father used to be.

Page 151　Exercise S: *Have You Heard?*
Listen and complete the sentences.

1. When are you going to wash . . .
2. You're right.
3. Someday . . .
4. My answer is long.
5. That's light.
6. It's time to watch . . .
7. Have you hurt . . .
8. I hate chopping . . .
9. My brother's voice . . .
10. I've heard . . .
11. Why haven't you written . . .
12. Alexander brushes . . .

Page 153　Exercise E
Listen and complete the sentences.

Ex. I'm sorry I drove past your house. I must have had my mind on something else. If I hadn't had my mind on something else, . . .

1. If I hadn't taken a walk yesterday, . . .
2. I can't believe I deleted all my files. I must have hit the wrong key. If I hadn't hit the wrong key, . . .
3. I'm sure you'd get tired of going dancing . . .
4. If I had known your relatives were visiting, . . .
5. If I weren't on my way to a concert, . . .

ACTIVITY WORKBOOK ANSWER KEY

UNIT 1

WORKBOOK PAGE 2

A. For Many Years

1. swims
   He's swum
2. takes
   She's taken
3. drives
   He's driven
4. speak
   I've spoken
5. sing
   We've sung
6. writes
   He's written
7. rides
   She's ridden
8. draws
   He's drawn
9. flies
   She's flown
10. grows
    He's grown

WORKBOOK PAGE 3

B. A Little While Ago

1. Have, gone
   they have, They went
2. Has, taken
   she has, She took
3. Have, done
   I have, I did
4. Have, eaten
   we have, We ate
5. Has, given
   he has, He gave
6. Has, written
   she has, She wrote
7. Have, fed
   I have, I fed
8. Has, seen
   he has, He saw

C. Listening

1. a   3. a   5. b   7. b   9. b
2. b   4. b   6. a   8. a

WORKBOOK PAGE 4

D. In a Long Time

1. Have, taken
   we haven't, We haven't taken
2. Has, written
   she hasn't, She hasn't written
3. Has, gotten
   he hasn't, He hasn't gotten
4. Have, gone
   I haven't, I haven't gone
5. Have, swum
   they haven't, They haven't swum
6. Has, been
   it hasn't, It hasn't been
7. Have, seen
   we haven't, We haven't seen
8. Has, ridden
   she hasn't, She hasn't ridden
9. Have, eaten
   I haven't, I haven't eaten
10. Has, done
    he hasn't, He hasn't done

11. Have, given
    you haven't, You haven't given

WORKBOOK PAGE 6

F. What Are They Saying?

1. has, known
   He's known, for
2. has, had
   She's had, since
3. have, played
   I've played, for
4. have, owned
   They've owned, for
5. has, liked
   He's liked, since
6. has, wanted
   She's wanted, since
7. have, worked
   We've worked, for
8. have, been
   We've been, for

G. Listening

1. a   3. a   5. b   7. a   9. b
2. b   4. b   6. a   8. b

WORKBOOK PAGE 7

H. What's the Question?

1. How long have, had a toothache
2. How long has, wanted to be a teacher
3. How long has, been in the hospital
4. How long have, known how to swim
5. How long have, owned your own home

WORKBOOK PAGE 8

J. How Long?

1. He's been waiting for a taxi for
2. She's been practicing the piano since
3. I've been feeling sick for
4. You've been talking for
5. They've been going out since
6. It's been making strange noises for
7. I've been doing sit-ups for
8. He's been snoring since

K. Listening

1. b   2. b   3. a   4. b   5. a   6. b

WORKBOOK PAGES 9–10

L. What Are They Saying?

1. has she been crying
   She's been crying
2. has it been leaking
   It's been leaking
3. has he been fighting
   He's been fighting
4. has it been making
   It's been making
5. has it been raining
   It's been raining

Answers are not provided for the achievement tests. Complete test answer keys are included in *Side by Side Plus* Teacher's Guide 4 and Multilevel Activity & Achievement Test Book 4 (and its accompanying CD-ROM).

6. have they been barking
They've been barking

M. What Are They Saying?

1. I've been giving
I've given
2. I've been baking
I've, baked
3. We've been selling
We've, sold
4. They've been building
They've, built
5. I've been taking
I've, taken
6. She's been seeing
she's seen
7. You've been writing
You've, written
8. I've been making
I've, made
9. You've been doing
You've, done

N. They've Been Working Very Hard

1. has been washing, He's, washed
2. He's, been vacuuming, He's, vacuumed
3. has been hanging up, She's, hung up
4. She's, been making, She's, made
5. has been planting, He's, planted
6. He's, been throwing out, He's, thrown out
7. has been baking, She's, baked
8. She's, been writing, She's, written
9. has been singing, They've, sung
10. They've been looking, looked

O. They Had Done That Before

1. had put
had eaten
2. had snored
3. had been
4. had gone
5. had left
6. had, assembled
7. had had
8. had given
9. had seen
10. had spent
11. had worn
12. had taken
13. had made

P. By the Time

1. got, had, closed
2. did, had, gone
3. arrived, had, gotten
4. drove, had, sailed
5. brought, had, borrowed
6. called, had, taken
7. saw, had been
8. found, had, begun
9. dropped, had, left
10. stopped, had fallen

Q. What Had They Been Doing?

1. had been planning
2. had been going out
3. had been training
4. had been living
5. had been rehearsing
6. had been preparing
7. had been having
8. had been working
9. had been coming,
had been falling
10. had been looking
11. had been practicing

T. What Are _They_ _Saying_?

A. My bro_th_er _Th_eodore doesn't _th_ink he can go to _th_e _th_eater wi_th_ u_s_ tomorrow becau_s_e he ha_s_ a _s_ore _th_roat.

B. Ano_th_er _s_ore _th_roat? _Th_at's terrible! Didn't he ju_s_t get over one la_s_t _Th_ursday?

A. _Th_at's right. Believe it or not, _th_is is _th_e _th_ird _s_ore _th_roat he_'s_ had _th_is mon_th_. My poor bro_th_er alway_s_ get_s_ _s_ick when _th_e wea_th_er i_s_ very cold.

B. I hope it i_sn_'t _s_eriou_s_ _th_is time.

A. I don't _th_ink _s_o. _Th_eodore _s_ays hi_s_ _s_ore _th_roat isn't bo_th_ering him too much, but bo_th_ my mo_th_er and fa_th_er _s_ay he'll have to re_s_t in bed for at lea_s_t a few day_s_. _Th_ey're worried becau_s_e he i_sn_'t eating any_th_ing, and _th_ey don't _th_ink he look_s_ very heal_th_y.

B. _Th_en I gue_ss_ he won't be going to _th_e _S_unday concert ei_th_er.

A. Probably not. And he_'s_ very di_s_appointed. He really love_s_ cla_ss_ical mu_s_ic.

B. Well, I'm _s_orry our plan_s_ fell _th_rough. Plea_s_e tell _Th_eodore I hope he feel_s_ better _s_oon. Oh, I almo_s_t forgot. My little si_s_ter Mar_th_a is having a _s_mall bir_th_day celebration today at _th_ree _th_irty. Would you like to come?

A. Ye_s_, of cour_s_e. _Th_ank you very much.

A. What Should They Have Done?

1. should have gotten
2. should have taken
3. should have studied
4. should have had
5. should have gone
6. should have seen
7. should have spoken
8. should have sat
9. should have kept
10. should have bought

B. Good Advice

1. b   **2.** b   **3.** a   **4.** a   **5.** b   **6.** b

D. What Might Have Happened?

1. might have missed
2. may have eaten
3. may have broken
4. might have gone
5. may have been
6. might have forgotten
7. might have lost

E. What's the Answer?

1. a   **2.** b   **3.** a   **4.** a   **5.** b   **6.** a

WORKBOOK PAGE 22

F. I Don't Understand It!

1. could have watched
2. could have worn
3. could have married
4. could have ridden
5. could have become
6. could have skated
7. could have taken
8. could have been
9. could have made
10. could have named
11. could have painted
12. could have eaten
13. could have gone
14. could have written

WORKBOOK PAGE 24

H. What Happened?

1. must have gotten up
2. must have eaten
3. must have met
4. must have left
5. must have spoken
6. must have been
7. must have broken up
8. must have bought
9. must have had
10. must have cost
11. must have done

WORKBOOK PAGE 29

L. What's the Word?

1. should have
2. must have
3. couldn't have
4. might have, might have
5. could have
6. must have
7. couldn't have
8. should have
9. might have
10. shouldn't have, could have
11. must have

M. Listening

| 1. a | 3. b | 5. b | 7. b |
| 2. b | 4. a | 6. a | 8. a |

WORKBOOK PAGE 30

N. What Does It Mean?

1. a	5. c	9. a	13. b
2. c	6. b	10. c	14. a
3. c	7. b	11. c	15. c
4. b	8. a	12. a	16. b

WORKBOOK PAGE 31

P. Have You Heard?

1. a	5. a	9. b	13. a
2. b	6. b	10. a	14. b
3. a	7. a	11. b	15. b
4. b	8. b	12. a	16. a

UNIT 3

WORKBOOK PAGE 32

A. Who Did It?

1. was painted
2. were built
3. was served
4. was composed
5. was discovered
6. was written

7. was worn
8. was directed
9. was taken
10. was baked

WORKBOOK PAGES 33–34

B. You Decide: *At the Museum*

1. was owned
....
was made
....
....
3. was worn
....
was given
....
was left
5. was written
....
....
was, sent
was discovered

2. was flown
....
....
was designed
....
4. were found
....
....
were forgotten

6. was built
....
was begun
wasn't finished

7. ....
was composed
....
was sung
....

WORKBOOK PAGE 35

D. It's Too Late

1. they've, been done
2. it's, been set
3. they've, been ironed
4. it's, been made
5. They've, been taken down
6. it's, been swept
7. they've, been bought
8. It's, been hung up

E. Listening

| 1. a | 3. b | 5. a | 7. a | 9. a |
| 2. b | 4. a | 6. b | 8. b | |

WORKBOOK PAGE 36

F. Nothing Is Ready!

1. haven't been made
2. hasn't been swept
3. hasn't been prepared
4. hasn't been fed
5. haven't been put

G. At the Hospital

1. Has
2. been taken
3. has
4. been given
5. Has
6. been done
7. was done
8. Has
9. been told
10. He's
11. been sent

WORKBOOK PAGE 37

H. Can We Leave Soon?

1. has been stopped
2. have been turned off
3. Has
4. been set
5. has
6. been taken out

I. Crossword

WORKBOOK PAGE 38

J. Ernest Hemingway

1. a   2. c   3. b   4. a   5. b   6. c

WORKBOOK PAGE 39

K. A Robbery

1. were
2. robbed
3. was
4. stolen
5. was
6. left
7. wasn't
8. taken
9. given
10. was
11. seen
12. was
13. arrested
14. was
15. sent
16. were
17. returned
18. been
19. ripped

L. Listening

1. a   4. a   7. b   10. a
2. b   5. a   8. a   11. b
3. b   6. b   9. a   12. b

WORKBOOK PAGE 40

M. You Decide: A Famous Composer

1. ....
2. have
3. been
4. performed
5. ....
6. heard
7. ....
8. ....
9. was
10. given
11. ....
12. were
13. rejected
14. ....
15. were
16. recorded
17. ....
18. ....
19. was
20. appreciated
21. was
22. considered
23. was
24. understood
25. ....
26. respected
27. ....
28. was
29. used
30. have

31. been
32. played
33. ....
34. was
35. hurt
36. ....
37. was
38. chosen
39. was
40. invited

WORKBOOK PAGE 41

N. What Are They Saying?

1. It's being rewritten
2. It's, being repaired
3. It's, being baked
4. They're, being taken in
5. she's being promoted
6. It's, being set up
7. It's being washed
8. is being clipped

WORKBOOK PAGE 42

P. A Factory Tour

1. is
2. made
3. is
4. taken
5. is
6. put
7. is
8. mixed
9. is
10. poured
11. are
12. prepared
13. are
14. being
15. chopped
16. are
17. being
18. sliced
19. are
20. added
21. was
22. invented
23. is
24. kept
25. is
26. sent
27. be
28. enjoyed

WORKBOOK PAGE 43

Q. What Does It Mean?

1. a   6. a   11. c
2. c   7. c   12. b
3. a   8. b   13. c
4. b   9. a   14. b
5. b   10. c

R. Listening

1. a   3. b   5. b   7. b
2. b   4. a   6. a   8. a

WORKBOOK PAGES 44–45

CHECK-UP TEST: Units 1–3

A.

1. I've spoken
2. has ridden
3. haven't taken
4. haven't eaten
5. haven't written, wrote

6. have, been
7. has been
8. had seen
9. had, taken
10. had been going

B.

1. must have practiced
2. should have done
3. might have left, might have left
4. could have built
5. must have studied
6. shouldn't have worn
7. should have fed
8. could have fallen
9. might have spent, might have spent

C.

1. was drawn
2. It's, being repaired
3. has been given
4. be taught
5. They've, been done
6. They're, being taken in
7. was chosen
8. be made
9. hasn't been sent

D.

1. b   2. a   3. b   4. b   5. a

UNIT 4

WORKBOOK PAGE 46

A. They Didn't Say

1. where they're living now
2. where Janet is working
3. how their children are
4. when he'll be starting his new job
5. when they're going to come to New York
6. when their new house will be finished
7. what they've been doing
8. why they haven't e-mailed us
9. what their telephone number is

WORKBOOK PAGE 47

B. I'm Not the Person to Ask

1. what this painting means
2. why Robert always gets to school so early
3. when the ice cream truck came by
4. where Margaret works
5. how Sam broke his arm
6. why Alice rewrote her novel
7. when the concert begins
8. when the bank opens tomorrow
9. what we did in French class yesterday

10. where Mom and Dad went
11. how much a quart of milk costs

WORKBOOK PAGE 48

C. Too Many Questions!

1. when I learned to drive
2. why Grandma doesn't drive
3. why the sky is blue
4. how birds learn to fly
5. why clouds are white
6. what time the zoo opens tomorrow
7. where that mouse is now
8. ....
9. ....
10. ....
11. ....

WORKBOOK PAGE 49

D. What Are They Saying?

1. a   3. b   5. b   7. b   9. a
2. b   4. a   6. a   8. b   10. b

E. Listening

1. a   3. b   5. a   7. a
2. a   4. b   6. b   8. b

WORKBOOK PAGES 50–51

G. You Decide: *What Are They Saying?*

1. how much this bicycle costs
....
2. where the nearest clinic is
....
3. whose cell phone this is
....
4. why you've been late to work all week
....
5. when my dog will be ready
....
6. how long we've been driving
....
7. why Johnny is sitting in a puddle
....
8. when the post office opens
....
9. what's in the "Chicken Surprise Casserole"
....
10. when you'll be getting out of here
....

WORKBOOK PAGE 53

I. What Are They Saying?

1. a   3. a   5. a   7. a   9. a
2. b   4. b   6. a   8. b   10. a

J. Listening

1. a	**3.** b	**5.** a	**7.** b	**9.** a
2. a	**4.** a	**6.** b	**8.** b	

WORKBOOK PAGE 54

L. Renting an Apartment

1. if it's been rented yet
2. if there's an elevator in the building
3. if the kitchen has a microwave
4. if pets are allowed
5. if there's a bus stop nearby
6. if the landlord lives in the building
7. if the apartment has an Internet connection
8. ....
9. if I can see the apartment today.

WORKBOOK PAGES 55–56

M. You Decide: *The College Visit*

1. how many students go to your school
2. if I have to take any special examinations
3. how I get an application form
4. if the classes are difficult
5. if the dormitories are noisy
6. what kind of food you serve in the cafeteria
7. what students do on weekends
8. how much your school costs
9. ....
10. ....

UNIT 5

WORKBOOK PAGE 57

A. If

1. b	**3.** b	**5.** a	**7.** b	**9.** a
2. a	**4.** b	**6.** a	**8.** b	**10.** b

B. Scrambled Sentences

1. If Barbara has a lot to do, she'll work late at the office tonight.
2. If Tom feels energetic, he'll clean his attic this weekend.
3. If I decide to forget about my diet, I'll have cake for dessert.
4. If the weather isn't nice tomorrow, I'll stay home and fill out my income tax forms.
5. If I still have a cold tomorrow, I'll go to the clinic and see Dr. Lopez.

WORKBOOK PAGE 58

D. Listening

1. b	**6.** b	**11.** a
2. a	**7.** a	**12.** b
3. a	**8.** a	**13.** a
4. b	**9.** b	**14.** a
5. b	**10.** b	

WORKBOOK PAGES 60–61

F. They Might

1. a	**3.** a	**5.** b	**7.** a
2. b	**4.** a	**6.** b	**8.** b

G. You Decide: *What Might Happen?*

1. you drink, . . .	**5.** you practice, . . .
2. you put, . . .	**6.** you stay, . . .
3. we send, . . .	**7.** you go hiking, . . .
4. you skip, . . .	**8.** you get married, . . .

WORKBOOK PAGE 63

I. What's the Polite Answer?

1. b	**3.** a	**5.** b	**7.** b
2. b	**4.** b	**6.** a	

J. Listening

1. a	**3.** b	**5.** a	**7.** b	**9.** a	**11.** a
2. b	**4.** b	**6.** b	**8.** a	**10.** b	**12.** b

WORKBOOK PAGE 64

K. Hopes

1. it rains	**3.** it's
we have to cancel	is
it doesn't rain	it isn't
2. it's cold	**4.** is
doesn't start	we don't have
it isn't cold	it isn't

WORKBOOK PAGE 65

L. The Exam

1. you	**3.** isn't	**4.** I
I'll	is	I
2. it's	she'll	I'll
I do		I'm
will be		I'll

WORKBOOK PAGE 66

M. What If?

1. b	**3.** b	**5.** b	**7.** b	**9.** a	**11.** a
2. a	**4.** a	**6.** a	**8.** b	**10.** a	**12.** b

N. Listening

1. b	**3.** b	**5.** b	**7.** a
2. a	**4.** a	**6.** b	**8.** a

WORKBOOK PAGE 69

Q. Matching

1. d	**3.** g	**5.** h	**7.** b	**9.** f	**11.** i
2. j	**4.** a	**6.** e	**8.** k	**10.** c	

WORKBOOK PAGES 71–72

S. If

1. she didn't want to get
   wouldn't work overtime

2. he weren't afraid
   wouldn't be hiding
3. she didn't want to win
   wouldn't run
4. he didn't love
   wouldn't wear
5. she weren't careless
   wouldn't make
6. he didn't want to lose
   wouldn't go
7. he didn't have
   wouldn't be
8. there weren't
   wouldn't be driving

WORKBOOK PAGES 74–75

X. *Norman*'s Broken Keyboard

1.

Dear A*m*y,

   I really e*n*joyed visiti*ng* you i*n* your *n*ew apart*m*e*n*t. It's o*n*e of the *n*icest apart*m*e*n*ts I've ever see*n*. I liked everythi*ng* about it: the *m*oder*n* kitche*n* a*n*d bathroo*m*, the elega*n*t livi*ng* roo*m* and di*n*i*ng* roo*m*, a*n*d the su*nn*y bedroo*m*s. I ca*n*'t believe there's eve*n* a garde*n* with le*m*o*n* and ora*n*ge trees i*n* fro*n*t of the buildi*ng*. I thi*n*k you'll be very happy i*n* your *n*ew *n*eighborhood. It's certai*n*ly very co*n*ve*n*ie*n*t to be so *n*ear a super*m*arket, a *m*ovie theater, a*n*d a trai*n* statio*n*.

   I'*m* looki*ng* forward to seei*ng* you agai*n* a*n*d *m*eeti*ng* your *n*ew *n*eighbors.

   Si*n*cerely,
   *N*or*m*an

2.

To Who*m* It *M*ay Co*n*cer*n*:

   I a*m* writi*ng* to reco*mm*e*n*d *M*ax *M*iller for the job of co*m*puter progra*mm*er at the ABC Co*m*puter Co*m*pa*n*y. Duri*ng* the *n*i*n*e years I've k*n*ow*n* him, he's bee*n* a*n* excelle*n*t e*m*ployee a*n*d a ki*n*d a*n*d ho*n*est frie*n*d. He's *n*ever *m*issed a day's work at our co*m*pa*n*y, a*n*d he's always bee*n* o*n* ti*m*e. But *m*ost i*m*porta*n*t, *M*ax *M*iller really u*n*dersta*n*ds what *m*akes a good co*m*puter progra*mm*er.

   Si*n*cerely,
   *N*or*m*an Brow*n*
   *M*a*n*ager
   XYZ Co*m*puter Co*m*pa*n*y

3.

Dear Bria*n*,

   I just fi*n*ished readi*ng* your *m*ost rece*n*t poe*m*s, a*n*d i*n* *m*y opi*n*io*n*, they're a*m*azi*ng*. The poe*m* about the e*n*viro*n*me*n*t is very origi*n*al, but *m*y favorite o*n*es are "*M*issi*ng* *M*y *M*other" a*n*d "U*n*der *M*y U*m*brella."

   Accordi*ng* to *m*y wife a*n*d frie*n*ds, you're beco*m*i*ng* fa*m*ous i*n* *m*a*n*y foreig*n* cou*n*tries, a*n*d your poe*m*s are bei*ng* tra*n*slated i*n*to Russia*n*, Chi*n*ese, Ger*m*a*n*, Spa*n*ish, a*n*d Japa*n*ese. I thi*n*k that's fa*n*tastic!

   Have you begu*n* writi*ng* your *n*ew *n*ovel yet? I wo*n*der whe*n* we'll be heari*ng* more about it.

   *N*or*m*an

4.

Dear *M*ichael,

   Re*m*e*m*ber whe*n* you explai*n*ed to *m*e how to *m*ake your *m*other's fa*m*ous chicke*n* a*n*d *m*ushroo*m* casserole? Well, I *m*ade so*m*e for di*nn*er last *n*ight, a*n*d I'*m* afraid so*m*ethi*ng* *m*ust have go*n*e wro*ng*. I *m*ight have bur*n*t the chicke*n*, or *m*aybe I did*n*'t put i*n* e*n*ough o*n*io*n*s a*n*d *m*ushroo*m*s. I do*n*'t k*n*ow what happe*n*ed, but I k*n*ow I *m*ust have *m*ade so*m*e *m*istakes because *n*obody e*n*joyed it very *m*uch. To*m* and *N*a*n*cy did*n*'t co*m*plai*n*, but they said yours was *m*uch *m*ore delicious.

   Do you thi*n*k you could se*n*d your *m*other's recipe to *m*e by e-*m*ail so I ca*n* try it again? Whe*n* you explai*n*ed it to *m*e, I should have writte*n* it dow*n*.

   *N*or*m*an

WORKBOOK PAGES 76–77

CHECK-UP TEST: Units 4–5

A.

1. when the next train will be leaving
2. if/whether Michael was at work yesterday
3. how much this suit costs
4. if/whether there's a laundromat nearby
5. why David got up so early
6. if/whether Martha took her medicine this morning
7. how long we've been waiting

B.

1. have
2. he'd be
3. she wouldn't go
4. don't get
5. you won't
6. it doesn't
7. wins
8. will be
9. fed

C.

1. didn't work, she wouldn't be
2. studied, he'd get
3. had, they'd get along
4. weren't, she wouldn't make

D.

1. b   2. a   3. b   4. a   5. b

UNIT 6

WORKBOOK PAGE 78

A. What's the Word?

1. b	3. b	5. a	7. b	9. a
2. a	4. b	6. a	8. a	10. b

B. If

1. were
2. went out
3. got lost
4. had
5. ate
6. lost
7. quit
8. sold

WORKBOOK PAGE 79

C. You Decide: *If*

1. ....
   she would, She'd be
2. ....
   he would, He'd be
3. ....
   he/she would, He'd/She'd be
4. ....
   they would, They'd be
5. ....
   he/she would, He'd/She'd be
6. ....
   she would, She'd be

WORKBOOK PAGE 80

D. What's the Word?

1. b	3. b	5. a	7. a	9. b	11. b
2. a	4. b	6. b	8. b	10. a	12. b

E. Listening

1. b	3. b	5. b	7. a	9. a	11. b
2. a	4. a	6. b	8. b	10. b	12. a

WORKBOOK PAGES 81–82

F. Personal Opinions

1. went, you'd, fall
2. I'd, He'd, tune it up
3. went, you'd, have
4. you painted, it would
5. wouldn't drive, you drove, you'd
6. wouldn't have, you had, would be
7. wouldn't see, you saw, you'd

8. were, you bought, it would
9. ....

WORKBOOK PAGE 83

H. What Do They Wish?

1. b	3. a	5. a	7. b	9. a
2. a	4. b	6. a	8. b	10. b

I. Listening

1. b	3. a	5. b	7. b	9. b	11. b
2. b	4. b	6. a	8. a	10. a	12. a

WORKBOOK PAGE 84

J. I Wish

1. I wish I felt
2. I wish, were 5:00
3. I wish I sang
4. I wish I taught
5. I wish, gave
6. I wish I had a dog.

WORKBOOK PAGE 85

L. Looking for a Job

1. I could
2. you could
3. you'd be
4. you could repair DVD players
5. would be
6. I could/I were able to
7. ....
8. ....
9. ....
10. you could ....
11. would be
12. could/were able to
13. you could/you were able to be
14. you wouldn't have
15. ....
16. ....
17. I'd
18. ....
19. I could/I were able to

WORKBOOK PAGE 86

M. Choose

1. a	3. c	5. a	7. a	9. a
2. b	4. b	6. c	8. b	10. c

N. Listening

1. a   2. b   3. a   4. b   5. b   6. a

WORKBOOK PAGE 88

Q. What Does It Mean?

1. a	5. c	9. b	13. c
2. b	6. a	10. a	14. b
3. c	7. c	11. b	15. a
4. b	8. b	12. a	16. c

WORKBOOK PAGE 89

R. Sound It Out!

1. gets
2. take
3. Ted
4. paid
5. vacation
6. Spain
7. when
8. friend

9. When my friend Ted gets paid, he'll take a vacation in Spain.

10. play
11. eight
12. tennis
13. let's
14. next
15. Wednesday
16. Fred

17. Let's play tennis with Fred next Wednesday at eight o'clock.

UNIT 7

WORKBOOK PAGES 90–91

A. What's the Answer?

1. a
2. a
3. b
4. b
5. a
6. b
7. a
8. b
9. a
10. a

B. Complete the Sentences

1. had been approved, would have been able
2. had rung, would have arrived
3. had won, would have been
4. had known, would have gotten
5. had practiced, would have learned
6. had taken, would have been
7. had noticed, would have stopped
8. had bought, would have had

WORKBOOK PAGE 93

D. What's the Answer?

1. a
2. b
3. a
4. b
5. a
6. b
7. b
8. a
9. b
10. b

E. Listening

1. b
2. a
3. b
4. b
5. a
6. b
7. a
8. b
9. a
10. b

WORKBOOK PAGE 94

F. How I Became a Basketball Player

1. hadn't taken me
2. hadn't bought me
3. hadn't sent me
4. hadn't played
5. hadn't gone
6. wouldn't have become

G. I'm Really Glad

1. I hadn't gone
2. wouldn't have
3. hadn't learned
4. wouldn't have gotten
5. hadn't gotten
6. wouldn't have been
7. hadn't been
8. wouldn't have
9. hadn't met
10. wouldn't have been

WORKBOOK PAGE 95

H. Why Didn't You Tell Me?

1. you had told
2. wouldn't have gone
3. hadn't gone
4. would have been
5. I had been
6. would have been
7. had been
8. would have
9. had fixed
10. had told
11. made/prepared
12. had made/ had prepared
13. there had been
14. wouldn't have gone
15. hadn't gone
16. wouldn't have gotten
17. hadn't gotten
18. wouldn't have
19. hadn't had
20. would have been
21. have done
22. had done
23. wouldn't have been

WORKBOOK PAGE 97

K. What's the Answer?

1. b
2. a
3. b
4. a
5. a
6. b
7. b
8. a

L. Complete the Sentences

1. I had taken
2. she had studied
3. he worked
4. I had had
5. I knew
6. I had seen
7. we didn't have to

WORKBOOK PAGE 98

M. Patty's Party

1. hadn't gone, had done
2. hadn't been, would have been
3. hadn't sung, played, hadn't sung, played, wouldn't have had
4. didn't, had remembered/hadn't forgotten, had, wouldn't have
5. had known, had known, wouldn't have been, wouldn't have felt

WORKBOOK PAGE 100

O. Hopes and Wishes

1. could tell, can tell
2. worked, get
3. had sung, sings
4. had studied, spoke
5. didn't, have, were
6. weren't, lose

WORKBOOK PAGE 101

Q. Wish or Hope?

1. wish
2. wishes
3. hope
4. wishes
5. hopes
6. wish
7. hope
8. wishes
9. wishes

WORKBOOK PAGE 102

R. Listening

1. a
2. a
3. b
4. a
5. b
6. b

S. Listening: *Hopes and Wishes*

1. b	**6.** b	**11.** b
2. a	**7.** a	**12.** a
3. b	**8.** a	**13.** b
4. b	**9.** b	**14.** a
5. a	**10.** a	

WORKBOOK PAGE 103

U. Have You Heard?

1. b	**5.** a	**9.** b	**13.** a
2. a	**6.** a	**10.** a	**14.** a
3. b	**7.** b	**11.** a	**15.** b
4. b	**8.** a	**12.** b	**16.** b

UNIT 8

WORKBOOK PAGE 104

A. What Did They Say?

1. he was having
2. they couldn't come
3. she would visit
4. he had forgotten
5. she was planning
6. he hadn't written
7. she was, she had
8. was, could pick
9. had seen, hadn't seen
10. she would be, she wouldn't
11. she had been working, needed

WORKBOOK PAGES 105–107

B. Messages

1. she had gotten an "A" on her biology test
2. he was home from the hospital and he was feeling much better
3. they had seen the Colosseum, but they hadn't gone to the Vatican yet
4. he hoped I could visit him when I came to Japan this summer
5. she was sorry, but I wasn't the right person for the job
6. he was very busy, and he couldn't repair our dishwasher this week
7. they loved Hawaii, and they were thinking of buying a condominium
8. he had been hoping to send me more money for college, but he wouldn't be able to because he was having financial problems
9. ....
10. ....
11. ....

WORKBOOK PAGE 108

D. What's the Answer?

1. b	**3.** b	**5.** b	**7.** a
2. a	**4.** a	**6.** b	**8.** a

E. Listening

1. b	**3.** a	**5.** a	**7.** a	**9.** b
2. a	**4.** b	**6.** b	**8.** a	**10.** a

WORKBOOK PAGE 109

F. You Decide: *What Happened While Paula Wilson Was Away?*

1. he had gotten married	7.	....
2. she was in the hospital	8.	....
3. she had been	9.	....
4. had had	10.	....
5. had been	11.	....
6. was going to become	12.	....

WORKBOOK PAGE 110

G. You Won't Believe It!

1. b	**3.** a	**5.** a	**7.** b	**9.** b
2. a	**4.** b	**6.** a	**8.** a	**10.** a

H. Listening

1. b	**3.** c	**5.** c	**7.** c
2. c	**4.** b	**6.** b	**8.** a

WORKBOOK PAGES 111–112

I. What Did They Ask?

1. if/whether he had delivered her letter to Santa Claus yet
2. how much time I had spent on my homework
3. if/whether she could have another piece of his delicious cake
4. why they always made so much noise
5. if/whether the operation would hurt
6. when the lecture was going to end
7. if he still loved her
8. why there were so many grammar rules in English
9. ....
10. ....

WORKBOOK PAGE 114

K. What Did They Tell You?

1. to speak confidently
2. not to drive too fast
3. to work quickly
4. not to eat too much candy
5. not to play loud music

L. What's the Answer?

1. a	**3.** b	**5.** b	**7.** a
2. a	**4.** a	**6.** b	**8.** a

M. Everybody Always Tells Him What to Do

1. to hurry
   my breakfast was getting cold
2. not to forget my umbrella
   it was going to rain later
3. not to walk so slowly
   we would be late for school
4. to be quiet
   I was disturbing the class
5. ....
   ....
6. ....
   ....
7. ....
   ....
8. ....
   ....
9. ....
   I would fail my math test if I didn't study
10. ....
    I had to get up early for school

N. Today at School

1. to study, not to study
2. to write, not to forget
3. to read, not to use
4. to answer, not to answer
5. to practice, not to look
6. ....
   ....
7. ....
   ....
8. ....
   ....
9. was expected, would be

P. Choose the Right Word

1. escaped		13. advice
2. casserole		14. away
3. anxious		15. sale
4. lock		16. break
5. bride		17. falling
6. flu		18. into
7. prevent		19. annoyed
8. know		20. qualified
9. poodle		21. dictionaries
10. grease		22. whether
11. reassured		23. engaged, married
12. taxes		

R. Who Is the Best?

Many pessimists don't trust dentists because they're scared the worst will happen. However, Dr. West's patients are all optimistic. They think Dr. West is the best dentist in Boston.

1. Stuart likes Dr. West.

   Not only is he honest, but he's the cheapest and the most reliable dentist in Boston.

2. Stuart's sister also thinks Dr. West is wonderful.

   Dr. West works very fast and never makes mistakes. He's the best dentist on State Street.

3. Mr. Jackson can't stand any other dentist.

   I go to Dr. West because I almost never feel any pain when I'm in his special dentist's chair. I could stay and rest there all day.

4. Betsy always talks about Dr. West.

   What I like most about Dr. West is that he doesn't ask a lot of questions when a patient's mouth is full of dental instruments.

5. Dr. West's Spanish-speaking patients are especially pleased.

   Dr. West studies Spanish in his spare time. We won't see any specialist but Dr. West.

6. Margaret is very enthusiastic about Dr. West.

   One day I got the hiccups in his office. Dr. West just stopped and stood there waiting patiently. He didn't make me feel stupid at all!

7. Patty thinks Dr. West is the hardest working dentist she knows.

   Dr. West never quits working all day. He even skips his lunch!

8. Steve also likes Dr. West.

   When I broke my leg playing basketball last spring, I missed two appointments. Dr. West wasn't upset at all. He even visited me in the hospital. We discussed politics and sports. That's when I discovered that Dr. West likes to ski and skate.

CHECK-UP TEST: Units 6–8

A.

1. he were	4. she had gotten
2. she had taken	5. I spoke
3. he drove	6. you hadn't eaten

B.

1. had been, would have enjoyed
2. didn't eat, wouldn't be
3. hadn't missed, she wouldn't have arrived
4. I could type, I wouldn't be
5. had been paying, wouldn't have made
6. understood, wouldn't look

C.

1. she had gotten
2. what my name was
3. if/whether I had seen her
4. she was sorry she had forgotten
5. he wouldn't be able to visit
6. to brush, not to eat
7. when he would be
8. why I was leaving, if/whether I was in a hurry

D.

1. a	2. b	3. a	4. b	5. a

UNIT 9

WORKBOOK PAGE 124

A. What Are They Saying?

1. won't she
2. can't I
3. don't you
4. didn't you
5. aren't I
6. haven't we
7. won't he
8. weren't you
9. isn't it
10. aren't you

WORKBOOK PAGE 125

B. What's the Tag?

1. a	3. b	5. b	7. a
2. a	4. a	6. b	8. b

C. I Think I Know You

1. aren't you
2. I am
3. haven't you
4. I have
5. didn't you
6. I did
7. don't you
8. I do
9. isn't it
10. isn't

WORKBOOK PAGE 126

D. What Are They Saying?

1. has it
2. are you
3. do you
4. did I
5. am I
6. will you
7. have we
8. does it
9. was it
10. is it

WORKBOOK PAGES 127–128

E. That's What I Thought

1. is it
   it isn't
2. do I
   you don't

3. have you
   I haven't
4. is there
   there isn't
5. has it
   it hasn't
6. will I
   you won't
7. did it
   it didn't
8. are they
   they aren't
9. was it
   it wasn't
10. can I
    you can't
11. are they
    they aren't

F. What's the Tag?

1. a	6. b	11. a
2. b	7. a	12. b
3. a	8. b	13. a
4. b	9. b	14. b
5. b	10. a	

WORKBOOK PAGE 129

G. Listening

1. b	3. a	5. a	7. b	9. b	11. a
2. b	4. b	6. a	8. a	10. b	12. b

H. You Decide: *A Good Father*

1. aren't I
2. don't I
3. am I
4. aren't I
5.–16. ....
17. aren't I

WORKBOOK PAGE 131

J. Surprises

1. have you
   I have
   You have
2. isn't she
   she isn't
   She isn't
3. will he
   he will
   He will
4. doesn't it
   it doesn't
   It doesn't
5. didn't you
   I didn't
   You didn't
6. does he
   he does
   He does

WORKBOOK PAGE 132

K. What Are They Saying?

1. weren't you
   you had been expecting
2. don't you
   you had
3. hasn't she
   she had been
4. is he
   he wasn't going to be
5. can't we
   we could leave
6. isn't it
   was
7. do I
   I didn't
8. won't you
   you would **marry**

L. Listening

1. b	3. a	5. a	7. b	9. a
2. a	4. b	6. b	8. a	10. b

M. High School Reunion

1. You did, didn't
   marry, did you
   I did
2. You do
   don't, have
   do you
   I do
3. You are, aren't
   are you
   I am
4. She was, wasn't
   chosen, was she
   she was
5. She did, didn't
   win, did she
   she did

6. ....
   He did, didn't
   did he
   he did
7. do you
   ....
   ....
   He can, can't
   can he
   he can
8. ....
   She is, isn't
   ...., is she

N. What Are They Saying?

1. have, haven't I
2. shouldn't, should we
3. did have, didn't they
4. aren't, are they
5. is, isn't he
6. does taste, doesn't it
7. was, wasn't I
8. will, won't we
9. haven't, have we
10. does look, doesn't it
11. did drive, didn't I

O. You Decide: *Why Shouldn't They Break Up?*

1. is
2. isn't he
3. does
4. send
5. doesn't he
6. ....
7. ....
8. isn't he
9. ....
10. did
11. ....
12. ....
13. didn't he
14. was
15. wasn't I
16. has
17. given
18. hasn't he
19. ....
20. ....
21. does he
22. ....
23. ....
24. ....
25. would
26. wouldn't he

Q. Beverly Wilson's Broken Keyboard

1.

Dear Betty,

You've probably heard from Bob about the terrible robberies we've been having in our neighborhood. (There have been seven robberies in five weeks!) Of course, everybody's been very worried because they still haven't discovered who the robbers are.

Last Wednesday, my neighbor's bicycle was stolen from his basement. The next evening, somebody broke into a building on Brighton Boulevard and took several silver bracelets, a wallet, and two wedding rings.

Then last weekend, believe it or not, the Reliable Bank was robbed. I'll always remember the evening of the robbery. I was taking a bath, and my husband, Bill, was reading his favorite novel in bed when Rover began barking. He must have heard the robbers driving away. By the time I got out of the bathtub, everybody in the neighborhood was talking about the robbers' escape.

Well, ever since the bank robbery last weekend, we've all been very nervous. Some of the neighbors are so worried that they're thinking about moving away. Bill and I have been wondering what we should do.

Love,

Beverly

2.

Dear Betsy,

We're having a wedding anniversary celebration on Wednesday for my brother-in-law, Barry, and his wife, Roberta, and we would love it if you and your husband, Walter, were there. It won't be a very big celebration, just a few relatives, William, Vincent, Elizabeth, Steve, and of course my brothers and their wives.

We've heard that your brother's little boy Bobby is visiting you this week. Why don't you bring him along with you when you come over on Wednesday?

Love,

Beverly

3.

> Dear Albert,
>
>   We're having a wonderful time on our vacation in Boston, but we wish you and your wife were here with us. I'm positive both you and Barbara would love it here. Barbara would love the Boston Public Garden and the boats on the Charles River. And you would have a wonderful time visiting the universities and the Boston Public Library. We're staying with Bill's relatives while we're in Boston. They live in a very modern high-rise building with a beautiful view of the river. We've been very lucky. Bill's relatives drive us everywhere.
>
>   The weather in Boston was very warm when we arrived, but now it's windy. I wish we had brought warmer clothes to wear.
>
>   By the way, Bill and I went to a lively baseball game last Wednesday, and we've been to the ballet twice. We've also been very busy buying presents for everybody at home and souvenirs for ourselves. (Unfortunately, we weren't able to buy the watch your brother Walter wanted.)
>
>   Love,
>
>   Beverly

UNIT 10

WORKBOOK PAGE 139

A. What's the Answer?

1. b	**3.** b	**5.** b	**7.** a	**9.** a
2. a	**4.** a	**6.** b	**8.** a	**10.** b

B. What Are They Saying?

1. eating, ate
2. you'd, going, went
3. watching, hadn't watched, I'd
4. done/washed, doing/washing, to do/to wash

WORKBOOK PAGE 140

C. What Are They Saying?

1. to see
2. seeing
3. seen
4. saw
5. seeing
6. wouldn't see
7. seeing
8. seeing
9. to see
10. going
11. going
12. going
13. went
14. to go/going
15. to go/going
16. went
17. going
18. go
19. to go

E. They Never Would Have Done That!

1. she hadn't hit
   would have deleted
2. he hadn't been
   would have driven
3. I hadn't had
   would have gotten
4. we hadn't misunderstood
   would have been
5. he hadn't decided
   would have forgotten
6. she hadn't thought
   would have put
7. they hadn't mixed up
   would have erased

WORKBOOK PAGE 144

H. What Are They Saying?

1. has he been
   For
2. has it had
   Since
3. have you been having trouble
   Since
4. have you been feeling
   Since
5. have they hurt
   For
6. has it been
   Since
7. have they been
   For
8. has she wanted to buy
   Since

WORKBOOK PAGE 145

I. What's Wrong?

1. since
2. for
3. since
4. For
5. since
6. since
7. for
8. for
9. since
10. for

J. Listening

1. a	**3.** a	**5.** a	**7.** b	**9.** b
2. b	**4.** b	**6.** a	**8.** a	

WORKBOOK PAGE 146

K. What's the Answer?

1. a	**3.** b	**5.** a	**7.** b	**9.** a
2. b	**4.** a	**6.** b	**8.** a	**10.** b

L. Complete the Sentences

1. didn't have to
2. were
3. putting, weren't
4. hadn't
5. weren't, I'd
6. figuring, I'd
7. weren't, to, I'd
8. were having, had known, were having, would have

N. What's the Word?

1. to	11. by
2. by	12. with
3. on	13. about, to
4. up	14. of
5. into	15. in
6. out	16. past
7. about	17. at
8. of	18. off
9. in, with	19. from
10. up	20. on

O. What's the Word?

1. balance	10. allergic
2. passport	11. quit
3. wallpaper	12. misunderstood
4. suspect	13. hamster, mess
5. tie	14. scrap
6. slipped	15. unemployed
7. ingredients	16. tournament
8. wisdom	17. rewind
9. move out	18. delete, files

P. Listening

1. b	2. a	3. b	4. b
5. b	6. a	7. b	8. b

Q. Out of Place

1. date	9. usher
2. snowman	10. promoted
3. mural	11. assemble
4. apology	12. aggressive
5. poodle	13. register
6. customer	14. accident
7. discovered	15. confused
8. cactus	

S. Have You Heard?

1. b	3. b	5. a	7. b	9. b	11. a
2. a	4. a	6. b	8. a	10. b	12. b

CHECK-UP TEST: Units 9–10

A.

1. has it	6. will they
2. didn't you	7. did you
3. were there	8. can't you
4. do we	9. aren't I
5. doesn't he	10. won't you

B.

1. She hasn't called in a long time, has she!
2. That was a boring movie, wasn't it!
3. You're right. She does work hard, doesn't she!
4. He will be a fine doctor someday, won't he!
5. They do taste wonderful, don't they!

C.

1. Where will you be staying?
2. When did you get engaged?
3. How much did you spend?
4. How long has he been cooking?
5. How many times did she mention me?
6. What were you assembling?
7. Why does he go to the gym?

D.

1. seeing	4. saw
2. seeing	5. hadn't seen
3. seen	6. to see

E.

1. a	2. b	3. b	4. a	5. b

Correlation Key

STUDENT TEXT PAGES	ACTIVITY WORKBOOK PAGES	STUDENT TEXT PAGES	ACTIVITY WORKBOOK PAGES
Chapter 1		**Chapter 6**	
2	2	84–85	78–79
3	3	86	80–82
4	4–5	87	83–84
5	6–7	89	85
7	8–10	90–91	86–89
8–9	11–12		T31–T36 (Test)
10	13	**Chapter 7**	
11	14	96–97	90–92
12	15–17	98–99	93–96
	T1–T6 (Test)	102–103	97–99
Chapter 2		106–107	100–103
16	18		T37–T42 (Test)
17	19–20	**Chapter 8**	
20	21	110–111	104–107
22	22–23	112–113	108–109
23	24–25	116–118	110–113
24–25	26–28	120–121	114–121
26–27	29–31		T43–T48 (Test)
	T7–T12 (Test)	**Check-Up Test**	**122–123**
Chapter 3		**Chapter 9**	
32–33	32–34	130	124–125
34–35	35–37	131	126–130
36–37	38–40	132–133	131–132
40–41	41–42	134–135	133–134
43	43	136–137	135–138
	T13–T18 (Test)		T49–T54 (Test)
Check-Up Test	**44–45**	**Chapter 10**	
Chapter 4		146–147	139–141
52	46	148–149	142–143
53	47–48	152–153	144–145
54–55	49–52	154–155	146–151
58–59	53–54		T55–T60 (Test)
62–63	55–56	**Check-Up Test**	**152–153**
	T19–T24 (Test)		
Chapter 5			
66	57–59		
67	60–62		
68	63		
69	64–65		
72–73	66–68		
74–75	69–73		
77	74–75		
	T25–T30 (Test)		
Check-Up Test	**76–77**		

SIDE by SIDE Activity Workbook Audio Program

The *Side by Side* Activity Workbook Audio CDs contain all workbook listening activities and GrammarRaps for entertaining language practice through rhythm, stress, and intonation. Students can use the Audio Program to extend their language learning through self-study outside the classroom.

Audio Program Contents